POINTS *of* DEPARTURE

CROSS-ROADS

CLASSIC THEMES IN YOUNG ADULT LITERATURE

FOREWORD BY
ROBERT CORMIER

ScottForesman
A Division of HarperCollinsPublishers

EDITORIAL OFFICES: Glenview, Illinois
REGIONAL OFFICES: Sunnyvale, California · Tucker, Georgia
· Glenview, Illinois · Oakland, New Jersey · Dallas, Texas

FOREWORD
Robert Cormier

CONSULTANTS
Kay Parks Bushman, *language arts teacher and department chair,* Ottawa High
School, Ottawa, Kansas • **Montserrat Fontes,** *writer and English teacher,*
University High School, Los Angeles, California • **Dierdre Glenn-Paul,** *assistant
professor of reading and educational media,* Montclair State University, Upper
Montclair, New Jersey • **Arnetta Harris,** *social studies teacher,* Richwoods High
School, Peoria, Illinois • **Steve Loach,** *language arts teacher,* Middleton Middle
School of Technology, Tampa, Florida • **Jack Matsumoto,** *middle school teacher,*
Edison Regional Gifted Center, Chicago, Illinois • **Linda Runyon,** *English teacher,*
Alief Hastings High School, Houston, Texas • **Gary Salvner,** *professor of English
and secondary education,* Youngstown State University, Youngstown, Ohio •
Elizabeth Sawyer-Cunningham, *English teacher,* Belmont High School, Los
Angeles, California • **Pat Vazzana,** *English teacher,* Calvert Hall College High
School, Towson, Maryland

ISBN: 0-673-29425-0
Acknowledgments appear on pages 370-371. The acknowledgments section is an extension
of the copyright page.

10111213-DQ-04030201

CONTENTS

FOREWORD

by Robert Cormier

Know what I wish as I sit down to write an introduction to this marvelous anthology you hold in your hands?

I wish that when I was a kid there were writers like Robert Lipsyte and Lois Lowry and Walter Dean Myers and Cynthia Rylant around, publishing novels and short stories. These are only four of the writers appearing in this book—all of them are to be cherished.

My reading as a boy had a wide and ridiculous range—from the junk I found in the magazine racks at Lamothe's Drug Store on French Hill in Leominster, Massachusetts, where I grew up, to the formidable classics like *Silas Marner* and Shakespeare's *Julius Caesar* that I encountered in high school English classes. What a leap—from Batman and Robin to Brutus and Cassius. With no in between.

I am embarrassed when I am asked about the literary influences of my childhood and have to recall my pleasure in reading pulp magazines like *Argosy* (adventures on the high seas or exotic places); *Wings* (battles in the skies over No-Man's-Land during World War I); and *Rangeland Romances* (cowboys and Indians in a fabled West that never actually existed). I was about thirteen years old when Superman, for the first time, leaped from the pages of *Action Comics*, a dubious highlight of my literary youth.

My first eight years of education were spent at St. Cecilia's Parochial School in a French-Canadian parish. We spoke English in the morning and French in the afternoon. The conscientious but stern and strict nuns vigorously educated us in the basics of grammar and arithmetic but were oblivious to anything of a literary nature. We became experts at parsing sentences and dissecting paragraphs but our books were so pale and so lacking in literary quality that I can't remember a single story today. If all went well, with no discipline problems during the week—not many of us dared to become discipline problems—Sister Catherine read us a new chapter about Tom Playfair from the *Young Catholic Messenger* late on Friday afternoons. I grew to hate Tom Playfair by the time June came around but remember him fondly today as the only fictional character I encountered during my eight years at St. Cecilia's. (I can still recite my multiplication tables and know all the capitals of the United States, however.)

My situation was particularly poignant because I found myself at the age of twelve desperately wanting to be a writer. Desperation was a big part of my life in those days. I was desperate because of all the emotions churning within me and my desire to express them somehow on paper, afraid that I might literally explode otherwise. Desperate questions also haunted me: Why was loneliness such a constant in my life? Did anyone else feel the way I did? Why was I nostalgic for places and things I had never known? What was I doing here on the planet Earth, anyway, in a solar system filled with a lot of questions but no answers? I began to put tentative answers down on paper, forcing certain words to rhyme, spent long hours in quiet places away from my six brothers and sisters, scribbling and crossing out and scribbling again. I shared my poems only with my mother, who shook her head in wonder at my words and read them with the forgiving eyes of love. Finally, I mustered my courage and showed them to a stern judge, Sister Catherine, who looked at me as if for the first time. "Robert," she said, "you're a writer"—giving me, at last, an identity.

The question that stared me in the face:

Where do I go from here?

"Nobody but a reader ever became a writer."

Those are the words of Richard Peck but they could have been uttered by all the writers I've ever known through the years. Writers hang around bookstores and libraries the way ballplayers are drawn to the playing fields and actors go to the movies. A natural inclination like water seeking its own level.

I found myself at twelve years old with a hunger for the written word, sensing that there was more to reading than the pulp magazines at Lamothe's. How could I become a real writer if the world of literature lay beyond my horizons? Belatedly, I discovered the Leominster Public Library and invaded the Children's Section like a pirate after booty, but found no satisfaction there. To tell the truth, I don't remember any specific books I borrowed from those children's shelves. However, I also discovered the library's Reading Room, a hushed area of gleaming, sturdy tables, like no tables to be found in the tenement kitchens of French Hill. Polished brass lamps with green shades flooded the surface of those tables. Here I found *The New Yorker* and *Harper's* and *Atlantic Monthly*, marveling that such magazines existed.

All of which leads to a moment that altered the course of my life.

In a magazine called *Scribner's*, which contained no illustrations but impressive typographical canyons of prose, I encountered a story called "The Winter of Our Discontent," the first-person narrative of a young girl.

The opening words fastened my eyes and my heart to the page:

> *You would have loved Daddy. He was so wild and beautiful, everybody adored him. That was the trouble: things came too easy for him, he never had to work for anything.*
> *The year before he died, I was about sixteen. God, I was a beauty!—I was like peaches and cream, I don't think I've changed much. Don't you think I have a nice face? It's the same as it always was, people don't change much.*

This was a real voice, bringing the print alive, an authentic, soul-grabbing voice, using the plain words that were also my plain words, my only words, and instantly creating a vital, vivid personality.

Later in the story, asked to describe what moves her,

what fills her life, the girl replies:

". . . Sometimes it's a leaf, and sometimes it's the pocket of a coat, and sometimes it's a button or a coin, . . . or an old shoe on the floor. . . . Sometimes it's a little boy, . . . and sometimes it's an old woman with a funny hat. . . . Sometimes it's the way Sunday morning feels when you wake up and listen to it—you can smell it and feel it, and it smells like breakfast. . . . And sometimes it's like Sunday afternoon, with people coming from a concert—this feels terrible and makes you blue. Sometimes it's the way you feel at night when you wake up in Winter time and you know it's snowing, although you can't see or hear it. . . ."

My God, I thought, there's someone else in the world who sees and feels what I see and feel, who has captured on paper what I've been afraid to capture, the small everyday things that make up life. I had wondered about the simple things—the way our kitchen curtains filtered morning sunshine, the smell of my mother's pie crusts, the loneliness of Saturday afternoon when the movie was over and the neighborhood dozed . . . all of this moved me but was it the stuff of literature?

I had had no great experiences, possessed no vocabulary to speak of (English in the morning, French in the afternoon, master of neither language). All of this discouraged me. How could I hope to be a writer when my world was confined to the three-decker streets of French Hill? I thought that a writer had to acquire all kinds of college degrees, roam the country or the world, become "sophisticated," suffer life-or-death situations. But then, on paper, in a *Scribner's* magazine, were simple singing words that created a story and a character out of the everyday things, the same things that surrounded me.

Trying to renew my inspiration, I returned to the Reading Room later to read again that *Scribner's* story. That particular issue of the magazine was gone, replaced by a new one. With a terrible sense of loss, I realized that I didn't know the name of the story's author. It was lost to me forever. (I also didn't know that the library did not throw away old issues of magazines and that I could have asked to see it.)

ROBERT CORMIER **ix**

Although no one detained me from visiting the Reading Room, my Children's Card prevented me from entering the forbidden area called "The Stacks" behind the horseshoe-shaped circulation desk. That's where the Adult books marched across shelf after shelf after shelf. I watched with envy as grownups strolled casually into the stacks, to feast themselves on all the wonders I sensed would be found there. Finally, with proper timing and my timid soul, for once, teeming with courage, I slipped past the guardians of "The Stacks" at the circulation desk and entered that sweet territory. Took down book after book, scanning the pages. My invasion of "The Stacks" became a daily game. I'd sit on the floor, legs jackknifed, and begin to read a chapter or two at a time, always keeping an ear out for advancing footsteps.

Miss Florence Wheeler, our tiny, whispering librarian, eventually found me there. She didn't order me banned forever but actually began a conversation with me. About books, about reading. I can't remember what I told her but whatever I said was enough for her to usher me to the circulation desk where she issued my first adult library card, my passport to a world with riches beyond surpassing.

The library became my second home. In the following weeks and months, I discovered those writers who would be my everlasting heroes. Ernest Hemingway and John Steinbeck and William Saroyan. Mystery writers like Ellery Queen and Agatha Christie. Wonderful novels like James Hilton's *Lost Horizon*, revealing that lost and lovely land called Shangri-La, and John O'Hara's *Appointment in Samarra*, with its lid-prying prose about what went on in fancy houses I had never visited.

The novels created in me a rage to write, and I'd sit for long hours at the kitchen table, with stubs of pencils and lined yellow pads, trying to create my own worlds on paper, never knowing whether I was succeeding.

One September afternoon, I checked out, as usual, the "New Fiction" bookshelf at the library's entrance and saw a book entitled *The Web and the Rock*, by a writer, unknown to me, named Thomas Wolfe. I turned the pages, basking in mountain torrents of prose, wild and free prose that was filled with all the longings of youth—my own youth, my own longings, my own hungers. Here in a novel was a mirror in which I saw myself.

Later, at home, I came upon a chapter called "Penelope's Web" with the following words:

You would have loved Daddy. He was so wild and beautiful, everybody adored him. . . .

My lost chapter found again, my lost author speaking to me once more, doing what great writers had always done, igniting my desire to read.

The Web and the Rock became my literary bible, to which I still turn every springtime. I long ago stopped trying to imitate that Wolfian prose, finding my own voice at last, but his words still have the power to hustle my soul, as they did that stumbling, long-ago thirteen-year-old boy.

Looking back, I ponder that vacant stretch between the trash of my childhood reading and the wonderful books I found in "The Stacks" of the Leominster Public Library.

Young readers don't face that vacant period today—the in-between years are filled with the novels, short stories, essays, and poems that have become known as Young Adult literature, a genre that has created an avenue to the classics while remaining true to the times in which we live.

The genre is wonderfully alive in *Crossroads: Classic Themes in Young Adult Literature.* And, as the title suggests, the literature in this anthology may set one on a pathway leading to the great modern novels and the enduring classics. There are reminders of this throughout this anthology, that Todd Strasser's "On the Bridge" might lead a reader to William Golding's *Lord of the Flies*, that Gary Paulsen's "Stupid" might send another to the great outdoor stories of Hemingway. Instinct guides this kind of leap, and this collection is filled with stories and poems and reminiscences that spark those instincts.

How much I regret that I did not hold such a book in my hands during my lost, in-between years.

UNIT 1

All in the Family

When was the last time you thought about your family? When did you last really consider who your family is, or what your family means to you?

The characters in each of the following selections are forced, for one reason or another, to stop for a time and examine what their families mean to them. Some of the conclusions they draw may surprise you.

As you read the selections in this unit, pay close attention to what the characters have to say about family. Do their beliefs and experiences have anything in common with yours?

Growing Up

Now that Maria was a tenth-grader, she felt she was too grown-up to have to go on family vacations. Last year, the family had driven three hundred miles to see their uncle in West Covina. There was nothing to do. The days were hot, with a yellow sky thick with smog they could feel on their fingertips. They played cards and watched game shows on television. After the first four days of doing nothing while the grown-ups sat around talking, the kids finally got to go to Disneyland.

Disneyland stood tall with castles and bright flags. The Matterhorn had wild dips and curves that took your breath away if you closed your eyes and screamed. The Pirates of the Caribbean didn't scare anyone but was fun anyway, and so were the teacups and It's a Small World. The parents spoiled the kids, giving each of them five dollars to spend on trinkets. Maria's younger sister, Irma, bought a Pinocchio coloring book and a candy bracelet. Her brothers, Rudy and John, spent their money on candy that made their teeth blue.

Maria saved her money. She knew everything was overpriced, like the Mickey Mouse balloons you could get for a fraction of the price in Fresno. Of course, the balloon at Hanoian's supermarket didn't have a Mickey Mouse face, but it would bounce and float and eventually pop like any other balloon.

Maria folded her five dollars, tucked it in her red purse, and went on rides until she got sick. After that, she sat on a bench, jealously watching other teenage girls who seemed much better dressed than she was. She felt stricken by poverty. All the screaming kids in nice clothes probably came from homes with swimming pools in their backyards, she thought. Yes, her father was a foreman at the paper mill, and yes, she had a Dough-boy swimming pool in her backyard, but *still*, things were not the same. She had felt poor, and her sundress, which seemed snappy in Fresno, was out of style at Disneyland, where every other kid was wearing Esprit shirts and Guess jeans.

This year Maria's family planned to visit an uncle in San Jose. Her father promised to take them to Great America, but she knew that the grown-ups would sit around talking for days before they remembered the kids and finally got up and did something. They would have to wait until the last day before they could go to Great America. It wasn't worth the boredom.

"Dad, I'm not going this year," Maria said to her father. He sat at the table with the newspaper in front of him.

"What do you mean?" he asked, slowly looking up. He thought a moment and said, "When I was a kid we didn't have the money for vacations. I would have been happy to go with my father."

"I know, I know. You've said that a hundred times," she snapped.

"What did you say?" he asked, pushing his newspaper aside.

Everything went quiet. Maria could hear the hum of the refrigerator and her brothers out in the front yard arguing over a popsicle stick, and her mother in the backyard watering the strip of grass that ran along the patio.

Her father's eyes locked on her with a dark stare. Maria had seen that stare before. She pleaded in a soft daughterly voice, "We never do anything. It's boring. Don't you understand?"

"No, I don't understand. I work all year, and if I want to go on a vacation, then I go. And my family goes too." He took a swallow of ice water, and glared.

Words in Spanish
Chihuahua (p. 4) a state in northern Mexico
los chavalos (p. 4) the kids
Habla, con tu mocosa (p. 5) Talk to your little girl. *Mocosa* is a slang term that literally means "runny-nosed girl."
nina (p. 5) short for *madrina*, or godmother

"You have it too easy," he continued. "In Chihuahua, my town, we worked hard. You worked, even *los chavalos!* And you showed respect to your parents, something you haven't learned."

Here it comes, Maria thought, stories about his childhood in Mexico. She wanted to stuff her ears with wads of newspaper to keep from hearing him. She could recite his stories word-for-word. She couldn't wait until she was in college and away from them.

"Do you know my father worked in the mines? That he

4   UNIT 1   ALL IN THE FAMILY

nearly lost his life? And today his lungs are bad." He pounded his chest with hard, dirt-creased knuckles.

Maria pushed back her hair and looked out the window at her brothers running around in the front yard. She couldn't stand it anymore. She got up and walked away, and when he yelled for her to come back, she ignored him. She locked herself in her bedroom and tried to read *Seventeen*, though she could hear her father complaining to her mother, who had come in when she had heard the yelling.

"*Habla, con tu mocosa,*" she heard him say.

She heard the refrigerator door open. He was probably getting a beer, a "cold one," as he would say. She flipped through the pages of her magazine and stopped at a Levi's ad of a girl about her age walking between two happy-looking guys on a beach. She wished she were that girl, that she had another life. She turned the page and thought, I bet you he gets drunk and drives crazy tomorrow.

M ARIA'S MOTHER WAS PUTTING AWAY A PITCHER OF Kool-Aid the boys had left out. She looked at her husband, who was fumbling with a wadded-up napkin. His eyes were dark, and his thoughts were on Mexico, where a father was respected and his word, right or wrong, was final. "Rafael, she's growing up; she's a teenager. She talks like that, but she still loves you."

"Sure, and that's how she shows her love, by talking back to her father." He rubbed the back of his neck and turned his head trying to make the stiffness go away. He knew it was true, but he was the man of the house and no daughter of his was going to tell him what to do.

Instead, it was his wife, Eva, who told him what to do. "Let the girl stay. She's big now. She don't want to go on rides no more. She can stay with her *nina.*"

The father drank his beer and argued, but eventually agreed to let his daughter stay.

The family rose just after six the next day and was ready to go by seven-thirty. Maria stayed in her room. She wanted to apologize to her father but couldn't. She knew that if she said, "Dad, I'm sorry," she would break into tears. Her father wanted to come into her room and say, "We'll do something really special this vacation. Come with us, honey." But it was hard for him to show his emotions around his children, especially when he tried to make up to them.

The mother kissed Maria. "Maria, I want you to clean the house and then walk over to your *nina*'s. I want no monkey business while we're gone, do you hear me?"

"*Sí*, Mama."

"Here's the key. You water the plants inside and turn on the sprinkler every couple of days." She handed Maria the key and hugged her. "You be good. Now, come say goodbye to your father."

Reluctantly, she walked out in her robe to the front yard and, looking down at the ground, said goodbye to her father. The father looked down and said goodbye to the garden hose at his feet.

After they left, Maria lounged in her pajamas listening to the radio and thumbing through magazines. Then she got up, fixed herself a bowl of Cocoa Puffs, and watched "American Bandstand." Her dream was to dance on the show, to look at the camera, smile, and let everyone in Fresno see that she could have a good time, too.

But an ill feeling stirred inside her. She felt awful about arguing with her father. She felt bad for her mother and two brothers, who would have to spend the next three hours in the car with him. Maybe he would do something crazy, like crash the car on purpose to get back at her, or fall asleep and run the car into an irrigation ditch. And it would be her fault.

She turned the radio to a news station. She listened for half an hour, but most of the news was about warships in the Persian Gulf and a tornado in Texas. There was no mention of her family.

Maria began to calm down because, after all, her father was really nice beneath his gruffness. She dressed slowly, made some swishes with the broom in the kitchen, and let the hose run in a flower bed while she painted her toenails with her mother's polish. Afterward, she called her friend Becky to tell her that her parents had let her stay home, that she was free—for five days at least.

"Great," Becky said. "I wish my mom and dad would go away and let me stay by myself."

"No, I have to stay with my godmother." She made a mental note to give her *nina* a call. "Becky, let's go to the mall and check out the boys."

"All right."

"I'll be over pretty soon."

Maria called her *nina*, who said it was OK for her to go shopping, but to be at her house for dinnertime by six. After hanging up, Maria took off her jeans and T-shirt, and changed into a dress. She went through her mother's closet to borrow a pair of shoes and drenched her wrists in Charlie perfume. She put on coral-pink lipstick and a smudge of blue eyeshadow. She felt beautiful, although a little self-conscious. She took off some of the lipstick and ran water over her wrists to dilute the fragrance.

While she walked the four blocks to Becky's house, she beamed happiness until she passed a man who was on his knees pulling weeds from his flower bed. At his side, a radio was reporting a traffic accident. A big rig had overturned after hitting a car near Salinas, twenty miles from San Jose.

A wave of fear ran through her. Maybe it was *them*. Her smile disappeared, and her shoulders slouched. No, it couldn't be, she thought. Salinas is not that close to San Jose. Then again, maybe her father wanted to travel through Salinas because it was a pretty valley with wide plains and oak trees, and horses and cows that stared as you passed them in your speeding car. But maybe it did happen; maybe they had gotten in an awful wreck.

By the time she got to Becky's house, she was riddled with guilt, since it was she who would have disturbed her father and made him crash.

"Hi," she said to Becky, trying to look cheerful.

"You look terrific, Maria," Becky said. "Mom, look at Maria. Come inside for a bit."

Maria blushed when Becky's mother said she looked gorgeous. She didn't know what to do except stare at the carpet and say, "Thank you, Mrs. Ledesma."

Becky's mother gave them a ride to the mall, but they'd have to take a bus back. The girls first went to Macy's, where they hunted for a sweater, something flashy but not too flashy. Then they left to have a Coke and sit by the fountain under an artificial tree. They watched people walk by, especially the boys, who, they agreed, were dumb but cute nevertheless.

They went to The Gap, where they tried on some skirts, and ventured into The Limited, where they walked up and down the aisles breathing in the rich smells of 100-percent wool and silk. They were about to leave, when Maria heard once again on someone's portable radio that a family had been killed in an auto accident near Salinas. Maria stopped smiling for a moment as she pictured her family's overturned Malibu station wagon.

Becky sensed that something was wrong and asked, "How come you're so quiet?"

Maria forced a smile. "Oh, nothing. I was just thinking."

" 'bout what?"

Maria thought quickly. "Oh, I think I left the water on at home." This could have been true. Maria remembered pulling the hose from the flower bed, but couldn't remember if she had turned the water off.

Afterward they rode the bus home with nothing to show for their three hours of shopping except a small bag of See's candies. But it had been a good day. Two boys had followed them, joking and flirting, and they had flirted back. The girls gave them made-up telephone numbers, and turned away and laughed into their hands.

"They're fools," Becky said, "but cute."

Maria left Becky when they got off the bus, and started off to her *nina*'s house. Then she remembered that the garden hose might still be running at home. She hurried home, clip-clopping clumsily in her mother's shoes.

THE GARDEN HOSE WAS ROLLED NEATLY AGAINST THE trellis. Maria decided to check the mail and went inside. When she pushed open the door, the living room gave off a quietness she had never heard before. Usually the TV was on, her younger brothers and sister were playing, and her mother could be heard in the kitchen. When the telephone rang, Maria jumped. She kicked off her shoes, ran to the phone, and picked up the receiver only to hear a distant clicking sound.

"Hello, hello?" Maria's heart began to thump. Her mind went wild with possibilities. An accident, she thought, they're in an accident, and it's all my fault. "Who is it? Dad? Mom?"

She hung up and looked around the room. The clock on the television set glowed 5:15. She gathered the mail, changed into jeans, and left for her *nina*'s house with a shopping bag containing her nightie and a toothbrush.

Her *nina* was happy to see her. She took Maria's head in her hands and gave it a loud kiss.

"Dinner is almost ready," she said, gently pulling her inside.

"Oh, good. Becky and I only had popcorn for lunch."

They had a quiet evening together. After dinner, they sat on the porch watching the stars. Maria wanted to ask her *nina* if she had heard from her parents. She wanted to know if the police had called to report that they had gotten into an accident. But she just sat on the porch swing, letting anxiety eat a hole in her soul.

The family was gone for four days. Maria prayed for them, prayed that she would not wake up to a phone call saying that their car had been found in a ditch. She made a list of the ways she could be nicer to them: doing the dishes without being asked, watering the lawn, hugging her father after work, and playing with her youngest brother, even if it bored her to tears.

At night Maria worried herself sick listening to the radio for news of an accident. She thought of her uncle Shorty and how he fell asleep and crashed his car in the small town of Mendota. He lived confined to a motorized wheelchair and was scarred with burns on the left side of his face.

"Oh, please, don't let anything like that happen to them," she prayed.

IN THE MORNING SHE COULD BARELY LOOK AT THE newspaper. She feared that if she unfolded it, the front page would feature a story about a family from Fresno who had flown off the roller coaster at Great America. Or that a shark had attacked them as they bobbed happily among the white-tipped waves. Something awful is going to happen, she said to herself as she poured Rice Krispies into a bowl.

But nothing happened. Her family returned home, dark from lying on the beach and full of great stories about the Santa Cruz boardwalk and Great America and an Egyptian museum. They had done more this year than in all their previous vacations.

"Oh, we had fun," her mother said, pounding sand from her shoes before entering the house.

Her father gave her a tight hug as her brothers ran by, dark from hours of swimming.

Maria stared at the floor, miffed. How dare they have so much fun? While she worried herself sick about them, they had splashed in the waves, stayed at Great America until nightfall, and eaten at all kinds of restaurants. They even went shopping for fall school clothes.

Feeling resentful as Johnny described a ride that dropped straight down and threw your stomach into your mouth, Maria turned away and went off to her bedroom, where she kicked off her shoes and thumbed through an old *Seventeen*. Her family was alive and as obnoxious as ever. She took back all her promises. From now on she would keep to herself and ignore them. When they asked, "Maria, would you help me," she would pretend not to hear and walk away.

"They're heartless," she muttered. "Here I am worrying about them, and there they are having fun." She thought of the rides they had gone on, the hours of body surfing, the handsome boys she didn't get to see, the restaurants, and the museum. Her eyes filled with tears. For the first time in years, she hugged a doll, the one her grandmother Lupe had stitched together from rags and old clothes.

"Something's wrong with me," she cried softly. She turned on her radio and heard about a single-engine plane that had crashed in Cupertino, a city not far from San Jose. She thought of the plane and the people inside, how the pilot's family would suffer.

She hugged her doll. Something was happening to her, and it might be that she was growing up. When the news ended, and a song started playing, she got up and washed her face without looking in the mirror.

That night the family went out for Chinese food. Although her brothers fooled around, cracked jokes, and spilled a soda, she was happy. She ate a lot, and when her fortune cookie said, "You are mature and sensible," she had to agree. And her father and mother did too. The family drove home singing the words to "La Bamba" along with the car radio.

About Gary Soto

Gary Soto is now a well-known author and college teacher, but as a child he had little interest in reading or writing: "I don't think I had any literary aspirations when I was a kid . . . . We didn't have books, and no one encouraged us to read."

Soto first became interested in writing in college, where he discovered that he enjoyed reading poetry. About writing, he says, "It's a clean yet terrifying job. And I mean 'clean' because I don't have to stuff my body in work clothes, and 'terrifying' because I have to continuously scratch at experience for subjects and the imagination that will make the subjects live."

Although Gary Soto's Mexican American background has influenced his writing, he says that most of his work explores themes, such as family and poverty, that affect people of all ethnic backgrounds. Two of Soto's collections of short stories are *Baseball in April* and *Local News*.

Responding

1. **Personal Response** While her family is on vacation, Maria is sure something will happen to them. Would you have the same fear if your family went on vacation without you? Why do you think Maria feels that way?

2. **Literary Analysis** Maria's father is an important *character* in the story. Maria thinks he is "really nice beneath his gruffness." Do you agree with this description? Present evidence from the story that supports your opinion.

3. Theme Connection How do Maria's feelings toward her family change by the end of the story? Why do they change?

Language Workshop

Sentence Variety Author Gary Soto makes his writing more interesting by varying his sentences. Here's how you can do the same in your writing:

• Begin some sentences with an introductory phrase, a prepositional phrase, a question, or a quote.

• Include shorter and longer sentences. Sometimes you can combine short, choppy sentences together.

• Use interrogative, exclamatory, and imperative sentences as well as declarative ones.

Look at the last paragraph from "Growing Up." Observe how the sentences vary. Then write a brief description of a family you know and use tips from this workshop to make your writing more interesting.

Writer's Portfolio

Imagine that Becky's family invited Maria to go camping with them. How do you think Maria would feel while she was away from her family? Put yourself in Maria's place and write about your first vacation away from your home and family.

COLBY   RODOWSKY

Mildred

MY NAME IS MILLY, WHICH IS SHORT FOR MILDRED, which is short for "Mil-dred." To my way of thinking *nobody* should be named Mildred except that my father's mother was and I guess he thought it was a good idea to name me after her. I never knew her, though, because she died before I was born. There's *another* name that's big in our family: Susan—which isn't terrific but it is better than Mildred. Anyway, it's my maternal grandmother's name . . . my mother's name . . . and of course my sister's name. Susan Marie Phelps. Susie. A name you can live with . . . be proud of . . . make proud of *you*. Which Susie hasn't exactly done. But that may be a prejudiced opinion.

Susie's always been a thorn in my side which my mother likes to believe is "perfectly normal sibling rivalry" except that I have friends who experience "perfectly normal sibling rivalry" almost daily and they don't have to put up with what I've put up with from Susie through the years.

Susie was thirteen when I was born and in some ways it was as though we were in two different families except that we had the same mother and father and both grew up in the same rambling house with the big wraparound front porch. One would think that having only one sister, and her that much older, would be sort of like being an only child except that even when Susie wasn't there, she was. I mean we could never stop thinking about her.

The one time I referred to her as a "bad seed," my mother cried and my father stared moodily out the window and the air in the room got heavy with unsaid things. Susie didn't do anything because as usual Susie was gone. Her "goneness" was a fact of life. Hers, mostly, but mine, too, because whatever Susie did seemed to spread over to me like milk spilled on a tabletop.

For example. The first birthday party I remember—the one where Amanda Shultz brought me the goldfish in the bowl—Susie was gone. I know because Nana (Grandmother Susan) came over and ran the party while Mom and Dad huddled upstairs next to the telephone, and then later on a policeman came and even a little kid knows that you can have a clown at a birthday party but never a policeman. Susie came back that time at Christmas and Mom and Dad pretended nothing had happened and I got a pain in my stomach on account of their pretending so hard. She left another time the night of my piano recital when I was the only one of Mrs. Cole's students to play "The Skater's Waltz" and I lost my place twice just looking at the door to see if my parents'd gotten there yet (and afterward they told me how good I was and tried to pretend they'd been there all along. And I let them.) Then there was my sixth birthday when she disappeared between the time Mom left to take seven little girls to the movies and when we got back for cake and ice cream. And I'll never forget the year we were finally going to New England for our vacation and Susie turned up on the doorstep just as Dad and I were loading the car and we had to unload it and carry everything back inside and wait three days while Mom and Dad and Susie had long and heartfelt talks.

We repeated this boomerang pattern forever: Susie leaving, Susie coming back, and, in between, me leading some average everyday kind of life. It's not that Susie deliberately set out to ruin all the great occasions of my life—it just worked out that way. Anyhow, this isn't an exercise in feeling sorry for myself (the way Great-Aunt

Words to Know

boomerang (p. 16) a curved piece of wood that, when thrown, returns to the thrower

defense mechanism (p. 17) a self-protective reaction

Zen (p. 17) a Japanese form of Buddhism that emphasizes meditation and intuition as a means of achieving spiritual enlightenment

est (p. 17) Erhard Seminar Training, a program of psychological therapy developed by Werner Erhard that stresses self-fulfillment

Hilda used to do and which we all found grossly unattractive) but rather a statement of fact. And also to explain what happened later, along with what Nana refers to as my smart-aleck attitude toward life and what Mom calls my defense mechanism.

THE LAST TIME SUSIE LEFT, WHEN SHE WAS TWENTY-three and I was ten (the day of my class trip to Mount Vernon, naturally, when Mom was supposed to chaperone but couldn't) Mom and Dad confronted her at the breakfast table and said that enough was enough; that Susie was certainly old enough to be on her own; to live her life as she saw fit; that it was better, since she obviously couldn't live by their standards, that she live somewhere else; but that they'd always be there for her. I don't think any of us knew how *there* they were going to have to be. The thing is that when someone leaves the way Susie left (with her clothes in a plastic leaf bag thrown into the back of a friend's Volkswagen) and slamming the door behind her, she's sometimes more *there* than if she'd never left in the first place.

I mean it's hard to tell which were worse: the months when we didn't hear *anything*, or the frantic phone calls, usually asking for money, that came late at night or early in the morning because Susie somehow never managed to handle the difference in time zones. In between there were occasional postcards or letters telling how she was experiencing life to the fullest; that she was into Zen, or est; was working as a waitress, a puppeteer, a ticket taker at a wildlife preserve, a deckhand on a fishing boat. The letters themselves were short and somehow skimpy looking but Mom saved them all, storing them away in the top drawer of the desk in the living room. Sometimes when no one else was home I'd take them out and reread them, as if trying to piece together my sister.

THEN, EVEN FOR SUSIE, SHE OUTDID HERSELF. AND I WAS the one who got the message. On the answering machine.

Since Mom and Dad both work, I usually beat them home in the afternoon and the first thing I do (after getting something to eat) is to check the answering machine. I mean, even though I've just left practically everyone I know at school, there's something about that glowing red light that makes me have to "rewind" and "replay." The weird thing was that with *that* particular message all set to uncurl one would definitely think the red light would've given off an ominous sort of glow. Which it didn't.

"Hi, Mom. Hi, Dad." The tape sounded garbled because it was worn and nobody'd thought to get a new one. "I'm living the ultimate experience. I'm pregnant and I'm heading home. See you soon."

My first thought was to "erase." My second was that there was no way I was going to give *that* message to my parents. And my third was to escape. So I rewound the tape, retraced my steps out of the house, and headed for the library, where I slumped down in a chair and started into *Rebecca* for about the seventeenth time except that the whole time I was trying to read Susie's voice kept sounding inside my head: . . . ultimate experience . . . pregnant . . . coming home . . . .

I stayed at the library so long, I was afraid my parents would begin to worry, but when I got home I saw I needn't have bothered. I mean, they were worrying, all right, but not about me. "Do you know what she's done now?" my mother said.

"Who's *she*?" I said. "Princess Di? Fergie?" My voice sounded wooden, the way thinking about Susie sometimes made me feel.

"Your sis-ter," said Mom.

I wanted to say, "I don't have a sister," but when I looked at my mother's face something pinched inside of me like a too-tight shoe.

"What?" I said instead, turning away and trying to act

like I didn't know what she was going to say next.

"She's pregnant."

"Pregnant?" The surprise in my voice sounded fake, but Mom didn't seem to notice.

"Don't say that word in front of the child," my father said. And since my father prides himself on being an open and forthright kind of person (and since I'm fifteen and definitely not a child), that gives some idea how deep he was into denial.

"That's what she said," my mother went on. "Pregnant." And it was as if she had trouble getting her mouth around the shape of the word. "Maybe she's married. Maybe she just wants to surprise us."

"Mar-ried?" said my father, his voice cracking somewhere between the two *r*'s. "Did she say anything about a husband? Did she say anything about a father? No, she did not. I'll tell you what she said—she said she was experiencing a—the—"

"She said she was living the ultimate experience," said Mom, going to stand by the window and looking out into the dark.

SUSIE CAME HOME BY BUS AND WALKED UP FROM the station with a canvas tote bag slung on her shoulder. She looked pale and haggard and older than the twenty-eight years I knew her to be. For a minute I almost felt sorry for her—until I looked at my mother and father and *they* looked paler and even more haggard.

"Well, Susan," my father began. But whatever speech he had planned fizzled out and after a minute he wrapped Susie in an enormous bear hug.

"Yes, well, Susie," my mother began. "It's not the way we planned it—I mean the way we thought it would be," she said, dabbing at her eyes.

"But that's just the point," the old Susie said, extricating herself from my father's arms. "It's the way *I* planned it. I mean, I'm not getting any younger and I've always felt that giving birth is life's ultimate experience. And I want it all."

"But—but—but—" My father was fairly sputtering. "What about the father?"

"What do you see as his role in all this?" my mother said.

"I don't see him as having a role. In fact, I plain don't see him at all anymore," my sister answered in a voice that clearly said that that was all the explanation we were going to get.

And it was all the explanation we *did* get.

IT WAS THEN THAT I ENTERED MY LIFE-ON-THE-OTHER-SIDE-of-the-door phase. The door was any door, with Mom, Dad, and Susie on one side and me crouched, head against the wood, on the other. I got used to hearing in phrases: ". . . stay here until . . ." ". . . up for adoption . . ." ". . . best for the child . . ." ". . . sense of responsibility . . ."

And always, after a while, Susie shouting out, "I want this baby. I'm going to keep it."

Then there would be another door and another set of phrases: ". . . mother's raised *her* children . . ." ". . . a job, and day care . . ." ". . . here till you get on your feet . . ." ". . . give you all the help we can but . . ."

And again, Susie: ". . . leave if you don't want me here . . ." "I've changed . . ." and "I want this baby."

THE THING IS, SUSIE DID GET A JOB (JUST AS SOON AS she stopped throwing up). It was a job in an office and you could tell she didn't think it could compare to being a waitress, a puppeteer, a ticket taker at a wildlife preserve, or a deckhand on a fishing boat. And she didn't leave. Though the truth is that there were times, in the middle of the night, or even in Latin class, when I wished she would. I mean (and I have to say this in a whisper, even to myself) there were times when my sister Susie seemed like more of a stranger than a stranger would've been.

"Is she going to *stay* here?" I asked my mother one night when we were doing the dishes.

"Of course she is," said Mom. "This is her home the same as it's yours."

"What about the kid? It won't even have a name."

"Of course it will," snapped Mom. "Its name will be Phelps."

"But that's *my* name," I heard myself whine (just like Great-Aunt Hilda used to do).

"It's our *family* name," my mother said, scrubbing at the broiler pan. And then, after a minute, "Mil-dred, I'd hate to think you were embarrassed about your own sister."

Which is exactly what I was. I mean, there we were in the midst of the sexual revolution and I was embarrassed. Besides that, all of a sudden Susie was looking like Lucille Ball when she was pregnant on the *Lucy* show. She waddled. She lumbered. And when my friends came over they'd all sneak little glances at her from the side and then pretend not to notice.

It seemed like my whole family was into being what Mom called "supportive." She bought Susie a new robe to take to the hospital, a bunch of baby clothes, and a stuffed bear. Dad got the old crib out of the attic and scrubbed it down. Nana made curtains for the nursery.

Correction: My whole family except me was into being supportive. When Susie and I were alone in a room together there still didn't seem to be anything to say, and the night she told me she was dying of boredom and could we please go the movies I told her I had a headache. And then hated the way I felt afterward.

WHEN SUSIE WENT TO CHILDBIRTH CLASSES MOM WENT with her. A couple of times my mother tried to get me to go, saying that it would help me to be a part of things (which I definitely didn't want to be a part of), but I always managed to get out of it until one night after dinner when Mom tried again and I said no again and Dad said, "Mil-dred . . . it would be a help to your mother," in that no-nonsense voice of his. And all of a sudden there I was in this big room with pregnant women all over the floor, along with husbands, significant others, and *my mother*. While Mom helped Susie breathe (helped her breathe?) I sat in the corner and tried to pretend I'd just stopped in to get out of the rain. Which is what I did for all the rest of the classes, though I guess my mother didn't notice, because when they were finished Mom sighed a big sigh and said, "Well, now, I certainly feel better that there're two of us prepared to help Susie."

Prepared? To help her do what? I mean, *I* wasn't the one having a baby. In fact, I wasn't even sure I *liked* babies all that much.

AND THEN MOM GOT A TOOTHACHE. NOT A LITTLE TWINGY run-of-the-mill toothache but a huge, throbbing kind that needed a root canal and kept her up all night and sent her out to an emergency dentist appointment early the next morning.

"Wow," said Susie, waddling into the kitchen just as Dad and Mom pulled out of the driveway.

"Wow what?" I said, trying not to look at her standing there in her pink pajamas with the pants scooping down under her enormous belly.

"Another one," said Susie.

"Another what?"

"Pain. Another pain," said Susie.

"What do you mean another pain?" I shrieked at her. "Has there been one before?"

"All night," my sister said, turning a funny gray color and hanging on to the door frame.

"Why didn't you tell Mom? Call her," I said running to

the kitchen window as if I thought the car might still be in the driveway. "We'll call her at the dentist . . . we'll—"

"No," said Susie. "There isn't time. And besides, she has to get that tooth taken care of. We'll take a taxi."

"A *taxi?*" I said. "We can't take a taxi. I only have a dollar."

"In Mom's top dresser drawer," said Susie turning and heading for the stairs, walking as though she were stepping on eggs, and calling back over her shoulder, "There's money there. Mom told me. In case I was ever here alone and needed a cab."

IN THE HOSPITAL THERE WERE PEOPLE WHO TOOK information and blood and who examined Susie to see how things were going and then said that they were going fine. And quickly. Then Susie and I were alone in a room together, except for the people coming in and out, and she rocked and sang and rested some. She groaned and grunted and moaned. She laughed a lot and showed me how to rub her back and when she looked tense I told her to relax and when she said she couldn't stand it anymore I said she could and that she was.

Then it was as if everything went into fast forward and there was someone handing me a funky green gown and all of a sudden we were in another room with bright lights and tile on the walls. A nurse told me to stay out of the way and if I felt faint to sit down, but Susie called for me and I went to stand by her head. Her face was sweaty and twisted and smiling all at the same time and suddenly there was a thin watery cry as if from far away and someone plunked this ugly, slimy, beautiful baby across Susie's chest and said, "It's a girl . . . a girl . . . a girl . . . " in a voice that seemed to sing out loud.

I wiped my sister's face and after she had looked the baby all over she said, "We'll call Mom and Dad and tell them now. About the baby, and the name."

"Name?" I said, as if it were news to me that babies

had them.

And then she said it. Susie, my sister, said that this baby—this niece—was going to be named Mildred.

For a minute I started to tell her that that was a rotten thing to do to some unsuspecting kid. Then I caught myself. I mean, I stood there looking at the baby with its funny spiky hair, stark naked with its screwed-up face and its fists flailing, and thought how already she looked tough and precocious and incredibly smart, and definitely ready for the challenge. Because if there's one thing that makes life interesting it's the challenge.

If you don't believe it, ask Susie; ask me; or wait a few years and ask Mildred Marie Phelps.

About Colby Rodowsky

Like fifteen-year-old Mildred, many of the characters in Colby Rodowsky's books face difficult family situations involving challenges such as

loneliness, teenage pregnancy, illness, and death. Yet her characters find ways to grow and express themselves in spite of, or perhaps because of, their problems.

Rodowsky knew she wanted to be a writer at an early age. As an only child, she was alone much of the time reading and writing. After college, she married and spent many busy years teaching and raising her six children. It wasn't until she was in her forties that she found time to start writing again and publish her first book.

Rodowsky's advice to young people interested in writing is "Read, read, read. And read some more." Her award-winning books include *What About Me?*; *A Summer's Worth of Shame*; *H, My Name is Henley*; *Julie's Daughter, Sydney, Herself*; and *Lucy Peale*.

Responding

1. **Personal Response** How would you feel if you had a sister like Susie? Explain.

2. **Literary Analysis** The author has chosen to tell this story from Mildred's *point of view.* How does this affect the way you understand events in the story?

3. **Theme Connection** How do you think Mildred will feel about her family when Susie and the baby are home from the hospital?

Language Workshop

Descriptive Adjectives and Adverbs Adjectives modify nouns and pronouns. Adverbs modify verbs, adjectives, and adverbs. In "Mildred," Colby Rodowsky uses vivid adjectives and adverbs to help describe her characters and the events in the story. Consider these examples:

. . . the air in the room got <u>heavy</u> with <u>unsaid</u> things . . .
. . . my father stared <u>moodily</u> out the window . . .
. . . Susie looked <u>pale</u> and <u>haggard</u> . . .

What do the adjectives and adverbs add to each of these descriptions?

Add adjectives or adverbs to the following sentences to make them more descriptive.

1. As we walked through the woods, we saw birds.

2. The band played songs for the crowd.

3. The runner ran toward the finish line.

Writer's Portfolio

How would Mildred's sister describe the events in the story? Retell the story from Susie's point of view.

Hum It Again, Jeremy

CHARACTERS

JEREMY BOTKIN, a young man about sixteen

ROSALIE BOTKIN, his mother

DAN BOTKIN, his father

DARRELL WASHINGTON, Jeremy's best friend

SETTING

TIME: *An evening in May.*

PLACE: *Cleveland, Ohio.*

> *An asphalt basketball court on a dimly lit playground, center stage, in front of an apartment building. It is littered with cans and papers. There is one streetlight above the hoop. As the curtain rises, we see* DARRELL WASHINGTON, *a sixteen-year-old young man dressed in jeans and a T-shirt, shooting baskets alone on the court. It is eight o'clock.*

DARRELL: Where you been, man? *(Irritated, he pivots and makes a sharp chest shot to* JEREMY BOTKINS *who bursts on the court, out of breath. He is a tall, gangly sixteen-year-old, dressed in jeans and a Cleveland Cavaliers T-shirt.)*

JEREMY *(Catches ball, jarred backward a bit by its unexpected force. He tucks ball under his arm and makes "time out" signal.):* Time. *(He throws ball underarm like a referee to* DARRELL.)

DARRELL *(accusingly):* It's dark.

JEREMY *(holding hands up, shaking his head):* Not you too— I can't handle it.

DARRELL *(Pauses, irritated. He looks around the court, dribbling the ball hard. Then sighs, resignedly.):* Okay. *(He bounces the ball once, catches it, and pauses again.)* Let's play.

Basketball Words
dribble (p. 28) to bounce the basketball
guard (p. 28) to try to keep the other team from scoring
rebound (p. 28) a ball that bounces off the backboard or basket rim after a shot
slam dunk (p. 29) to slam the ball through the basket from above the basket

JEREMY *(guarding* DARRELL, *who dribbles toward basket):* Thanks for waiting. *(*DARRELL *shoots, guarded by* JEREMY, *then* JEREMY *shoots, guarded by* DARRELL. DARRELL *shoots, guarded by* JEREMY.):* Nice shot.
[*Substitute* "Almost . . . nice shot" *if ball doesn't go in.*]

DARRELL *(guarding* JEREMY, *who takes shot):* I figured it was your mom, your old man, or Renee.

JEREMY: All of the above. *(Guards* DARRELL, *who shoots. He gets* DARRELL'*s rebound, then shoots and misses, and* DARRELL *gets the ball.)*

DARRELL: It's the Jam Man. *(Dribbles to basket, goes up, and slam dunks in the air a foot below the basket. JEREMY cracks up at the air dunk. DARRELL passes to JEREMY.)*

JEREMY *(dribbling toward basket as DARRELL guards):* You know what would be great?

DARRELL *(guarding JEREMY):* What?

JEREMY *(Shoots, catches his own rebound, and dribbles ball in place.):* If you could do a trade. In your family—like it was a team. I'd get a power father. My present one doesn't come to play—as they say. *(Passes ball to DARRELL.)* So I'd just trade him.

DARRELL *(dribbling toward basket as JEREMY guards):* For money? Or another player?

JEREMY: My mom would want the money. She's into the green. It's all she talks about, but this is my deal, see? I'd trade him for another player. *(Shooting)* I'd trade him for Bill Cosby.

DARRELL *(shouting excitedly):* All right! My mom for Tina Turner!

JEREMY *(bending down to tie his shoe):* That's not the idea, man. You never see Tina Turner with kids or anything like that. See—you scout a different kind of talent for this trade. Like, take Bill Cosby. Everyone knows he loves his kids—

DARRELL *(holding ball, snapping fingers and singing Tina Turner song):* "What's love got to do, got to do with it?"

JEREMY *(Stands up, takes ball from* DARRELL. *Flatly):*
Sometimes—I wonder. *(Dribbles toward basket. Freezes
as set becomes black.)*

*Earlier the same day. Spots light the living room of the
Botkin apartment, which is set on risers on the left of the
stage. Furnished with a worn couch and matching chair, it
is a small L-shaped room with a formica dinette set in the
end of the room next to the adjoining small kitchen, which is
offstage. On an end table next to the chair is a phone with a
long extension cord that can
reach around the corner to the
kitchen offstage. An exercise bike
is in the corner of the room
facing a television set. Over the
television is a macramé wall
hanging, and on the wall behind
the dinette set is a plate
commemorating the wedding of Prince Charles and Princess
Di. There is a large plant in the corner of the living room,
many of its leaves brown and dying. On the formica coffee
table in front of the sofa is an arrangement of plastic flowers
and a Walkman radio.* ROSALIE BOTKIN *is riding the exercise
bike and watching the shopping channel on TV. She is a
short, chunky woman with obviously dyed auburn hair.
Dressed in pink sweats, she is scowling and puffing as she
pedals the bike.*

Theater Words
freeze (p. 30) become motionless
spot (p. 30) a spotlight, a bright light
riser (p. 30) a long, low platform
offstage (p. 30) away from or behind the stage

ROSALIE *(shouting):* Jeremy! Don't leave this apartment
without talking to me. *(She pedals laboriously and begins
to pant before shouting again, louder.)* I have to talk to
you, Jeremy. *(JEREMY enters, leans against top of each chair,
holding car keys.)*

JEREMY: I gotta go, Mom. After I have dinner with him—
I'm supposed to meet Darrell. *(Heads for the door.)*

ROSALIE: Just tell him to give me the check. (*She runs a hand through her hair, then wipes her forearm across her brow.*) I want that check, Jeremy. (*Carefully, she gets off the bike rubbing her thighs, then slowly goes to the chair and flops down in it as the phone rings.*) Stay right here—I'm not through. (*While* ROSALIE *answers the phone,* JEREMY *dribbles and shoots an imaginary basketball.*) Hello . . . Yeah, he's here. (*Covering the mouthpiece*) It's that girl. Why don't you bring her to meet me? She's forward enough to call you, she ought to meet your mother. (*She hands the phone to* JEREMY.) Here.

JEREMY (*taking the phone, angrily mouthing*): Shhhhhh. (*He disappears into the kitchen around the corner with the phone.*)

ROSALIE (*nagging, as* JEREMY *disappears to kitchen*): And if you want to know, I still don't think it's right for girls to be calling boys. (*She lies on the floor, begins doing sit-ups; after four sit-ups* JEREMY *enters and heads for door. She sits up.*) You were the one card I had, Jeremy. If he didn't pay—I wouldn't let him see you. So—now you're driving a car, you're a big guy, you go see the jerk whenever you please. You think we don't need the money or something? Don't you give a damn about my feelings?

JEREMY (*impatiently, jiggling the car keys*): Listen Mom—

ROSALIE: No, you listen! Because of you I don't have any control over this situation. Not unless I want to go to some lawyer, and those greedy slobs won't even talk to me unless I give 'em a hundred bucks up front. Now if I had an extra hundred bucks lying around, I wouldn't need a lawyer, would I?

JEREMY *(nodding, defeatedly):* Yeah, Mom. *(Quietly, mumbling)* Yeah.

ROSALIE *(softening):* Look, this is strictly business. Why can't you see that you're the only leverage I've got? I'm not trying to make you hate him, Jeremy.

> ### Words to Know
>
> **leverage** (p. 32) bargaining power
> **. . . call his lines . . .** (p. 33) call his buyers, or customers
> **garnish** (p. 33) withhold part of a paycheck to pay a debt

JEREMY: You know . . .
(He pauses, leaning back against door.)
It's beyond me how the two of you ever got together.

ROSALIE *(quietly, shaking her head):* You aren't the only one to wonder that.

JEREMY: What d'you mean, Mom?

ROSALIE *(Stands and gets on exercise bike.):* Oh—just that no one ever looked at me. I was just known as Elaine's kid sister. *(Starts pedaling.)* So when Dan Botkin came around for me, I thought it was a mistake. And then— when he actually wanted to marry me—me, Rosalie— well . . . *(She pauses.)* I thought I'd died and gone to heaven.

JEREMY: Some heaven.

ROSALIE *(bitterly):* Yeah. Some heaven. I shoulda known better. Like ya been told, your grandfather was a drunk—just as well you didn't know that bum—but your father didn't touch the stuff—and that impressed me. In fact, I thought I was the luckiest girl on the block. *(Sighs.)* But for all the good he did us, he might as well've been a drunk like his old man. Dan's great disappearing act. Now you see him—now you don't. When I think about it, the only thing he ever did for me *(pausing)* was for one brief moment in my life *(pausing again, leaning forward on handlebars)* he made me feel beautiful. *(She shakes her head, starts pedaling.)* I guess that's something.

JEREMY *(embarrassed):* I gotta go, Mom.

ROSALIE *(fiercely):* Jeremy, you tell your father that if he doesn't come up with that check, I got a lawyer who'll call his lines and garnish his pay. You tell him that, Jeremy!

JEREMY: See you later, Mom. *(Turns toward door.)*

ROSALIE *(Stops pedaling. Tenderly, as* JEREMY *exits):* Drive carefully, Jeremy. *(Gets off bike, goes to door and shouts after him.)* Jeremy! You damn well better come back here with that check!

Set becomes black.
Lights come back up on basketball court. JEREMY *and* DARRELL *are sitting on the ground leaning back against the apartment wall that borders the court.*

JEREMY: You see the Cavs last night?

DARRELL: A little, before I had to go to work. They didn't look that bad in the first quarter.

JEREMY: They sure blew it in the fourth. It was pitiful. I shoulda gone over to Renee's instead of watching 'em. I oughta give up on those clowns.

DARRELL: How's Renee?

JEREMY *(depressed):* Mr. Sanduzi wouldn't let me see her.

DARRELL: That's cold.

JEREMY *(sarcastically):* Yeah. Tell me about it. *(He stands and bounces the ball.)* I stop by her apartment on my way to see my dad. She'd even called and asked me to come by. So I get there, I buzz their apartment, and Mr. Sanduzi comes on the intercom. He says *(mimicking a low growling voice)* "Renee's got to help her mother, Botkin. Don't come up here." *(He passes the ball to* DARRELL, *who stands in place and dribbles it.* JEREMY *picks up a can and throws it against the brick wall of the apartment building.)*

DARRELL: It was bad with your dad too—huh?

JEREMY: Yeah. Like I said—he doesn't come to play.

Set darkens.
Earlier that evening. *Spots light* DAN BOTKIN's *apartment bedroom, which is set on risers on the right of stage. It is furnished with a double bed, a dresser, a chair, and an end table that holds a phone and a lamp. A closet is across from the bed; next to the chair is a window. The furnishings are sparse and cheap in contrast to the appearance of* DAN BOTKIN, *a balding, middle-aged man; he is a sharp dresser, wearing a silk sport coat. He has several large gold rings on his fingers.* DAN *is packing his suitcase while* JEREMY *stands by the window, looking out.*

DAN *(cheerily):* Who d'ya think'll make the playoffs, Jeremy?

JEREMY *(looking out the window, turning away from* DAN*)*:
I dunno.

DAN: Sonics are looking good.

JEREMY *(sadly):* Yeah.

DAN: Bullets have a shot. *(Chuckles.)* Little joke there,
Jeremy. *(He pauses, waiting for a response from* JEREMY,
who silently stares out the window.) Hey—not even a
courtesy laugh?

JEREMY: I don't feel like laughing.

DAN: Look—I told you I was sorry about tonight. We'll do
it some other time.

JEREMY *(mumbling, voice fading):* Like always—

DAN: What? Speak up, wouldya?

JEREMY *(shouting):* It's always some other time!

DAN: Listen, kid. You don't have it so bad. Name one time
I ever laid a hand on you, Jeremy.

JEREMY *(expressionless):* You never laid a hand on me, Dad.

DAN: See this watch? Read that name. R-O-L-E-X. Best
watch money can buy, and I earned every damn dime
to pay for it. My old man couldn't blink at a watch like
this. You know, Jeremy—when I wear this watch
(pausing) I feel like somebody. It's insurance, too. I've
never had to—but if I ever got in a jam—it's liquid—
instant cash. But so far *(knocking on dresser)* the Lord
willin' and the river don't rise—I've never had to.

JEREMY *(coldly):* Mom says she needs the check.

DAN *(defensively):* Look, Jeremy, my lines aren't paying me. They're slime. Take it from me, don't ever be a rep in the rag business—it's not worth it. They're supposed to pay me next week. *(Angrily, slamming suitcase shut)* Tell your mother I'm doing the best I can.

JEREMY: When'll you be back?

DAN: This week I've got Akron, Salem, Columbus, and Cincinnati. Probably the end of the week—but I know a gal in Cincinnati, so—might be the first of next if I get lucky. She's pretty—but I got my eyes open. You can't trust pretty women. You want one that'll stick around. I'm sure what led my old man to the bottle was when my mother took off. *(Lifts suitcase off bed.)* You know, the only thing I remember about her is bright-red lips and she smelled like cigarettes and soap. Funny, huh?

JEREMY: Yeah.

DAN: And a little song she used to sing. Only you know what, Jeremy?

JEREMY *(sadly):* What?

DAN: I even forgot the song. *(Gets trench coat from the closet.)* So—tell your mother—next week. *(Takes out wallet and hands JEREMY a five-dollar bill.)* Sorry about dinner. Get yourself something to eat with this, okay?

JEREMY *(taking bill, looking at floor):* Can I see you next week?

DAN: Sure kid—I'll call you.

> *Set becomes black.*
> *Scenes alternate among the basketball court,* JEREMY's *apartment, and* DAN BOTKIN's *apartment.*

JEREMY *(holding ball under his arm):* Beats me why I don't give up on the jerk.

DARRELL *(shrugging):* Maybe for the same reason we don't give up on the Cavs.

JEREMY: Yeah. Every season we think this'll be the year they put it all together. *(Pauses.)* You know— sometimes I feel like this damn ball.

> *Bounces ball four times. Set becomes black. Spot on stage left.*

ROSALIE: *(rapidly):* Tell your father—

> *Ball bounces once, punctuating. Spot on stage right.*

DAN: Tell your mother—

> *Ball bounces once. Spot on stage left.*

ROSALIE: Tell your father—

> *Ball bounces once. Spot on stage right.*

DAN: Tell your mother—

Ball bounces once. Spot on stage left.

ROSALIE: Tell your father—

Ball bounces once. Spot on stage right.

DAN: Tell your mother—

Ball bounces once. Set darkens. Spot on basketball court.

DARRELL *(dribbling toward basket as* JEREMY *guards):* Who was the greatest forward?

JEREMY *(going up for rebound and getting it):* All-time?

DARRELL *(guarding* JEREMY*):* All-time.

JEREMY *(shooting):* Elgin Baylor.

DARRELL *(getting rebound as* JEREMY *guards him):* The Bird Man.

JEREMY *(Catches ball that* DARRELL *passes to him. They pass it back and forth, taking a break from the game):* The greatest guard?

DARRELL: Magic.

JEREMY: Michael Jordan.

DARRELL: Jerry West.

JEREMY: Oscar Robertson.

DARRELL: Gail Goodrich. *(Dribbles toward basket and shoots as* JEREMY *guards.)*

JEREMY (*Getting rebound, takes ball out and shoots, while* DARRELL *guards.*): Center?

DARRELL (*Bounce passes to* JEREMY, *who returns it as they punctuate each player they name with a pass.*): Kareem.

JEREMY: Bill Russell.

DARRELL: Wilt Chamberlain.

JEREMY: Akeem Olajuwon.

DARRELL: Soon to be the greatest?

JEREMY: Mark Eaton. (*Dribbles the ball toward basket. Stops. There is a pause as he holds ball and looks straight at* DARRELL.) Know who I'd like to be?

DARRELL (*standing under basket, leaning against pole*): Who, man?

JEREMY (*quietly*): Denny.

DARRELL: Denny? Who—Denny Crum? Coach at Louisville?

JEREMY (*Bounces ball once, then holds it again.*): Nope.

DARRELL: You mean baseball? That Tigers pitcher Denny McClain?

JEREMY (*Walks across court and sits down, leaning back against the brick wall of the apartment building.*): Denny. The guy that owns all those restaurants. Makes people happy. You know, Denny's. It's open all night. All day.

You can get pancakes and stuff—everybody likes to go there. That Denny.

DARRELL (*Walks to edge of court.* JEREMY *tosses him the ball. He sits down next to* JEREMY.): Yeah. That'd be nice.

JEREMY: You know who else I'd like to be?

DARRELL: Ronald McDonald?

JEREMY: No, man. The guy at the games, all the games—basketball, football, baseball—you name it. The guy that plays "The Star-Spangled Banner."

DARRELL: You serious? How come you wanna be that guy?

JEREMY: Because when he plays that song, all the people in the whole place stand up. All he does is play that one song, and all those thousands of people stand up. God, I think that'd be so great.

Set becomes black.
The Botkin apartment. Nine-thirty the same night. JEREMY *is sitting at the table near the kitchen, eating a sandwich and drinking a glass of milk.*

ROSALIE (*Enters through door off living room. She is dressed in a faded bathrobe and is rubbing cream on her face.*): I thought you had dinner. (*She sits across from him at the table.*)

JEREMY (*not looking at her, taking a bite of the sandwich*): He had to—

ROSALIE *(interrupting him):* Don't talk with your mouth full, Jeremy.

JEREMY *(Slowly chews sandwich. Takes a gulp of milk. Wipes his arm across his mouth.):* We didn't have dinner. He had to leave. *(Continues to finish eating sandwich.)*

ROSALIE *(angrily):* Typical. *(She leans back and folds her arms across her chest and glares at him. Demandingly)* Did you get the check? *(*JEREMY *picks up empty plate and glass and goes to kitchen.* ROSALIE *stands up and calls after him.)* I gotta have that check, Jeremy!

JEREMY *(Returns from kitchen, opens wallet, and takes out five-dollar bill and hands it to* ROSALIE.*):* He gave me this.

ROSALIE *(Grabs money, holds out bill, and looks at it disgustedly.):* That's all you came back with? *(Stares at bill, then stuffs it in her bathrobe pocket and crosses room to door.* JEREMY *stands, holding back of chair, looking helpless. She calls over her shoulder, before exit to bedroom.)* You're as worthless as he is!

Lights dim. JEREMY *sits at table. One elbow is on the table and he props his forehead against his hand. He sits like this for a minute, then gets up and goes to the living room and grabs his Walkman from the coffee table. He puts on the earphones, fiddles with the dial, and returns to the kitchen. He sits again, leaning forward, elbows on the table, with his chin propped in his hands. After a few minutes he takes off the earphones and goes to the kitchen. He disappears for a minute, then returns holding phone, pulling cord, and leaning against the kitchen wall. Set darkens. A spot is on* JEREMY. *At the end of the stage another spot is on* DARRELL, *sitting in a chair, holding a phone.*

JEREMY: Darrell?

DARRELL: Hi, man. How's it goin'?

JEREMY *(pausing a moment, then, defeatedly):* It's air balls— my life's just air balls. *(A pause. Hopelessly)* Nothing I do goes in.

DARRELL *(not really understanding):* Hmmm.

JEREMY *(flatly):* Mr. Sanduzi won't let me near Renee. My dad gives me five bucks and splits. I give it to my mom. She tells me I'm as worthless as he is. *(A pause. He pounds his thigh. Turns toward wall.)* Sometimes— some . . . *(His voice catches.)*

DARRELL: Jeremy?

JEREMY *(Holding phone, he leans his forehead against the wall, his back to the audience. His shoulders shake as he begins to cry quietly. After a few minutes, he takes a deep breath and wipes the back of his hand across his eyes. A long pause. Quietly):* Sometimes I just wanna go to Lake Erie and walk off in the water. It'd be so cold, you'd just feel nothing. Just close your eyes and the water'd come all around and it'd be cold and you'd just feel nothing. *(A long silence.)*

DARRELL: Hum, Jeremy.

JEREMY: What?

DARRELL: I said hum, man. Hum "The Star-Spangled Banner." *(A pause. Forcefully)* DO IT, MAN! JUST DO IT!

Hesitantly, JEREMY *starts to hum the first few bars of "The Star-Spangled Banner," then stops, then starts again.*

DARRELL *(Stands up.):* I'm standing up, Jeremy. (JEREMY *stops humming, half smiles.)* Hum it again, Jeremy. I'm standing up. (JEREMY *hums as the light dims and the curtain drops slowly.)*

CURTAIN

About Jean Davies Okimoto

Jean Davies Okimoto says she decided to be a writer in sixth grade when she and a friend started their own neighborhood newspaper. Since the days of the *Broxton Blab*, Okimoto has gone on to write articles, plays, and novels.

As a child, Jean Davies Okimoto was very close to her grandfather. Not surprisingly, friendship between young and elderly people is a common theme in her books. She also frequently writes about family problems involving divorce and remarriage. Okimoto says, "I have a theory that writers are often people who, as children, felt they weren't heard. Perhaps they develop a strong need to express themselves and tell everybody what they think and how they feel about things."

Ms. Okimoto's books include *Who Did It, Jenny Lake?*; *Jason's Women*; and *Molly By Any Other Name*. She currently lives in Seattle, Washington, where she works as a writer and psychotherapist.

Responding

1. **Personal Response** What would you like to say to Jeremy's mother and father? Why do you think they act the way they do?

2. **Literary Analysis** A *metaphor* describes one thing by seeming to say it is something else. How does the playwright use basketball as a metaphor for Jeremy's life in this play?

3. **Theme Connection** Does this play have a message about family life? If so, what is the message? Explain.

Language Workshop

Commas with Items in a Series Commas are
punctuation marks used to indicate pauses between words
and groups of words. Notice how commas are used in this
sentence from the play:

*It is furnished with a double bed, a dresser, a chair, and an end
table that holds a phone and a lamp.*

When you list more than two items in a series, use
commas between each item. In the following sentences,
add commas where needed.

1. Jeremy has problems talking to his mother his father
and his girlfriend.

2. Dan Botkin travels to cities like Akron Salem Columbus
and Cincinnati.

3. Jeremy and Darrell discuss whether Magic Johnson
Michael Jordan Jerry West Oscar Robinson or Gail
Goodrich is the all-time greatest guard.

Writer's Portfolio

You are a famous advice columnist. Jeremy has written
to you for help. What advice do you have for him? Tell
him in a letter.

BUDGE WILSON

Be-ers and Doers

Mom was a little narrow wisp of a woman. You wouldn't have thought to look at her that she could move a card table; even for me it was sometimes hard to believe the ease with which she could shove around an entire family. Often I tried to explain her to myself. She had been brought up on the South Shore of Nova Scotia. I wondered sometimes if the scenery down there had rubbed off on her—all those granite rocks and fogs and screeching gulls, the slow, laboring springs, and the quick, grudging summers. And then the winters—grayer than doom, and endless.

> **Words to Know**
>
> **conformist** (p. 46) someone who goes along with the rules
>
> **malleable** (p. 46) easily shaped or influenced
>
> **buck the system** (p. 46) to rebel, refuse to go along

I was the oldest. I was around that house for five years before Maudie came along. They were peaceful, those five years, and even now it's easy to remember how everything seemed calm and simple. But now I know why. I was a conformist and malleable as early as three years old; I didn't buck the system. If Mom said, "Hurry, Adelaide!" I hurried. If she said to me, at five, "Fold that laundry, now, Adie, and don't let no grass grow under your feet," I folded it fast. So there were very few battles at first, and no major wars.

Dad, now, he was peaceful just by nature. If a tornado had come whirling in the front door and lifted the roof clear off its hinges, he probably would have just scratched the back of his neck and said, with a kind of slow surprise, "Well! Oho! Just think o' that!" He had been born in the

Annapolis Valley, where the hills are round and gentle, and the summers sunlit and very warm.

"Look at your father!" Mom would say to us later. "He thinks that all he's gotta do is *be*. Well, bein' ain't good enough. You gotta *do*, too. Me, I'm a doer." All the time she was talking, she'd be knitting up a storm, or mixing dough, or pushing a mop—hands forever and ever on the move.

Although Mom was fond of pointing out to us the things our father didn't do, he must have been doing something. Our farm was in the most fertile part of the Valley, and it's true that we had the kind of soil that seemed to make things grow all of their own accord. Those beets and carrots and potatoes just came pushing up into the sunshine with an effortless grace, and they kept us well fed, with plenty left over to sell. But there was weeding and harvesting to do, and all those ten cows to milk—not to mention the thirty apple trees in our orchard to be cared for. I think maybe he just did his work so slowly and quietly that she found it hard to believe he was doing anything at all. Besides, on the South Shore, nothing ever grew without a struggle. And when Dad was through all his chores, or in between times, he liked to just sit on our old porch swing and watch the spring unfold or the summer blossom. And in the fall, he sat there smiling, admiring the rows of vegetables, the giant sunflowers, the golden leaves gathering in the trees of North Mountain.

Maudie wasn't Maudie for the reasons a person is a Ginny or a Gertie or a Susie. She wasn't called Maudie because she was cute. She got that name because if you've got a terrible name like Maud, you have to do something to rescue it. She was called after Mom's Aunt Maud, who was a miser and had the whole Bank of Nova Scotia under her mattress. But she was a crabby old thing who just sat around living on her dead husband's stocks and bonds. A be-er, not a doer. Mom really scorned Aunt Maud and hated her name, but she had high hopes that our family would sometime cash in on that gold mine under the mattress. She hadn't counted on Aunt Maud going to Florida one winter and leaving her house in the care of a dear old friend. The dear old friend emptied the contents of the mattress, located Aunt Maud's three diamond rings, and took off for Mexico, leaving the pipes to freeze and the cat to die of starvation. After that, old Aunt Maud couldn't have cared less if everybody in the whole district had been named after her. She was that bitter.

Maudie was so like Mom that it was just as if she'd

> ### Words to Know
>
> **miser** (p. 48) someone who loves money and hates to share it
>
> **clone** (p. 49) an exact copy of an original form
>
> **Member of Parliament** (p. 49) an elected official who serves on Parliament, the national lawmaking body of Canada

been cut out with a cookie cutter from the same dough. Raced around at top speed all through her growing-up time, full of projects and sports and hobbies and gossip and nerves. And mad at everyone who sang a different tune.

But this story's not about Maudie. I guess you could say it's mostly about Albert.

Albert was the baby. I was eight years old when he was born, and I often felt like he was my own child. He was special to all of us, I guess, except maybe to Maudie, and when Mom saw him for the first time, I watched a slow soft tenderness in her face that was a rare thing for any of us to see. I was okay because I was cooperative, and I knew she loved me. Maudie was her clone, and almost like a piece of herself, so they admired one another, although they were too similar to be at peace for very long. But Albert was something different. Right away, I knew she was going to pour into Albert something that didn't reach the rest of us, except in part. As time went on, this scared me. I could see that she'd made up her mind that Albert was going to be a perfect son. That meant, among other things, that he was going to be a fast-moving doer. And even when he was three or four, it wasn't hard for me to know that this wasn't going to be easy. Because Albert was a be-er. *Born* that way.

As the years went by, people around Wilmot used to say, "Just look at that family of Hortons. Mrs. Horton made one child—Maudie. Then there's Adelaide, who's her own self. But Albert, now. Mr. Horton made him all by himself. They're alike as two pine needles."

And just as nice, I could have added. But Mom wasn't either pleased or amused. "You're a bad influence on that boy, Stanley," she'd say to my dad. "How's he gonna get any ambition if all he sees is a father who can spend up to an hour leanin' on his hoe, starin' at the Mountain?" Mom had it all worked out that Albert was going to be a lawyer or a doctor or a Member of Parliament.

My dad didn't argue with her, or at least not in an

angry way. "Aw, c'mon now, Dorothy," he might say to her, real slow. "The vegetables are comin' along jest fine. No need to shove them more than necessary. It does a man good to look at them hills. You wanta try it sometime. They tell you things."

"Nothin' *I* need t'hear," she'd huff, and disappear into the house, clattering pans, thumping the mop, scraping the kitchen table across the floor to get at more dust. And Albert would just watch it all, saying not a word, chewing on a piece of grass.

Mom really loved my dad, even though he drove her nearly crazy. Lots more went on than just nagging and complaining. If you looked really hard, you could see that. If it hadn't been for Albert and wanting him to be a four-star son, she mightn't have bothered to make Dad look so useless. Even so, when they sat on the swing together at night, you could feel their closeness. They didn't hold hands or anything. Her hands were always too busy embroidering, crocheting, mending something, or just swatting mosquitoes. But they liked to be together. Personal chemistry, I thought as I grew older, is a mysterious and contrary thing.

One day, Albert brought his report card home from school, and Mom looked at it hard and anxious, eyebrows knotted. " 'Albert seems a nice child,' " she read aloud to all of us, more loudly than necessary, " 'but his marks could be better. He spends too much time looking out the window, dreaming.' " She paused. No one spoke.

"Leanin' on his hoe," continued Mom testily. "Albert!" she snapped at him. "You pull up your socks by Easter or you're gonna be in deep trouble."

Dad stirred uneasily in his chair. "Aw, Dorothy," he mumbled. "Leave him be. He's a good kid."

"Or could be. *Maybe*," she threw back at him. "What he seems like to me is rock-bottom lazy. He sure is slow-moving, and could be he's slow in the head, too. Dumb."

Albert's eyes flickered at that word, but that's all. He just stood there and watched, eyes level.

"But I love him a lot," continued Mom, "and unlike you, I don't plan t'just sit around and watch him grow dumber. If it's the last thing I do, I'm gonna light a fire under his feet."

Albert was twelve then, and the nagging began to accelerate in earnest.

"How come you got a low mark in your math test?"

"I don't like math. It seems like my head don't want it."

"But do you *work* at it?"

"Well, no. Not much. Can't see no sense in workin' hard at something I'll never use. I can add up our grocery bill. I pass. That's enough."

"Not for me, it ain't," she'd storm back at him. "No baseball practice for you until you get them sums perfect. Ask Maudie t'check them." Maudie used to drum that arithmetic into him night after night. She loved playing schoolteacher, and that's how she eventually ended up. And a cross one.

One thing Albert was good at, though, was English class. By the time he got to high school, he spent almost as much time reading as he did staring into space. His way of speaking changed. He stopped dropping his *g*'s. He said *isn't* instead of *ain't*. His tenses were all neated up. He wasn't putting on airs. I just think that all those people in his books started being more real to him than his own neighbors. He loved animals, too. He made friends with the calves and even the cows. Mutt and Jeff, our two grey cats, slept on his bed every night. Often you could see him out in the fields, talking to our dog, while he was working.

"Always messin' around with animals," complained Mom. "Sometimes I think he's three parts woman and one part child. He's fifteen years old, and last week I caught him bawlin' in the hayloft after we had to shoot that male calf. Couldn't understand why y' can't go on feedin' an animal that'll never produce milk."

"Nothing wrong with liking animals," I argued. I was home for the weekend from my secretarial job in Wolfville.

"Talkin' to dogs and cryin' over cattle is not what I'd call a short cut to success. And the cats spend so much time with him that they've forgotten why we brought them into the house in the first place. For mice."

"Maybe there's more to life than success or mice," I said. I was twenty-three now, and more interested in Albert than in conformity.

Mom made a "huh" sound through her nose. "Adelaide Horton," she said, "when you're my age, you'll understand more about success and mice than you do now. Or the lack of them." She turned on her heel and went back in the house. "And if you can't see," she said through the screen door, "why I don't want Albert to end up exactly like your father, then you've got even less sense than I thought you had. I don't want any son of mine goin' through life just satisfied to *be*." Then I could hear her banging around in the kitchen.

I looked off the verandah out at the front field, where Dad and Albert were raking up hay for the cattle, slowly, with lots of pauses for talk. All of a sudden they stopped, and Albert pointed up to the sky. It was fall, and four long wedges of geese were flying far above us, casting down their strange muffled cry. The sky was cornflower blue, and the wind was sending white clouds scudding across it. My breath was caught with the beauty of it all, and as I looked at Dad and Albert, they threw away their rakes and lay down flat on their backs, right there in the front pasture, in order to drink in the sky. And after all the geese had passed over, they stayed like that for maybe twenty minutes more.

We WERE ALL HOME FOR CHRISTMAS THE YEAR Albert turned eighteen. Maudie was having her Christmas break from teaching, and she was looking skinnier and more tight-lipped than I remembered her. I was there with my husband and my new baby, Jennifer, and Albert was even quieter than usual. But content, I thought. Not making any waves. Mom had intensified her big campaign to have him go to Acadia University in the fall. "Pre-law," she said, "or maybe teacher training. Anyways, you gotta go. A man has to be successful." She avoided my father's eyes. "In the fall," she said. "For sure."

"It's Christmas," said Dad, without anger. "Let's just be happy and forget all them plans for a few days." He was sitting at the kitchen table breaking up the bread slowly, slowly, for the turkey stuffing. He chuckled. "I've decided to be a doer this Christmas."

"And if the doin's bein' done at that speed," she said, taking the bowl from him, "we'll be eatin' Christmas dinner on New Year's Day." She started to break up the bread so quickly that you could hardly focus on her flying fingers.

Christmas came and went. It was a pleasant time. The food was good; Jennifer slept right through dinner and didn't cry all day. We listened to the Queen's Christmas message; we opened presents. Dad gave Mom a ring with a tiny sapphire in it, although she'd asked for a new vacuum cleaner.

"I like this better," she said, and looked as though she might cry.

"We'll get the vacuum cleaner in January," he said, "That's no kind of gift to get for Christmas. It's a work thing."

She looked as if she might say something, but she didn't.

It was on December 26th that it happened. That was the day of the fire.

It was a lazy day. We all got up late, except me, of course, who had to feed the baby at two and at six. But when we were all up, we just sort of lazed around in our dressing gowns, drinking coffee, admiring one another's presents, talking about old times, singing a carol or two around the old organ. Dad had that look on him that he used to get when all his children were in his house at the same time. Like he was in temporary possession of the best that life had to offer. Even Mom was softened up, and she sat by the grate fire and talked a bit, although there was still a lot of jumping up and down and rushing out to the kitchen to check the stove or cut up vegetables. Me, I think that on the day after Christmas you should just eat up leftovers and enjoy a slow state of collapse. But you can't blame a person for feeding you. It's handy to have a Martha or two around a house that's already equipped with three Marys. Albert was the best one to watch, though. To me, anyway. He was sitting on the floor in his striped pajamas, holding Jennifer, rocking her, and singing songs to her in a low, crooning voice. Tender, I thought, the way I like a man to be.

Albert had just put the baby back in her carriage when a giant spark flew out of the fireplace. It hit the old nylon carpet like an incendiary bomb, and the rug burst into flames. Mom started waving an old afghan over it, as though she was blowing out a match, but all she was doing was fanning the fire.

While most of us stood there in immovable fear, Albert had already grabbed Jennifer, carriage and all, and rushed out to the barn with her. He was back in a flash, just in time to see Maudie's dressing gown catch fire. He pushed her down on the floor and lay on top of her to smother the flames, and then he was up on his feet again, taking charge.

"Those four buckets in the summer kitchen!" he yelled. "Start filling them!" He pointed to Mom and Dad, who obeyed him like he was a general and they were the privates. To my husband he roared, "Get out to th' barn

---

Words to Know

Martha and Mary (p. 54) Two sisters who appear in the New Testament of the Bible. Martha worked hard to take care of her houseguests while Mary preferred to relax and enjoy their company.

incendiary bomb (p. 54) a bomb that is made to start fires

afghan (p. 54) a shawl or blanket that is knitted or crocheted

immovable (p. 54) cannot be moved

and keep that baby warm!"

"And you!" He pointed to me. "Call the fire department. It's 825-3131." In the meantime, the smoke was starting to fill the room and we were all coughing. Little spits of fire were crawling up the curtains, and Maudie was just standing there, shrieking.

Before Mom and Dad got back with the water, Albert was out in the back bedroom hauling up the carpet. Racing in with it over his shoulder, he bellowed, "Get out o' the way!" and we all moved. Then he slapped the carpet over the flames on the floor, and the fire just died without so much as a protest. Next he grabbed one of the big cushions off the sofa, and chased around after the little lapping flames on curtains and chairs and table runners, smothering them. When Mom and Dad appeared with a bucket in each hand, he shouted,

"Stop! Don't use that stuff! No need t'have water damage too!"

Then Albert was suddenly still, hands hanging at his sides with the fingers spread. He smiled shyly.

"It's out," he said.

I rushed up and hugged him, wailing like a baby, loving him, thanking him. For protecting Jennifer—from smoke, from fire, from cold, from heaven knows what. Everyone opened windows and doors, and before too long, even the smoke was gone. It smelled pretty awful, but no one cared.

When we all gathered again in the parlor to clear up the mess, and Jennifer was back in my bedroom asleep, Mom stood up and looked at Albert, her eyes ablaze with admiration—and with something else I couldn't put my finger on.

"Albert!" she breathed, "We all thank you! You've saved the house, the baby, all of us, even our Christmas presents. I'm proud, proud, *proud* of you."

Albert just stood there, smiling quietly, but very pale. His hands were getting red and sort of puckered looking.

Mom took a deep breath. "And *that*," she went on, "is what I've been looking for, all of your life. Some sort of sign that you were one hundred percent alive. And now we all know you are. Maybe even a lick more alive than the rest of us. So!" She folded her arms, and her eyes bored into him. "I'll have no more excuses from you now. No one who can put out a house fire single-handed and rescue a niece and a sister and organize us all into a fire brigade is gonna sit around for the rest of his life gatherin' dust. No siree! Or leanin' against no hoe. Why, you even had the fire department number tucked away in your head. Just imagine what you're gonna be able to do with them kind o' brains! I'll never, never rest until I see you educated and successful. Doin' what you was meant to do. I'm just proud of you, Albert. So terrible proud!"

Members of the fire department were starting to arrive at the front door, but Albert ignored them. He was white now, like death, and he made a low and terrible sound. He didn't exactly pull his lips back from his teeth and growl, but the result was similar. It was like the sound a dog makes before he leaps for the throat. And what he said was *"You jest leave me be, woman!"*

We'd never heard words like this coming out of Albert, and the parlor was as still as night as we all listened.

"You ain't proud o' me, Mom," he whispered, all his beautiful grammar gone. "Yer jest proud o' what you want me t'be. And I got some news for you. Things I shoulda tole you years gone by. *I ain't gonna be what you want.*" His voice was starting to quaver now, and he was trembling all over. "*I'm gonna be me.* And it seems like if that's ever gonna happen, it'll have t'be in some other place. And I plan t'do somethin' about that before the day is out."

Then he shut his eyes and fainted right there down onto the charred carpet. The firemen carted him off to the hospital, where he was treated for shock and second-degree burns. He was there for three weeks.

MY DAD DIED OF A STROKE WHEN HE WAS SIXTY-SIX. "Not enough exercise," said Mom, after she'd got over the worst part of her grief. "Too much sittin' around watchin' the lilacs grow. No way for his blood to circulate good." Me, I ask myself if he just piled up his silent tensions until he burst wide open. Maybe he wasn't all that calm and peaceful after all. Could be he was just waiting, like Albert, for the moment when it would all come pouring out. Perhaps that wasn't the way it was; but all the same, I wonder.

Mom's still going strong at eighty-eight. Unlike Dad's, her blood must circulate like a racing stream, what with all that rushing around; she continues to move as if she's being chased. She's still knitting and preserving and scrubbing and mending and preaching. She'll never get one of those tension diseases like angina or cancer or even arthritis, because she doesn't keep one single thing bottled up inside her for more than five minutes. Out it all comes like air out of a flat tire–with either a hiss or a bang.

Perhaps it wasn't growing up on the South Shore that made Mom the way she is. I live on that coast now, and I've learned that it's more than just gray and stormy. I know about the long sandy beaches and the peace that comes of a clear horizon. I've seen the razzle-dazzle colors of the low-lying scarlet bushes in the fall, blazing against the black of the spruce trees and the bluest sky in the world. I'm familiar with the way one single radiant summer day can make you forget a whole fortnight of fog—like birth after a long labor. You might say that the breakers out on the reefs are angry or full of threats. To me, though, those waves are leaping and dancing, wild with freedom and joyfulness. But I think Mom was in a hurry from the moment she was born. I doubt if she ever stopped long enough to take notice of things like that.

Albert left home as soon as he got out of the hospital.

He worked as a stevedore in Halifax for a number of years, and when he got enough money saved, he bought a little run-down house close to Digby, with a view of the Bay of Fundy. He's got a small chunk of land that's so black and rich that it doesn't take any pushing at all to make the flowers and vegetables grow. He has a cow and a beagle and four cats—and about five hundred books. He fixes lawn mowers and boat engines for the people in his area, and he putters away at his funny little house. He writes pieces for *The Digby Courier*, and *The Novascotian*, and last winter he confessed to me that he writes poetry. He's childless and wifeless, but he has the time of day for any kid who comes around to hear stories or to have a broken toy fixed. He keeps an old rocker out on the edge of the cliff, where he can sit and watch the tides of Fundy rise and fall.

About Budge Wilson

Budge Wilson and her husband Alan make their home in Nova Scotia, on the Atlantic coast of

Canada. The harshly beautiful province of Nova Scotia is the setting for *The Leaving*, the collection of short stories from which "Be-ers and Doers" is taken.

Wilson did not begin writing for young adults until the age of fifty. She has written several young adult novels, including *Breakdown*, which in 1988 received an award from the Canadian Children's Book Centre.

Responding

1. **Personal Response** Which character in the story do you think you are the most like? Tell why.

2. **Literary Analysis** Some of the characters in the story speak in *dialect,* a pattern of speech used by members of a particular group that differs from standard English. Find examples of dialect in the story. Tell why you think the author would have her characters speak this way.

3. **Theme Connection** Draw a diagram that shows how the members of the Horton family get along with each other. Then compare the Hortons to another family you have read about in this unit. Are any of the relationships similar? Which family seems to be happier?

Language Workshop

Direct Quotations When a speaker's exact words are written down, this is a *direct quotation.* When you use a direct quotation, place quotation marks before and after the speaker's exact words.

When the speaker is named after the quotation, you usually use a comma to set off the speaker from the words spoken. Example: *"Nothing wrong with liking animals,"* I argued. But if the quotation ends with a question mark or an exclamation point, no comma is used. Example: *"Look at your father!"* Mom would say to us later.

Add punctuation to the following.

1. I can't live at home anymore said Albert

2. Why is that boy so lazy Mom would always ask

3. Help said Maudie The rug is on fire

Writer's Portfolio

Are you a be-er or a doer? Are you a be-er in some situations and a doer in others? Write down your thoughts about whether be-ers or doers have a better attitude toward life.

The Last Word

"I did that," says my memory.
"I did not," says my pride; and
memory yields.
—Nietzsche, *Beyond Good and Evil*

My MOTHER OPENS THE PHOTO ALBUM TO A PICTURE of my father as a very young man in an army uniform. She says to me, "You had not met your father yet when this photograph was taken. He left for Panama when I was a couple of months pregnant with you, and didn't get back until you were two years old."

I have my own "memories" about this time in my life, but I decide to ask her a few questions, anyway. It is always fascinating to me to hear her version of the past we shared, to see what shades of pastel she will choose to paint my childhood's "summer afternoon."

"How did I react to his homecoming?" I ask my mother whose eyes are already glazing over with grief and affection for her husband, my father, dead in a car wreck now for over a decade. There are few pictures of him in middle age in her album. She prefers to remember him as the golden boy she married, forever a young man in military uniform coming home laden with gifts from exotic places for us.

"You were the happiest little girl on the island, I believe." She says smiling down at his picture. "After a

---

Words to Know

inseparable (p.61) constantly together
jarred (p.61) shocked
disparity (p.61) difference, being unalike
recollections (p.61) memories

few days of getting acquainted, you two were inseparable. He took you everywhere with him."

"Mother . . ." In spite of my resolve, I am jarred by the disparity of our recollections of this event. "Was there a party for him when he returned? Did you roast a pig out in the backyard? I remember a fire . . . and an accident . . . involving me."

She lifts her eyes to meet mine. She looks mildly surprised.

"You were only a baby . . . what is it that you think happened on that day?"

"I remember that I was put in a crib and left alone. I remember many people talking, music, laughter." I want her to finish the story. I want my mother to tell me that what I remember is true. But she is stubborn too. Her memories are precious to her and although she accepts my explanations that what I write in my poems and stories is mainly the product of my imagination, she wants certain things she believes are true to remain sacred, untouched by my fictions.

"And what is this accident you remember? What do you think happened at your father's homecoming party?" Her voice has taken on the deadly serious tone that has always made me swallow hard. I am about to be set straight. I decide to forge ahead. *This is just an experiment*, I tell myself. I am comparing notes on the past with my mother. This can be managed without resentment. After all, we are both intelligent adults.

"I climbed out of the crib, and walked outside. I think . . . I fell into the fire."

My mother shakes her head. She is now angry, and worse, disappointed in me. She turns the pages of the book until she finds my birthday picture. A short while after his return from Panama, my father is supposed to have spent a small fortune giving me the fanciest birthday party ever seen in our pueblo. He wanted to make up for all the good times together we had missed. My mother has told me the story dozens of times. There are many photographs documenting the event. Every time I visit a relative someone brings out an album and shows me a face I've memorized: that of a very solemn two-year-old dressed in a fancy dress sent by an aunt from New York just for the occasion, surrounded by toys and decorations, a huge, ornate cake in front of me. I am not smiling in any of these pictures.

My mother turns the album toward me. "Where were you burned?" she asks, letting a little irony sharpen the hurt in her voice. "Does that look like a child who was neglected for one moment?"

"So what really happened on that day, Mami?" I look

> ### Words in Spanish
>
> **pueblo** (p.62) small town
> **Mami** (p.62) Mom, Mother
> **Hija** (p.63) Daughter
> **un momentito, nada más, Hija** (p.63) no more than a moment, Daughter
> **pan-pan** (p.63) a spanking
> **Es la pura verdad** (p.63) It is the pure truth.

at the two-year-old's face again. There is a celebration going on around her, but her eyes—and my memory—tell me that she is not a part of it.

"There was a little accident involving the fire that day, Hija," my mother says in a gentler voice. She is the Keeper of the Past. As the main witness of my childhood, she has the power to refute my claims.

"This is what happened. You were fascinated by a large book your father brought home from his travels. I believe it was a foreign language dictionary. We couldn't pry it away from you, though it was almost as big as you. I took my eyes off you for one moment, *un momentito, nada más, Hija*, and you somehow dragged that book to the pit where we were roasting a pig, and you threw it in."

"Do you know why I did that, Mother?" I am curious to hear her explanation. I dimly recall early mentions of a valuable book I supposedly did away with in the distant past.

"Why do children do anything they do? The fire attracted you. Maybe you wanted attention. I don't know. But," she shakes her finger at me in mock accusation, "if you remember a burning feeling, the location of this fire was your little behind after I gave you some *pan-pan* to make sure you didn't try anything like that ever again."

We both laugh at her use of the baby word for a spanking that I had not heard her say in three decades.

"That is what really happened?"

"*Es la pura verdad*," she says. "Nothing but the truth."

But that is not how *I* remember it.

My Father in the Navy

Stiff and immaculate
in the white cloth of his uniform
and a round cap on his head like a halo,
he was an apparition on leave from a shadow-world
and only flesh and blood when he rose from below
the waterline where he kept watch over the engines
and dials making sure the ship parted the waters
on a straight course.
Mother, brother and I kept vigil
on the nights and dawns of his arrival,
watching the corner beyond the neon sign of a quasar
for the flash of white, our father like an angel
heralding a new day.
His homecomings were the verses
we composed over the years making up
the siren's song that kept him coming back
from the bellies of iron whales
and into our nights
like the evening prayer.

About Judith Ortiz Cofer

Judith Ortiz Cofer was born in a village in Puerto Rico.
After a few years, her family began living half of each

year in New Jersey, where her father was
stationed in the U.S. Navy. In her autobio-
graphical book *Silent Dancing*, Cofer writes
about her family life in two very different
cultures.

Judith Ortiz Cofer now lives in Georgia.
She has published books of poetry and a
novel, *Line of the Sun*.

Responding

1. **Personal Response** What do *you* think really happened at the homecoming party? Why?

2. **Literary Analysis** In her poem, Cofer says her father is "an apparition," "like an angel." What does this *figurative language* reveal about her relationship with him?

3. **Theme Connection** The author says her mother is "Keeper of the Past." What does this mean? What role does a "Keeper of the Past" play within a family?

Language Workshop

Word Families In "The Last Word," the author reflects on her childhood memories. The words *memory* and *remember* come from the Latin word *memoria*. Make a list of three or four words that belong to this word family. Write a brief definition of each word. You may want to consult a dictionary.

Writer's Portfolio

Write down your impressions of a memorable event from your childhood. Then ask someone in your family to write down his or her memories of the event. Compare the two accounts. Do you remember the same things about the event?

All in the Family

PROJECTS

Family Portrait

Each of the families you've read about is unique in one way or another. Working alone or in pairs, create a collage that captures that uniqueness. Use photographs, magazine cut-outs, your own sketches, three-dimensional objects— or anything that will create a vivid picture of the family you've chosen to portray.

Instant Replay

Every family experiences conflict of one form or another, and the families you've read about are no exception. In small groups, choose one story to reenact, offering a new version of how the central conflict might have been resolved. Perform your reenactment for the rest of the class. Is your version of the story more effective? How so? Let the rest of the class decide.

Writing About Families

Author Jean Davies Okimoto says that writers are people who, as children, felt they weren't heard. Well, here's your chance to be heard. Write an account of an event—real or imagined—that takes place within a family. Use vivid language to describe the experience, and let your audience know how individual family members react.

FURTHER READING

These novels have a lot to say about families. You may want to add a few of them to your reading list.

Where the Lilies Bloom by Bill and Vera Cleaver. When her father dies, 14-year-old Mary Call must take charge of her brother and sisters. Afraid they will be separated, the children hide their father's death from the outside world and struggle to survive a long winter in the mountains.

Jacob Have I Loved by Katherine Paterson. Living on a small island in Chesapeake Bay, Louise longs for a chance to pursue her dreams. But her twin sister Caroline always captures the spotlight—and the opportunities. As Louise struggles to find her place in the world, she learns to take a new look at those she loves.

A Raisin in the Sun by Lorraine Hansberry. In this play, an African American family living in a Chicago housing project hopes to escape from poverty by buying a home in the suburbs. But tensions within and outside the family threaten to destroy their fragile dream.

Unfinished Portrait of Jessica by Richard Peck. Jessica is spending the holidays in Mexico with her handsome, fascinating father. But even though Mexico seems like paradise, her father is not quite the wonderful man she has always believed in.

The Grapes of Wrath by John Steinbeck. The Joad family leaves their farm in the Oklahoma "dustbowl" in the hope of finding a better life. Their struggles do not grow easier, however, as they begin working as migrant farm laborers in California.

UNIT 2

Who Am I?

Who am I? What do I want from life, and how will I go about getting it?

Some people spend their whole lives trying to answer those questions. Right now, how would you respond? Do you find it a challenge to figure out who you are and what you want to become?

The characters in the following selections each ask the question "Who am I?" and then try their best to answer honestly. In fact, you might say that some of their answers are brutally honest. Are you ready to ask the same question? Are you ready to give an honest answer?

On the Bridge

"I BEAT THE CRAP OUT OF THIS GUY AT THE mall yesterday, " Adam Lockwood said. He was leaning on the stone wall of the bridge, smoking a cigarette and watching the cars speed by on the highway beneath him. His black hair fell down into his eyes.

"How come?" Seth Dawson asked, leaning on the stone wall next to him.

Adam shrugged. The turned-up collar of his leather jacket rose and fell along his neck. "He just bugged me, that's all. He was bigger, probably a senior. I guess he

thought he could take me 'cause I was smaller. But I don't let anyone push me around."

"What'd you do to him?" Seth asked. He too was smoking a cigarette. It was his first ever, and he wasn't really inhaling. Just holding the smoke in his mouth for a while and then blowing it out.

"I'm pretty sure I broke his nose," Adam said. "I couldn't hang around to find out because the guy in the pizza place called the cops. I'm already in enough trouble with them."

"What for?" Seth asked. He noticed that when Adam took a drag, he seemed to hold the smoke in his mouth and then blow it out his nose. But it was probably just a different way of inhaling. Adam definitely inhaled.

"They just don't like me," Adam said. "You know how it is."

Seth nodded. Actually, he didn't know how it was. But there was no way he'd admit that. It was just pretty cool to think that the cops didn't like you. Seth was pretty sure the

cops didn't even know who he was.

The two boys looked back down at the highway. It was a warm spring afternoon, and instead of taking the bus home after school, they'd decided to walk to the diner. There Adam had instructed Seth on how to feed quarters into the cigarette machine and get a pack of Marlboros. Seth had been really nervous about getting caught, but Adam told him it was no sweat. If the owner came out, you'd just tell him you were picking them up for your mother.

Words to Know

fraud (p. 72) a fake, a cheater

abutment (p. 73) the support for an arch or a bridge

span (p. 73) the part of a bridge that runs between the supports

overpass (p. 74) a bridge over a road or railroad

Now the pack of Marlboros was sticking out of the breast pocket of Seth's new denim jacket. It wasn't supposed to look new because he'd ripped the sleeves off and had washed it in the washing machine a hundred times to make it look old and worn. But somehow it had come out looking new and worn. Seth had decided to wear it anyway, but he felt like a fraud. Like a kid trying to imitate someone truly cool. On the other hand, Adam's leather jacket looked authentically old and worn. The right sleeve was ripped and the leather was creased and pliant. It looked like he'd been in a hundred fights with it. Seth had never been in a fight in his life. Not a serious punching fight, at least.

The other thing about Adam was, he wore the leather jacket to school every day. Adam wasn't one of these kids who kept their cool clothes in their lockers and only wore them in school because their parents wouldn't let them wear them at home. Seth had parents like that. His mother would have had a fit if she ever saw him wearing his sleeveless denim jacket, so he had to hide it in the garage every day before he went into the house. Then in the morning when he left for school he'd go through the garage and pick it up.

Seth leaned forward and felt the smooth cold granite of the bridge with his fingers. The bridge was old and made of large granite blocks. Its heavy stone abutments stood close to the cars that sped past on the highway beneath it. Newer bridges were made of steel. Their spans were longer and the abutments were farther from the road.

On the highway, a red Fiat convertible approached with two girls riding in the front seat. Adam waved, and one of the girls waved back. A second later the car shot under the bridge and disappeared. He turned to Seth and grinned. "Maybe they'll get off on the exit ramp and come back," he said.

"You think?" Seth asked. Actually, the thought made him nervous. "They must be old enough at least to drive."

"So?" Adam asked. "I go out with older girls all the time."

"Really?" Seth asked.

"Sure," Adam said. He took another drag off his cigarette and blew the smoke out of his nose. Seth wanted to try that, but he was afraid he'd start to cough or do something else equally uncool.

"What do you do with them?" Seth asked.

Adam glanced at him with a sly smile. "What do you think I do with them?"

"I mean, do you go out?"

"Sure, if they want to take me out, we go out. Otherwise sometimes we just hang around and make out."

Seth was awestruck. At a party once he'd played spin the bottle and pass the orange and had kissed a few girls in the process. But he'd never seriously made out.

In the distance a big semitrailer appeared on the highway. Adam raised his arm in the air and pumped his fist up and down. The driver responded with three loud blasts of his air horns. A moment later the semi rumbled under them and disappeared.

"Let me try that," Seth said. Another truck was coming and he leaned over the stone ledge and jerked his arm up and down. But the trucker ignored him.

Adam laughed.

"How come it didn't work?" Seth asked.

"You gotta do it a special way," Adam told him.

"Show me," Seth said.

"Can't, man," Adam said. "You just have to have the right touch. It's something you're born with."

Seth smirked. It figured. It was just his luck to be born without the touch that made truckers blow their horns.

The traffic was gradually getting thicker as the afternoon rush hour approached. Many of the drivers and passengers in the cars seemed unaware of the two boys on the overpass. But a few others stared up through their windshields at them.

"Bet they're wondering if we're gonna drop something on them," Adam said. He lifted his hand in the air as if he was holding an imaginary rock. On the highway more of the people in the cars were watching now. Suddenly Adam threw his arm forward. Even though there was nothing in his hand, a woman driving a blue Toyota put her hands up in fear. Her car swerved momentarily out of its lane.

Seth felt his jaw drop. He couldn't believe Adam had done that. If the car had been going faster it might have gone out of control and crashed into the stone abutment next to the highway.

Meanwhile Adam grinned at him. "Scared the crap out of her."

"Maybe we ought to go," Seth said, suddenly worried that they were going to get into trouble. What if a cop had seen them? Or what if the woman was really mad?

"Why?" Adam asked.

"She could get off and come back here."

Adam shrugged. "Let her," he said. "The last person in

the world I'd be afraid of is some old lady." He took a drag off his cigarette and turned away to watch the cars again.

Seth kept glancing toward the exit ramp to see if the woman in the blue Toyota had gotten off. He was really tempted to leave, but he stayed because he liked being with Adam. It made him feel good that a cool guy like Adam let him hang around.

A few minutes passed and the blue Toyota still did not appear on the exit ramp. Seth relaxed a little. He had smoked his Marlboro almost all the way down to the filter and his mouth tasted awful. Smoke kept getting in his eyes and making them water. He dropped the cigarette to the sidewalk and crushed it under his sneaker, relieved to be finished with it.

"Here's the way to do it," Adam said. He took the butt of his cigarette between his thumb and middle finger and flicked it over the side of the bridge and down into the traffic. With a burst of red sparks it hit the windshield of a black Camaro passing below. Adam turned and grinned. Seth smiled back uncomfortably. He was beginning to wonder just how far Adam would go.

Neither of them saw the black Camaro pull off onto the exit ramp and come up behind them on the bridge. Seth didn't notice it until he heard a door slam. He turned and saw three big guys getting out of the car. They were all wearing nylon sweatsuits, and they looked strong. Seth suddenly decided that it was time to go, but he quickly realized that the three guys had spread out, cutting off any way to escape. He and Adam were surrounded.

"Uh, Adam." Seth nudged him with his elbow.

"Wha—?" Adam turned around and looked shocked. In the meantime the three big guys were coming closer. Seth and Adam backed against the bridge wall. Seth felt his stomach tighten. His heart began to beat like a machine gun. Adam looked pretty scared too. Was it Seth's imagination, or was his friend trembling?

"Which one of you twerps flicked that butt on my car?" The question came from the husky guy with a black moustache and long black hair that curled behind his ears.

Seth and Adam glanced at each other. Seth was determined not to tell. He didn't believe in squealing on his friends. But suddenly he noticed that all three guys were staring at him. He quickly looked at Adam and saw why. Adam was pointing at him.

Before Seth could say anything, the husky guy reached forward and lifted him off the ground by the collar of his jacket. His feet kicked in the air uselessly for a second and then he was thrown against the front fender of the Camaro. He hit with a thud and lost his breath. Before he had a chance to recover, the guy grabbed him by the hair and forced his face toward the windshield.

"Lick it off," he grumbled.

Seth didn't know what he was talking about. He tried to raise his head, but the husky guy pushed his face closer to the windshield. God, he was strong.

"I said, lick it."

Lick what? Seth wanted to shout. Then he looked down at the glass and saw the little spot of gray ash where Adam's cigarette had hit. Oh, no. He stiffened. The thought made him sick. He tried to twist his head around, but the guy leaned his weight against Seth and pushed his face down again.

"Till it's clean," the guy said, pressing Seth's face down until it was only an inch from the smooth tinted glass. Seth stared at the little spot of ash. With the husky guy's weight on him, he could hardly breathe. The car's fender was digging into his ribs. Where was Adam?

The husky guy leaned harder against him, squeezing Seth painfully against the car. He pushed Seth's face down until it actually pressed against the cool glass. Seth could feel a spasm in his chest as his lungs cried for air. But he clamped his mouth closed. He wasn't going to give the guy the satisfaction of seeing him lick that spot.

The husky guy must have known it. Suddenly he pulled Seth's head up, then slammed it back down against the windshield. *Wham!* Seth reeled backwards, his hands covering his nose and mouth. Everything felt numb, and he was certain his nose and some teeth were broken. He slipped and landed in a sitting position, bending forward, his throbbing face buried in his hands.

A second passed and he heard someone laugh. Looking up he saw the three guys get back into the Camaro. The car lurched away, leaving rubber.

"You're bleeding." Adam was standing over him. Seth took his hand away from his mouth and saw that it was covered with bright red blood. It was dripping down from his nose and chin onto his denim jacket, leaving red spots. He tilted his head back, trying to stop the bleeding. At the same time he squeezed the bridge of his nose. It hurt, but somehow he knew it was not broken after all. He touched his front teeth with his tongue. They were all still there, and none felt loose.

"You want a hand?" Adam asked.

Seth nodded and Adam helped pull him up slowly. He was shaky on his feet and worried that his nose was going to start bleeding again. He looked down and saw that his denim jacket was covered with blood.

"I tried to help you," Adam said, "but one of them held a knife on me."

Seth glanced at him.

"It was a small knife," Adam said. "I guess he didn't want anyone to see it."

Seth felt his nose again. It was swollen and throbbed painfully. "Why'd you point at me?" he asked.

"I figured I could jump them if they made a move at you," Adam said. "How could I know they had knives?"

Seth shook his head. He didn't believe Adam. He started to walk toward home.

"You gonna make it okay?" Adam asked.

Seth nodded. He just wanted to be alone.

"I'll get those guys for you, man," Adam said. "I think I once saw one of them at the diner. I'm gonna go back there and see. Okay?"

Seth nodded again. He didn't even turn to watch Adam go.

On the way to his house, Seth stopped near some garbage cans a neighbor had put on the curb for collection. He looked down at his denim jacket. The spots of blood had turned dark. If he took it home and washed it now, the stains would probably make it look pretty cool. Like a jacket that had been worn in tons of fights. Seth smirked. He took it off and threw it in the garbage can.

About Todd Strasser

Todd Strasser says he writes about young adults because he is still trying to resolve conflicts from  his own youth. The teenagers in many of his books face personal challenges and learn the importance of honesty and "standing up for one's friends, self, and beliefs."

Strasser has written many award-winning books, including *Friends Till the End, The Wave, Angel Dust Blues,* and *Turn It Up!* Strasser also runs his own fortune cookie business.

Responding

1. **Personal Response** What would you like to say to Seth? to Adam?

2. **Literary Analysis** Is Adam a believable *character?* Tell why or why not.

3. **Theme Connection** Why does Seth throw away his jacket? Why does he "smirk" as he does it?

Language Workshop

Sentence Fragments A sentence fragment is punctuated like a sentence but does not express a complete thought. Writers usually avoid sentence fragments, but in "On the Bridge," author Todd Strasser uses them on purpose, as in this example:

If he took it home and washed it now, the stains would probably make it look pretty cool. Like a jacket that had been worn in tons of fights.

Can you identify the sentence fragment? Why would Strasser use a sentence fragment here? What effect does he create by using sentence fragments?

Read these quotations from the story. Identify whether each is a sentence or sentence fragment.

1. "Seth had decided to wear it anyway, but he felt like a fraud."

2. "Like a kid trying to imitate someone truly cool."

3. "Seth had never been in a fight in his life."

4. "Not a serious punching fight, at least."

Writer's Portfolio

At the beginning of the story, Seth thinks Adam is "pretty cool," but by the end, he's not so sure. Describe a time when you changed your mind about someone. Compare what you first believed about that person with what you later concluded about him or her.

ALICE WALKER

Beauty: When the Other Dancer Is the Self

It is a bright summer day in 1947. My father, a fat, funny man with beautiful eyes and a subversive wit, is trying to decide which of his eight children he will take with him to the county fair. My mother, of course, will not go. She is knocked out from getting most of us ready: I hold my neck stiff against the pressure of her knuckles as she hastily completes the braiding and then beribboning of my hair.

My father is the driver for the rich old white lady up the road. Her name is Miss Mey. She owns all the land for miles around, as well as the house in which we live. All I remember about her is that she once offered to pay my mother thirty-five cents for cleaning her house, raking up piles of her magnolia leaves, and washing her family's clothes, and that my mother —she of no money, eight children, and a chronic earache—refused it. But I do not think of this in 1947. I am two and a half years old. I want to go everywhere my daddy goes. I am excited at the prospect of riding in a car. Someone has told me fairs are fun. That there is room in the car for only three of us doesn't faze me at all. Whirling happily in my starchy frock, showing off my biscuit-polished patent-leather shoes and lavender socks, tossing

> ### Beauty Words
>
> **biscuit-polished** (p. 80) polished with a biscuit. The lard in the biscuit is especially good for shining patent leather.
>
> **sassiness** (p. 82) pertness, self-confidence
>
> **womanishness** (p. 82) acting too old for her age
>
> **mess** (p. 82) cute, stylish, extraordinary

my head in a way that makes my ribbons bounce, I stand, hands on hips, before my father. "Take me, Daddy," I say with assurance, "I'm the prettiest!"

Later, it does not surprise me to find myself in Miss Mey's shiny black car, sharing the back seat with the other lucky ones. Does not surprise me that I thoroughly enjoy the fair. At home that night I tell the unlucky ones all I can

remember about the merry-go-round, the man who eats live chickens, and the teddy bears, until they say: that's enough, baby Alice. Shut up now, and go to sleep.

It is EASTER SUNDAY, 1950. I AM DRESSED IN A green, flocked, scalloped-hem dress (handmade by my adoring sister, Ruth) that has its own smooth satin petticoat and tiny hot-pink roses tucked into each scallop. My shoes, new T-strap patent leather, again highly biscuit-polished. I am six years old and have learned one of the longest Easter speeches to be heard that day, totally unlike the speech I said when I was two: "Easter lilies / pure and white / blossom in / the morning light." When I rise to give my speech I do so on a great wave of love and pride and expectation. People in the church stop rustling their new crinolines. They seem to hold their breath. I can tell they admire my dress, but it is my spirit, bordering on sassiness (womanishness), they secretly applaud.

"That girl's a little *mess*," they whisper to each other, pleased.

Naturally I say my speech without stammer or pause, unlike those who stutter, stammer, or, worst of all, forget. This is before the word "beautiful" exists in people's vocabulary, but "Oh, isn't she the *cutest* thing!" frequently floats my way. "And got so much sense!" they gratefully add . . . for which thoughtful addition I thank them to this day.

It was great fun being cute. But then, one day, it ended.

I AM EIGHT YEARS OLD AND A TOMBOY. I HAVE A cowboy hat, cowboy boots, checkered shirt and pants, all red. My playmates are my brothers, two and four years older than I. Their colors are black and green, the only difference in the way we are dressed. On Saturday nights we all go to the picture show, even my mother; Westerns are her favorite kind of movie. Back home, "on the ranch," we pretend we are Tom Mix, Hopalong Cassidy, Lash LaRue (we've even named one of our dogs Lash LaRue); we chase each other for hours rustling cattle, being outlaws, delivering damsels from distress. Then my parents decide to buy my brothers guns. These are not "real" guns. They shoot "BBs," copper pellets my brothers say will kill birds. Because I am a girl, I do not get a gun. Instantly I am relegated to the position of Indian. Now there appears a great distance between us. They shoot and shoot at everything with their new guns. I try to keep up with my bow and arrows.

One day while I am standing on top of our makeshift

"garage"—pieces of tin nailed across some poles—holding my bow and arrow and looking out toward the fields, I feel an incredible blow in my right eye. I look down just in time to see my brother lower his gun.

Both brothers rush to my side. My eye stings, and I cover it with my hand. "If you tell," they say, "we will get a whipping. You don't want that to happen, do you?" I do not. "Here is a piece of wire," says the older brother, picking it up from the roof; "say you stepped on one end of it and the other flew up and hit you." The pain is beginning to start. "Yes," I say. "Yes, I will say that is what happened." If I do not say this is what happened, I know my brothers will find ways to make me wish I had. But now I will say anything that gets me to my mother.

Confronted by our parents we stick to the lie agreed upon. They place me on a bench on the porch and I close my left eye while they examine the right. There is a tree growing from underneath the porch that climbs past the railing to the roof. It is the last thing my right eye sees. I watch as its trunk, its branches, and then its leaves are blotted out by the rising blood.

I am in shock. First there is intense fever, which my father tries to break using lily leaves bound around my head. Then there are chills: my mother tries to get me to eat soup. Eventually, I do not know how, my parents learn what has happened. A week after the "accident" they take me to see a doctor. "Why did you wait so long to come?" he asks, looking into my eye and shaking his head. "Eyes are sympathetic," he says. "If one is blind, the other will likely become blind too."

> ## Words to Know
>
> **sympathetic** (p. 83) responsive to another's pain
>
> **cataract** (p. 84) a cloudy film in the eye
>
> **throes** (p. 84) agony, anguish

This comment of the doctor's terrifies me. But it is really how I look that bothers me most. Where the BB pellet struck there is a glob of whitish scar tissue, a hideous cataract, on my eye. Now when I stare at people—a favorite pastime, up to now—they will stare back. Not at the "cute" little girl, but at her scar. For six years I do not stare at anyone, because I do not raise my head.

Years LATER, IN THE THROES OF A MID-LIFE CRISIS, I ask my mother and sister whether I changed after the "accident." "No," they say, puzzled. "What do you mean?"

What do I mean?

I am eight, and, for the first time, doing poorly in school, where I have been something of a whiz since I was four. We have just moved to the place where the "accident" occurred. We do not know any of the people around us because this is a different county. The only time I see the friends I knew is when we go back to our old church. The new school is the former state penitentiary. It is a large stone building, cold and drafty, crammed to overflowing with boisterous, ill-disciplined children. On the third floor there is a huge circular imprint of some partition that has been torn out.

"What used to be here?" I ask a sullen girl next to me on our way past it to lunch.

"The electric chair," says she.

At night I have nightmares about the electric chair, and about all the people reputedly "fried" in it. I am afraid of the school, where all the students seem to be budding criminals.

"What's the matter with your eye?" they ask, critically.

When I don't answer (I cannot decide whether it was an "accident" or not), they shove me, insist on a fight.

My brother, the one who created the story about the wire, comes to my rescue. But then brags so much about "protecting" me, I become sick.

After months of torture at the school, my parents decide to send me back to our old community, to my old school. I live with my grandparents and the teacher they board. But there is no room for Phoebe, my cat. By the time my grandparents decide there *is* room, and I ask for my cat, she cannot be found. Miss Yarborough, the boarding teacher, takes me under her wing, and begins to teach me to play the piano. But soon she marries an African—a "prince," she says—and is whisked away to his continent.

At my old school there is at least one teacher who loves me. She is the teacher who "knew me before I was born" and bought my first baby clothes. It is she who makes life bearable. It is her presence that finally helps me turn on the one child at the school who continually calls me "one-eyed bitch." One day I simply grab him by his coat and beat him until I am satisfied. It is my teacher who tells me my mother is ill.

My mother is lying in bed in the middle of the day, something I have never seen. She is in too much pain to speak. She has an abscess in her ear. I stand looking down on her, knowing that if she dies, I cannot live. She is being treated with warm oils and hot bricks held against her cheek. Finally a doctor comes. But I must go back to my grandparents' house. The weeks pass but I am hardly aware of it. All I know is that my mother might die, my father is not so jolly, my brothers still have their guns, and I am the one sent away from home.

> **Words to Know**
>
> **abscess** (p. 85) a collection of fluid resulting from an infection
>
> **abuse** (p. 86) use harsh and insulting language about
>
> **rant and rave** (p. 86) scold violently

"You did not change," they say.

Did I imagine the anguish of never looking up?

I am twelve. When relatives come to visit I hide in my room. My cousin Brenda, just my age, whose father works in the post office and whose mother is a nurse, comes to find me. "Hello," she says. And then she asks, looking at my recent school picture, which I did not want taken, and on which the "glob," as I think of it, is clearly visible, "You still can't see out of that eye?"

"No," I say, and flop back on the bed over my book.

That night, as I do almost every night, I abuse my eye. I rant and rave at it, in front of the mirror. I plead with it to clear up before morning. I tell it I hate and despise it. I do not pray for sight. I pray for beauty.

"You did not change," they say.

I AM FOURTEEN AND BABY-SITTING FOR MY BROTHER Bill, who lives in Boston. He is my favorite brother and there is a strong bond between us. Understanding my feelings of shame and ugliness he and his wife take me to a local hospital, where the "glob" is removed by a doctor named O. Henry. There is still a small bluish crater where the scar tissue was, but the ugly white stuff is gone. Almost immediately I become a different person from the girl who does not raise her head. Or so I think. Now that I've raised my head I win the boyfriend of my dreams. Now that I've raised my head I have plenty of friends. Now that I've raised my head classwork comes from my lips as faultlessly as Easter speeches did, and I leave high school as valedictorian, most popular student, and *queen*, hardly believing my luck. Ironically, the girl who was voted most beautiful in our class (and was) was later shot twice through the chest by a male companion, using a "real" gun, while she was pregnant. But that's another story in itself. Or is it?

"You did not change," they say.

IT IS NOW THIRTY YEARS SINCE THE "ACCIDENT." A beautiful journalist comes to visit and to interview me. She is going to write a cover story for her magazine that focuses on my latest book. "Decide how you want to look on the cover," she says. "Glamorous, or whatever."

Never mind "glamorous," it is the "whatever" that I hear. Suddenly all I can think of is whether I will get enough sleep the night before the photography session: if I don't, my eye will be tired and wander, as blind eyes will.

At night in bed with my lover I think up reasons why I should not appear on the cover of a magazine. "My meanest critics will say I've sold out," I say. "My family will now realize I write scandalous books."

"But what's the real reason you don't want to do this?" he asks.

"Because in all probability," I say in a rush, "my eye won't be straight."

"It will be straight enough," he says. Then, "Besides, I thought you'd made your peace with that."

And I suddenly remember that I have.

I remember:

I am talking to my brother Jimmy, asking if he remembers anything unusual about the day I was shot. He does not know I consider that day the last time my father, with his sweet home remedy of cool lily leaves, chose me, and that I suffered and raged inside because of this. "Well," he says, "all I remember is standing by the side of the highway with Daddy, trying to flag down a car. A white man stopped, but when Daddy said he needed somebody to take his little girl to the doctor, he drove off."

I remember:

I am in the desert for the first time. I fall totally in love with it. I am so overwhelmed by its beauty, I confront for the first time, consciously, the meaning of the doctor's words years ago: "Eyes are sympathetic. If one is blind, the other will likely become blind too." I realize I have dashed about the world madly, looking at this, looking at that, storing up images against the fading of the light. *But I might have missed seeing the desert!* The shock of that possibility—and gratitude for over twenty-five years of sight—sends me literally to my knees. Poem after poem comes—which is perhaps how poets pray.

ON SIGHT

I am so thankful I have seen
The Desert
And the creatures in the desert
And the desert Itself.

The desert has its own moon
Which I have seen
With my own eye.
There is no flag on it.

Trees of the desert have arms
All of which are always up
That is because the moon is up
The sun is up
Also the sky
The stars
Clouds
None with flags.

If there *were* flags, I doubt
the trees would point.
Would you?

> *But mostly, I remember this:*
> I am twenty-seven, and my baby daughter is almost three. Since her birth I have worried about her discovery that her mother's eyes are different from other people's. Will she be embarrassed? I think. What will she say? Every day she watches a television program called "Big Blue

Marble." It begins with a picture of the earth as it appears from the moon. It is bluish, a little battered-looking, but full of light, with whitish clouds swirling around it. Every time I see it I weep with love, as if it is a picture of Grandma's house. One day when I am putting Rebecca down for her nap, she suddenly focuses on my eye. Something inside me cringes, gets ready to try to protect myself. All children are cruel about physical differences, I know from experience, and that they don't always mean to be is another matter. I assume Rebecca will be the same.

But no-o-o-o. She studies my face intently as we stand, her inside and me outside her crib. She even holds my face maternally between her dimpled little hands. Then, looking every bit as serious and lawyerlike as her father, she says, as if it may just possibly have slipped my attention: "Mommy, there's a *world* in your eye." (As in, "Don't be alarmed, or do anything crazy.") And then, gently, but with great interest. "Mommy, where did you *get* that world in your eye?"

For the most part, the pain left then. (So what, if my brothers grew up to buy even more powerful pellet guns for their sons and to carry real guns themselves. So what, if a young "Morehouse man" once nearly fell off the steps of Trevor Arnett Library because he thought my eyes were blue.) Crying and laughing I ran to the bathroom, while Rebecca mumbled and sang herself off to sleep. Yes indeed, I realized, looking into the mirror. There *was* a world in my eye. And I saw that it was possible to love it: that in fact, for all it had taught me of shame and anger and inner vision, I *did* love it. Even to see it drifting out of orbit in boredom, or rolling up out of fatigue, not to mention floating back at attention in excitement (bearing witness, a friend has called it), deeply suitable to my personality, and even characteristic of me.

That night I dream I am dancing to Stevie Wonder's song "Always" (the name of the song is really "As," but I hear it as "Always"). As I dance, whirling and joyous, happier than I've ever been in my life, another bright-faced dancer joins me. We dance and kiss each other and hold each other through the night. The other dancer has obviously come through all right, as I have done. She is beautiful, whole and free. And she is also me.

About Alice Walker

Alice Walker grew up in Georgia, the youngest of eight children. She began keeping a notebook at the early age of eight: "Books became my world because the world I was in was very hard. My mother was working as a maid, so she was away from six-thirty in the morning until after dark. . . . I was twelve, coming home to an empty house and cleaning and fixing dinner . . . I missed my mother very much."

 About writing, Ms. Walker says, "If you're silent for a long time, people [characters] just arrive in your mind. It makes you believe the world was created in silence." The experience Ms. Walker writes about in "Beauty: When the Other Dancer Is the Self" actually happened to her as a child.

Ms. Walker has won numerous awards for her novels, short stories, and poems. Her books for young adults include *To Hell with Dying* and *Finding the Green Stone*.

Responding

1. **Personal Response** What emotions did you feel as you read this essay? Compare your reactions with a classmate's.

2. **Literary Analysis** Alice Walker repeats the line "'You did not change,' they say" several times throughout the story. What is her *purpose* for doing this? What point is she trying to make?

3. **Theme Connection** At the end of the essay, Walker describes a dream about a dancer. What do you think is the significance of the dream?

Language Workshop

Sequence The *sequence*, or order of events, may be difficult to figure out in a selection that uses flashbacks, such as "Beauty: When the Other Dancer Is the Self." List these events from the reading in the order that they happened.

1. Alice Walker is asked to appear on a magazine cover.

2. Walker's little girl asks about her blinded eye.

3. Alice Walker says her Easter speech without any mistakes.

4. Walker is blinded in one eye by a BB pellet.

5. The white scar tissue is removed from Walker's eye.

Writer's Portfolio

Alice Walker learns to accept and even love her blinded eye. Write about a time when you or someone you know experienced similar feelings about something that was at first hard to accept.

Beautiful & Cruel

from *The House on Mango Street*

I AM AN UGLY DAUGHTER. I AM THE ONE NOBODY comes for.

Nenny says she won't wait her whole life for a husband to come and get her, that Minerva's sister left her mother's house by having a baby, but she doesn't want to go that way either. She wants things all her own, to pick and choose. Nenny has pretty eyes and it's easy to talk that way if you are pretty.

My mother says that when I get older my dusty hair will settle and my blouse will learn to stay clean, but I have decided not to grow up tame like the others who lay their necks on the threshold waiting for the ball and chain.

In the movies there is always one with red red lips who is beautiful and cruel. She is the one who drives men crazy and laughs them all away. Her power is her own. She will not give it away.

I have begun my own quiet war. Simple. Sure. I am one who leaves the table like a man, without putting back the chair or picking up the plate.

Maybe

Tomorrow
may be the day
that you won't look
through me.

Instead
you'll stop
and look
into me.

LANGSTON HUGHES

I, Too

I, too, sing America.

I am the darker brother.
They send me to eat in the kitchen
When company comes,
But I laugh,
And eat well,
And grow strong.

Tomorrow,
I'll be at the table
When company comes.
Nobody'll dare
Say to me,
"Eat in the kitchen,"
Then.

Besides,
They'll see how beautiful I am
And be ashamed—

I, too, am America.

About Sandra Cisneros

Sandra Cisneros was born in Chicago, the daughter of a Mexican father and a Mexican American mother. She has worked as a visiting writer at numerous universities and currently lives in San Antonio, Texas. *The House on Mango Street*, from which "Beautiful & Cruel" is taken, is loosely based on the author's experiences growing up on Chicago's West Side.

About Eve Merriam

Eve Merriam started reading and writing poetry when she was very young. Although she wrote many kinds of books for all ages, her playfulness and ear for language are particularly evident in her poetry. She has said, "Whatever you do, find ways to read poetry. Eat it, drink it, enjoy it, and share it."

About Langston Hughes

Langston Hughes was a key figure during the Harlem Renaissance of the 1920s and is one of the most noted poets of the twentieth century. As in "I, Too," much of his work deals with the African American experience. Mr. Hughes wrote numerous books of poetry, short stories, novels, and plays, before his death in 1967.

Responding

1. **Personal Response** Which of these selections did you relate to the most? Tell why.

2. **Literary Analysis** The last sentence of "Beautiful & Cruel" contains a *simile*. Find the simile and explain what you think the author means by it.

3. **Theme Connection** What is the message of each of these selections? How are the messages the same? How are they different?

Language Workshop

It's or Its The contraction *it's* and the possessive pronoun *its* are frequently confused. Whenever you must decide between *it's* and *its*, ask yourself, "would it make sense to say 'it is' here?" If so, use *it's*, with an apostrophe. If not, use *its*, with no apostrophe.

Look at this sentence from "Beautiful & Cruel": *Nenny has pretty eyes and it's easy to talk that way if you are pretty.* *It's* is correct here because the writer means "it is easy." But look at this sentence: *My blouse has a stain on its sleeve.* In this case, *its* is correct, because "its sleeve" means "the blouse's sleeve," not "it is sleeve."

Add apostrophes where needed to the following.

1. Its not easy to find a true friend.

2. My life has had its share of ups and downs.

3. Its hard to believe, but being plain has its advantages.

Writer's Portfolio

These selections deal with self-image in different ways. Write a poem, a story, or a short essay that expresses your feelings about the importance of a person's self-image.

VICKIE SEARS

Dancer

TELL YOU JUST HOW IT WAS WITH HER. TOOK HER TO a dance not long after she come to live with us. Smartest thing I ever done. Seems like some old Eaglespirit woman saw her living down here and came back just to be with Clarissa.

Five years old she was when she come to us. Some foster kids come with lots of stuff, but she came with everything she had in a paper bag. Some dresses that was too short. A pair of pants barely holding a crotch. A pile of ratty underwear and one new nightgown. Mine was her third foster home in as many months. The agency folks said she was *so-cio-path-ic*. I don't know nothing from that. She just seemed like she was all full up with anger and scaredness like lots of the kids who come to me. Only she was a real loner. Not trusting nobody. But she ran just like any other kid, was quiet when needed. Smiled at all the right times. If you could get her to smile, that is. Didn't talk much, though.

Had these ferocious dreams, too. Real screamer dreams they were. Shake the soul right out of you. She'd be screaming and crying with her little body wriggling on

Words to Know

so-cio-path-ic (p. 98) sociopathic; being antisocial; having no sense of responsibility toward others

Assiniboin (p. 100) a Plains Indian tribe whose members now live primarily in Montana and the provinces of Alberta and Saskatchewan in Canada

fixated (p. 101) to be very interested in or attached to

the bed, her hair all matted up on her woody-colored face. One time I got her to tell me what she was seeing, and she told me how she was being chased by a man with a long knife what he was going to kill her with and nobody could hear her calling out for help. She didn't talk too much about them, but they was all bad like that one. Seemed the most fierce dreams I ever remember anybody ever having outside of a vision seek. They said her tribe was Assiniboin, but they weren't for certain. What was for sure was that she was a fine dark-eyed girl just meant for someone to scoop up for loving.

> ### More About Powwows
>
> At a Native American powwow, the focus is usually on dancing. A powwow often includes both social dances, open to all, and contest dances, where dancers compete for prizes. Contest dances may be "fancy"—fast-paced, with complicated steps—or "traditional"—slower, with simpler steps. Dancers wear brilliant hand-made costumes decorated with beadwork, feathers, buttons, fringe, or other materials.

Took her to her first dance in September, like I said, not long after she came. It wasn't like I thought it would be a good thing to do. It was just that we was all going. Me, my own kids, some nieces and nephews and the other children who was living with us. The powwow was just part of what we done all the time. Every month. More often in the summer. But this was the regular first Friday night of the school year. We'd all gather up and go to the school. I was thinking on leaving her home with a sitter cause she'd tried to kill one of the cats a couple of days before. We'd had us a big talk and she was grounded, but, well, it seemed like she ought to be with us.

Harold, that's my oldest boy, he and the other kids was mad with her, but he decided to show her around anyhow. At the school he went through the gym telling people, "This here's my sister, Clarissa." Wasn't no fuss or anything. She was just another one of the kids. When they was done meeting folks, he put her on one of the bleachers near the drum and went to join the men. He was in that place where his voice cracks but was real proud to be drumming. Held his hand up to his ear even, some of the time. Anyhow, Clarissa was sitting there, not all that interested in the dance or drum, when Molly Graybull come out in her button dress. Her arms was all stretched out, and she was slipping around, preening on them spindles of legs that get skinnier with every year. She was well into her seventies, and I might as well admit, Molly had won herself a fair share of dance contests. So it wasn't no surprise how a little girl could get so fixated on Molly. Clarissa watched her move around-around-around. Then all the rest of the dancers after Molly. She sure took in a good eyeful. Fancy dance. Owl dance. Circle dance. Even a hoop dancer was visiting that night. Everything weaving all slow, then fast. Around-around until that child couldn't see nothing else. Seemed like she was struck silent in the night, too. Never had no dreams at all. Well, not the hollering kind anyways.

Next day she was more quiet than usual only I could see she was looking at her picture book and tapping the old one-two, one-two. Tapping her toes on the rug with the inside of her head going around and around. As quiet as she could be, she was.

A few days went on before she asks me, "When's there gonna be another dance?"

I tell her in three weeks. She just smiles and goes on outside, waiting on the older kids to come home from school.

THE VERY NEXT DAY SHE ASKS IF SHE CAN LISTEN TO some singing. I give her the tape recorder and some of Joe Washington from up to the Lummi reservation and the Kicking Woman Singers. Clarissa, she takes them tapes and runs out back behind the chicken shed, staying out all afternoon. I wasn't worried none, though, cause I could hear the music the whole time. Matter of fact, it like to make me sick of them same songs come the end of three weeks. But that kid, she didn't get into no kind of mischief. Almost abnormal how good she was. Worried me some to see her so caught up but it seemed good too. The angry part of her slowed down so's she wasn't hitting the animals or chopping on herself with sticks like she was doing when she first come. She wasn't laughing much either, but she started playing with the other kids when they come home. Seemed like everybody was working hard to be better with each other.

Come March, Clarissa asks, "Can I dance?"

For sure, the best time for teaching is when a kid wants to listen, so we stood side to side with me doing some steps. She followed along fine. I put on a tape and started moving faster, and Clarissa just kept up all natural. I could tell she'd been practicing lots. She was doing real good.

Comes the next powwow, which was outside on the track field, I braided Clarissa's hair. Did her up with some ermine and bead ties, then give her a purse to carry. It was all beaded with a rose and leaves. Used to be my aunt's. She held it right next to her side with her chin real high. She joined in a Circle dance. I could see she was watching her feet a little and looking how others do their steps, but mostly she was doing wonderful. When Molly Graybull showed up beside her, Clarissa took to a seat and stared. She didn't dance again that night, but I could see there was dreaming coming into her eyes. I saw that fire that said to practice. And she did. I heard her every day in her room. Finally bought her her very own tape recorder so's the rest of us could listen to music too.

SOME MONTHS PASSED ON. ALL THE KIDS WAS getting bigger. Clarissa, she went into the first grade. Harvey went off to community college up in Seattle, and that left me with Ronnie being the oldest at home. Clarissa was keeping herself busy all the time going over to Molly Graybull's. She was coming home with Spider Woman stories and trickster tales. One night she speaks up at supper and says, right clear and loud, "I'm an Assiniboin." Clear as it can be, she says it again. Don't nobody have to say nothing to something that proud said.

Next day I started working on a wing dress for Clarissa. She was going to be needing one for sure real soon.

Comes the first school year powwow and everyone was putting on their best. I called for Clarissa to come to my room. I told her, "I think it's time you have something special for yourself." Then I held up the green satin and saw her eyes full up with glitter. She didn't say nothing. Only kisses me and runs off to her room.

Just as we're all getting out of the car, Clarissa whispered to me, "I'm gonna dance with Molly Graybull." I put my hand on her shoulder to say, "You just listen to your spirit. That's where your music is."

We all danced an Owl dance, a Friendship dance, and a couple of Circle dances. Things was feeling real warm and good, and then it was time for the women's traditional. Clarissa joined the circle. She opened her arms to something nobody but her seemed to hear. That's when I saw that old Eagle woman come down and slide right inside of Clarissa, scooping up that child. There Clarissa was, full up with music. All full with that old, old spirit, letting herself dance through Clarissa's feet. Then Molly Graybull come dancing alongside Clarissa, and they was both the same age.

About Vickie Sears

Vickie Sears is a Native American of Cherokee descent. She lives in Seattle, Washington, where she works as a writer, feminist therapist, and teacher.

In many of the stories in her book *Simple Songs: A Collection of Short Stories*, Sears portrays young girls or women who are struggling to find a sense of identity and self-esteem. As Native Americans, her characters experience the difficulty of living within a European American society that does not value or understand Native American culture. As in the story "Dancer," her characters often turn to their Native American cultural heritage to learn who they are.

In addition to short stories, Vickie Sears has written poems and essays that have appeared in a number of books and magazines.

Responding

1. **Personal Response** Would you like to have Clarissa for a sister? Tell why or why not.

2. **Literary Analysis** When you read "Dancer," it sounds like someone is telling the story out loud. Why would the author choose this *style* of writing? How does this style make the story more interesting?

3. **Theme Connection** How has dancing changed Clarissa? Why has it changed her?

Language Workshop

Double Negatives Negative words are words that mean "no" or "not." They include *neither, never, no, not, nothing, nobody, none,* and *nowhere.* When you want to say "no" in a sentence, only one negative word is needed. A *double negative* (two negative words) is incorrect.

In "Dancer," author Vickie Sears uses double negatives on purpose. For example: *But that kid, she <u>didn't</u> get into <u>no</u> kind of mischief.* Vickie Sears wants to make the narrator sound like a real person. But when you write, you should avoid double negatives—unless you invent a character who talks that way!

You can correct double negatives by substituting a positive word (like *any, anybody, anything, either,* or *ever*) for one of the negative words. You could correct the example above by saying: *But that kid, she didn't get into <u>any</u> kind of mischief.* Notice how the negative word *no* has been changed to the positive word *any.*

Correct the double negatives in the following sentences.

1. She never goes to no parties.

2. Nobody wants to listen to no music.

3. I didn't go nowhere interesting last summer.

Writer's Portfolio

Clarissa was proud that she belonged to the Assiniboin tribe. Write about an aspect of your cultural or family heritage that makes you feel proud.

PETER SIERUTA

Being Alive

EVERY TUESDAY AND THURSDAY AFTERNOON THE kid they called Kenny Wheels would come to watch our aerobics class. He'd sit against the wall, his face broken in half by a big smile, his fists banging double-time on the tray in front of him. Some people said he came just to watch the girls. It didn't matter to me; I wasn't particularly shy. And in a gym filled with girls in size-two pink, yellow, and orange leotards, I doubted he was paying much attention to a size twelve in a navy-blue sweatsuit like me. Besides, I was too busy with my own huffing and puffing to watch Kenny Wells in his wheelchair.

Until the day Kenny was kicked out of the gym.

Ms. Blair had just told us to pick up our jump ropes for the "aeropics" segment of the workout. A home-ec teacher by day, an exercise fiend by night, Ms. Blair was only a few years older than us seniors—but considered very sophisticated because she was rumored to have a live-in boyfriend. She claimed to have invented aeropics, and all the girls were so hung up on her that nobody questioned it. All I knew was that it was the hardest part of the workout, and the only reason I persisted at it was to burn up enough calories to justify buying a Moon Pie or pack of Twinkies on the way home without feeling guilty.

The music Ms. Blair played for the rope segment was especially irritating. It started off nice and slow, hop and pause and hop and pause, but steadily accelerated to hop-

hop-hop-hop-hop. By the time the song ended, most of the girls were on the floor, gasping. That particular day, two girls didn't stop jumping when the song ended: Kathi Weiss and Addie Haines. All through school Kathi had three things working for her: She was very pretty, very athletic, and had a name ending with *i*. Addie was also pretty and could run like the wind, but she had so much pride that if you threw a fifty-dollar bill at her feet, she wouldn't stoop to pick it up. It probably had something to do with the fact she was the only black girl at our entire high school.

Addie and Kathi were longtime rivals. For three years Addie had beaten Kathi in the girls' division of our school's 3-K Funrun. There was always some type of competition going on between them. That afternoon they continued jumping rope, facing each other, going faster and faster, until I wasn't sure their feet were even hitting the floor. Everyone was cheering, urging them on. When Kathi finally fell out of rhythm and tumbled to the floor, everyone laughed. Everyone including Kenny, whose laugh was loud and wheezy. Addie was too proud to even crack a smile over her victory; she just reached out a hand to help Kathi get up. But Kathi got up on her own, her face red and sweaty. She listened to the laughter, then whirled at Kenny. "Stop that!" she shrieked. "Stop that horrible laughing!"

He tried to stop, but the laugh kept burbling out of his chest.

"What are you doing here anyway?" Kathi shouted. "This class is for *girls only!* Ms. Blair, make him leave! He's disrupting . . . everything!"

"Oh, Kathi . . ." Ms. Blair began, then shrugged.

"I mean it! I mean it!" Kathi shouted, stamping her foot. I remembered Kathi's eleventh-birthday party when she threw the same kind of tantrum because she didn't win at pin the tail on the donkey.

Ms. Blair shrugged again, twisting the chains at her neck. "Well, maybe you're right, Kathi. I guess we should be a little more businesslike in this class. Maybe we shouldn't allow visitors. Kenny—"

But she didn't have to finish the sentence, because he was already rolling toward the door with his head down, the thumb of his right hand controlling the button on his electric wheelchair.

When Addie followed him across the gym, I thought she was just going to help him with the door. But she followed him right through it. "Addie? Addie, where are you going?" Ms. Blair called.

She came back and stood in the doorway, her thin brown arms folded across the front of her blue leotard. "I don't like discrimination, Ms. Blair. If we're not allowing people with handicaps in the gym today, I'm going outside to run the track."

"Discrimination? Handicaps? Addie, I'm not asking Kenny to leave because of—I'm asking him to leave because he's a boy, and this is an all-girls class."

Addie never looked away from Ms. Blair. "You didn't say anything when Mel Jacobs and the guys from the football team came in last week."

"But—"

"I don't want to hear any *buts!*" Addie Haines was the only person in the whole school who could get away with that kind of talk. "Okay, boys in wheelchairs aren't allowed today. Next week it might be black girls." She pointed to herself. "Or girls with blond hair." She pointed at Kathi. "Girls with sweatsuits." She pointed at me.

Then she walked out.

An hour later, when I left the gym, Addie was still running the outdoor track. She wasn't the only one out there, but she was definitely the fastest. I didn't realize Kenny was sitting under a tree until I heard him calling out, "Go! Go! Go!"

I said, "Kenny, I'm sorry about what happened in there."

He was leaning forward in his chair, following Addie's progress with his eyes. He shrugged. "Blair says— she invented— that aeropicise. What a liar." As always, he spoke with a lot of difficulty, twisting his head as if he were biting the words out of the air.

"Blair's a bitch," I said.

He laughed and clapped his hands over his mouth. His hands reminded me of lobster claws. The fingers on each hand all seemed to be glued together; his thumbs moved independently.

Addie raced by and raised a hand in greeting. "Go! Go! Go!" yelled Kenny.

"You like sports, huh?"

"Watching. Not really— participating," he said. He

was a little guy, but for some reason he had a large, round face, and when he smiled—like he did at that moment— he looked like a happy jack-o'-lantern. "Aerobics," he said. "This is— my— aerobics." He lifted his hand and bent his thumb up and down several times. "Whew. Tired." He wiped imaginary sweat from his forehead with the side of his arm.

Addie ran off the track and sat down on the grass. "How's that?" she asked Kenny.

"Super!"

"Listen, Addie," I said, touching her arm. She leaned forward to tie her shoe—her way of pulling away without making a big deal of it. "That was a neat thing you did. I wish I'd had the nerve to walk out like that."

"You could have," she said, then turned to Kenny: "Thanks for pacing me like that."

He smiled.

"It worked," she said. "I ought to hire you as my trainer for the Funrun."

"What's it— like?" he asked.

"Winning?"

"No. Running."

Resting her chin on her knee, Addie looked off at the track.

When she didn't answer, Kenny said, "I wonder— because I don't— run. Can't find— Adidas— to fit my— wheels."

Addie smiled, but continued staring off. Finally she said, "When you start off, it feels like God's hand is on your back, giving you that first push. And then you're alone. It feels like you're part of the air. You're running *toward* something . . . ." Her voice trailed off and she shrugged. "When I'm running, it feels the way being alive *should* feel." She looked at Kenny and added, "At least, it does for me."

She immediately got up and began doing stretching

exercises. Maybe she was a little embarrassed. But I wasn't. Because when she talked about running, for a moment I felt like I could run too. Kenny must have felt the same way, because he said, "I— want to feel it."

She was bent over, her right hand holding her left foot. She stayed that way for a moment. "Feel what, Kenny?"

"Like I'm part of the air."

"Okay," she said. "Let's go for a run."

She moved behind his chair and grasped the handles, but when she tried pushing, the wheels only moved a few feet. "How much does this thing weigh?"

"A lot," he said. "My chair— weighs— more than— I do."

I remembered back to when I was a sophomore and Kenny had just started attending our school. He used to wheel himself around on a nonmotorized chair. "Didn't you have another chair?" I said. "Before you got this one?"

"Antique," he said. "From when— I could use— my hands a lot."

"That would be easier to push," I said.

Addie said, "I'll tell you what, Kenny. Some night we'll come to the track with your other chair. I'll take you for a ride so fast your wheels will spark."

He bounced up in his seat. "Tonight?"

"WHERE ARE YOU GOING, NANCY?" MY YOUNGER sister asked that evening. My sister was a Kathi-Weiss-in-training, resembling Kathi in everything from her clothes and hairstyle to her stubborn refusal to call me "Nance." Nance was plain. It was me: Nance Sherman. Nancy sounded too much like Micki, Muffy, Buffy, and all the other names the girls at our school were called.

"Out," I said, letting her draw her own conclusions.

"With a *boy?*"

"Maybe," I said, and left for the school yard.

Kenny's mother was to drop him at the high school at

six-thirty P.M. No one had invited me to join them, but I went anyway. I guess I just wanted to see how Kenny enjoyed "running."

"Nance!" Kenny shouted, waving a claw in my direction.

Addie didn't seem surprised to see me. She was bent over, attaching Kenny's belt to the back of the wheelchair. Then she straightened and pushed the chair over to the track. No one else was running, but the big floodlights were still turned on because the football team had just finished practicing. The light caught Addie in profile, making her look like a proud African princess. "How fast— will we be— running?" Kenny asked.

"Like the wind," said Addie, and took off.

The light danced over and through the wheels, making Spirograph designs on the track. Feet pounded and wheels whirred, and then I heard it: Kenny's voice yelling, "Wheee!" His excitement pushed Kenny's voice into the upper register. It was the most amazing sound I'd ever heard. And that word! I couldn't remember saying "Wheee!" even as a child, but to hear a sixteen-year-old boy shout it just about broke my heart.

As they came around the last corner, facing me, I could see Kenny's face was completely split by that huge grin. Addie's breath was coming in little puffs of vapor, but—as always—she looked cool and aloof. I thought they'd pull over when they made a complete circle, but Addie kept going, around and around the track until something strange happened. The lights were set to go off automatically at seven o'clock, and when they did, the track went pitch dark. I couldn't see them at all, but I could hear the wheels, the feet, the breathing, the "Wheee!" and suddenly I felt I was there with them, running through the dark. First I felt I was Kenny being propelled through the night; then I was Addie, pounding the ground and pushing the chair in front of me. And then

I was part of the air. It lasted only a second—that feeling—but when Addie and Kenny finally came off the track, I felt as high as if I'd been running too. My heart was beating fast, I was taking deep gulps of air.

I could hear Kenny bouncing around in his chair, saying, "Super! Super! Super!"

In the dark we sat and talked. I asked Addie what made her start running. "What made me start breathing?" she replied. "I've always run, but I didn't get into competition until I got to this school. I guess I got tired of being an outcast."

"You're not an outcast!" I said, thinking cliques and social circles were the last thing Addie seemed interested in; she always seemed above that sort of thing. "Now if you want to talk about outcasts, let's talk about *me.* I've never fit into anything in my life—including my Levi's."

Addie said, "I started entering the races to show them that I may act like an outcast and look like an outcast, but, hey, I've got it!"

Words to Know
outcast (p. 113) a person who has been rejected by everyone
clique (p. 113) a small, exclusive group of people

"It?" said Kenny.

"It!" she said. "Whatever it takes to beat them. I'm showing them it's okay to be different."

"Outcasts, outcasts," said Kenny. "Am I the—only one here—who's always been an— average, normal guy?"

I wasn't sure how to take that until he started laughing. Then I laughed too. Addie's laugh was soft and low. I'd never heard her laugh before.

Kenny turned to me. "Don't you— run, Nance?"

"Only after Good Humor trucks," I said. "I mean, can you see this body in a race?"

"Why not?" said Addie.

"My sister calls me the Sherman tank," I said.

"I wish— I could run," said Kenny.

"You just did," said Addie.

"In a race," he said. "Run— in a race."

There was a long moment of silence. Then she said: "You can. You can run in a race. With me." It was too dark to see the expression on Addie's face. But I've always wondered what she looked like when she said those words.

THE NEXT DAY I APPROACHED HER AT SCHOOL. "You aren't serious about running with Kenny in the Funrun."

"I am."

"Don't get me wrong," I said. "It's nice and all that, but it also means you're going to *lose*."

"Winning doesn't make that much difference to me," she said. "Running does."

"But, Addie, they do have sports events for the handicapped. Maybe he could get into that sometime."

"No," she said forcefully. "He wants to feel like everyone else at this school, and I'm going to help him do it."

I said, "You don't have to run for him just because he can't."

"I'm not doing it *because he can't*," she said. "I'm doing it *because I can*."

"Because I can": That must have been Addie's motto. I remembered the first time I heard her say that, the year we were freshmen. Addie had just won her first Funrun, and Kathi—who had lost by fifty seconds—went up to congratulate her. She pressed her cheek against Addie's, but her eyes were burning with anger. Later, walking away from the awards stand, I heard Kathi say in her most patronizing voice, "Well, Addie, I guess you run because you're trying for a sports scholarship to college, right?"

Addie turned cold eyes upon her. "No. My father is a pediatrician, so I guess he can afford to send me just about anyplace I want to go." Kathi's mouth dropped open just a millimeter, and Addie stared at her. "Why do *you* run, Kathi?"

Kathi shrugged. "Because I'm good at it, I guess. Because I think I can win."

"Ah," said Addie, holding a long, dark finger in front of Kathi's nose. "You run because you want to win. I run because I can."

At the time I didn't understand what she meant—that she could run just for the joy of it. I knew how I'd feel if I ran: I'd want the awards. Even now I found it hard to believe Addie could pass up the chance to win.

I said, "But Addie, you're a senior. This will be your last chance for the Funrun. You won't be here next year."

She looked past me. "Kenny may not be here next year either."

"What do you mean? He's only a junior."

"I mean that I've been looking at some of my father's medical books," she said.

"I don't want to hear this," I said.

"Remember when he could talk more clearly than he does now? When he could wheel himself around in his chair? When he could move his fingers and take notes in class instead of carrying around that big tape recorder?"

"Don't tell me any more," I said, walking away.

I was always walking away from things I didn't want to hear. My father liked to tell about the time I was three years old and they brought my little sister home from the hospital. I hid under the bed, yelling, "Is it gone yet?" Maybe I hadn't changed much.

That night I ended up at the school yard. I knew I would. Again nobody had asked me to come.

Addie wheeled Kenny out to the track. "Keep your eye on the stopwatch," she told him.

"I can do that," I said.

"I'll keep you— going fast." He twisted his head around to look at her face. "I'll cheer— a lot."

"Sounds good," she said, and took off running.

"Go! Go! Go! Go!" I heard Kenny shout.

I watched the seconds tick around the stopwatch. When they came back, Addie said, "What was our time?"

I held up the watch, and she grimaced. "Well, usually I go about twice as fast as that," she muttered. "Let's try it again."

And that was how it went every night for the next three weeks. I'd leave the house—leaving my sister with the impression I was going on a date—and meet Addie and Kenny at the track. I'd hold the stopwatch as Addie ran and Kenny shouted encouragement. Sometimes I even felt like I was part of the air again.

Two nights before the race Addie ran the whole 3-K, just to make sure she could do it. She was wiped out when she got back, and their time wasn't that good. But it didn't seem to bother her. "We did it," she told Kenny. "We did run the whole three kilometers."

"We did it!" he shouted, and he looked happy, really happy.

ADDIE TOLD US TO MEET HER IN FRONT OF THE school at seven on Friday evening. For the first time she made a point of including me in the invitation. I thought she wanted me to time their last practice session, but when I got there, Addie was wearing a skirt instead of her usual leotard. "What's going on?" I asked. "Aren't you practicing tonight?"

"Not tonight," said Kenny.

Addie began pushing his chair down the sidewalk, and I ran to help her. "Where are we going?" I asked.

"Dinner," said Addie.

We walked the two blocks to a small restaurant I'd never noticed before. There were only a few people inside, all of them older than our parents. It was the type of restaurant most of the kids at our school would laugh at, but The Pasta Bowl—with its Italian songs on the jukebox and red plastic tablecloths—was my kind of place. People yelled their orders across the room and ran back and forth with trays of pizza and pitchers of beer.

I went to the counter for a pitcher of Coke, and when I returned, Addie was saying, "It's a good idea to load up on a lot of carbohydrates the night before a race. I usually eat spaghetti, but some people like pizza or pancakes."

"Oh, boy," said Kenny. "I want a— pizza."

"This is great," I said. "Next time my sister complains about my eating, I'm going to tell her I'm carbohydrate loading for a race."

Kenny tore open the end of his straw and blew the wrapper across the table at me; I shot mine back at him.

I realized it was the first time Addie, Kenny, and I had been together off the school track. All those nights we'd spent in training for the race were coming to an end. I didn't want to think about that. "Let's get a large pizza," I said.

Addie ordered a huge plate of spaghetti, and Kenny and I split the pizza. I sat there wolfing down my slices, and no one said, "Nancy, don't you think you've had enough?" or pushed salad at me. In fact, Addie offered me a taste of her spaghetti.

Kenny said, "Last year— when our homeroom won that prize— for best attendance— we had a pizza party." He paused to swipe at a strand of cheese hanging off his hand. "When I got my slice— Mrs. Pelton came over— and she wanted to— cut my pizza in small pieces."

"Why?" asked Addie.

"That's what I wonder," said Kenny. "She didn't want to cut— anyone else's."

I said, "That would make me really mad."

Kenny lowered his voice. "Pissed me off."

He reached forward with both hands and took another slice off the tray. "So when she was standing there beside my chair— I dropped my pizza. I dropped it right— on her skirt." He chewed for a few seconds, then added, "You know how sometimes— my hands don't work right." And he winked.

Addie and I burst out laughing, and Kenny joined in

with his loud, wheezy laugh.

When it was time to leave, we all wanted to pay the check ourselves. Kenny took out his wallet and counted dollar bills while I tried to grab the check from Addie's hand. "No," said Addie. "I invited you two out."

"Okay," I said. "But next time I'm paying."

It wasn't until I was home in bed that I thought about what I'd said: "Next time." No one had ever said there'd be a next time.

THE NEXT MORNING I WALKED TO THE FIELD IN THE early-morning cold. It was strange to see all the Kathis and Muffys and Phils and Chases of our town out on that track. For weeks it had been a private nighttime playground for Addie and Kenny and me.

When I finally found Addie and Kenny, they were in the middle of a confrontation with Kathi Weiss. "What do you think you're doing?" Kathi demanded.

"We're going to run," Addie replied calmly.

"Oh, no! Oh, no! You are *not* running with him."

"Try stopping us," said Addie.

"I just might! You better believe I just might! What is this, some hokey publicity stunt to get your name in the paper? Something to put on your college application?"

Kenny looked hurt for a second, and Addie moved in front of him—blocking Kathi from his view. "Listen, Weiss," she said. "Why don't you accept the fact that now you can win the girls' division—and just shut up."

Nobody ever told Kathi to shut up. She filled herself up with air to start yelling. But then a glimmer of understanding seemed to cross her face. She turned abruptly and walked away.

The race was almost ready to start. I only had time to say a quick "Good luck, you guys."

Addie smiled. Kenny stuck his thumb in the air.

"Runners, take your places," a voice boomed, and I ran off the track to stand in the crowd, never taking my eyes off them. His hands gripped the arms of the chair tightly. Her hands gripped the handles.

When the starting gun went off, seventy-two pairs of feet and one set of wheels went zipping across the line. The race course consisted of one lap around the track, then out onto the street for about a mile, and back to the track for another lap. Addie's legs were pumping like pistons, and the wheels of the chair spun so fast, I couldn't see the spokes. But by the time they had completed that first lap one thing was clear: They were going to lose.

Seeing Addie and Kenny about two-thirds of the way behind the leaders, I knew there was no hope. Of course we'd known it all along, but I guess I still harbored some secret hope for a miracle. But now I could see Bob Beechum, Gary Rosen, and Perry Astor were shoulder to shoulder at the front of the pack. Of the girls, Kathi Weiss wasn't too far behind them. I had never seen so much concentration on her face.

When Addie and Kenny passed me and started out toward the street, neither of them looked in my direction. Addie was still pumping hard, and Kenny was yelling, "Go! Go! Go!"

I was used to Addie and Kenny's usual pace, where I could eat a big bag of Cheetos before they finished one kilometer. But this was different. It didn't seem all that long before the first runners were coming back into the field. I wondered how far behind my friends were. Perry Astor crossed the finish line, winning the boys' medal, and a few minutes later Kathi Weiss bounded across the line, tears of pain or exhaustion or happiness streaming down her face.

The announcer was calling off the finishes as each kid crossed the line. "Thirty-eight, thirty-nine, forty, forty-one."

And then I saw them coming back onto the track— Addie kicking her feet into the air, puffing like an engine, Kenny urging her on. When they finally crossed the finish line, Kenny's fists were raised in the air. They had come in forty-fifth. Addie walked the chair to a slow stop, then moved away as people gathered around Kenny, shaking his hand, patting his back. Occasionally, above their congratulations, I heard his voice: "Wow! Super! Super!"

And I realized it didn't matter to Kenny whether they came in first, forty-fifth, or seventy-second. He was happy just to be part of it. I went looking for Addie and found her standing near the stage, watching Kathi and Perry receive their medals. Addie stood tall—as always—and her head was held high—as always. But there was something in her eyes I'd never seen before.

"Hi!" I shouted, moving toward her. My first impulse was to hug Addie. But as I got closer, the look in her eyes told me to back off.

"Congratulations!" I said, standing in front of her, not sure what to do.

"Thanks," she said, then turned to watch the medal presentation.

"You did great!"

"Nance, please! I'm trying to watch the presentation."

I saw a hand go up to her eye and realized she was crying. Despite all her talk, winning *had* been important to her. It was kind of ironic, considering it didn't matter to Kenny at all. Then it hit me: The reason Addie had run with Kenny was that no one else would. Anyone else could have run with him—Kenny wouldn't have cared— while Addie ran for the medal. I said to Addie, "I never thought of this until now, but you should have been running. Someone else could have run with Kenny. *I* could have tried."

"Yes," she said coldly. "You *could* have."

For the next twenty-four hours I was miserable. I was furious at myself for being so dim-witted, so self-centered that I'd cost Addie her chance to win the race. I was furious at Addie for being such a hypocrite— saying she didn't care about winning when she really did.

I was even mad at Kenny, because it seemed he was even more self-involved than I was. Didn't he realize Addie might have really wanted to run? Didn't he care that she was giving up her last chance just to give him a good time?

On Sunday evening I automatically put on my army jacket at six-fifteen. I didn't realize I'd done it until my younger sister said, "Off to meet Mr. Right?" and I realized I'd been a hypocrite myself—deliberately trying to look good in my sister's eyes by inventing a boyfriend. I said, "I don't have a boyfriend. I never did. I'm going out to find my two friends, Addie Haines and Kenny Wells!"

Then I crashed out the door. Behind me, my sister was shouting, "Kenny *Wheels?* The *cripple?* And that *black* girl?"

Of course, the field was dark, but I could hear her pounding footsteps on the track. I had never heard her run that fast before; I realized that all those weeks of pushing Kenny's chair had strengthened her, increased her speed. She ran for a long, long time, even though I was sure she knew I was there. Finally she came running off the track with a stopwatch in her hand and sat down beside me.

Now if she would only talk to me.

She held up the stopwatch and said, "My own private Funrun. I won. In fact, it was my best time ever." She didn't seem to be angry at me anymore.

I said, "Too bad I was the only one here to see it."

"Let's walk," she said, getting up.

We walked for a long time without talking. I think she was waiting for her breathing to level off before she spoke. Finally: "Yesterday was not one of my finer moments."

"Mine either," I admitted.

"I couldn't *believe* how bad it hurt to see Kathi Weiss with that medal around her neck. I couldn't *believe* how much I'd been lying to myself."

"I can't believe how dumb I've been," I said.

She continued, "I thought I was above that attitude, but I realized yesterday that I'm not. All yesterday and today I was down, down, down." Her voice dropped lower with each "down." "And then I thought to myself, Okay, Addie, so you're not perfect. You're petty and jealous and a hypocrite, so what? It's all part of being alive."

"I wish I could have that attitude," I began. "I can't stand myself."

"Neither can I sometimes," she admitted, and laughed.

We walked on in silence, heading for Kenny's house. We never said we were going there; we just did. And we ended up at the school a little while later, Addie on one side of the chair, me on the other, with Kenny between us, just taking a stroll down the track. Addie, Kenny, and me. Being alive.

About Peter Sieruta

Although Peter Sieruta has written plays for adult audiences, he says he prefers writing stories for and about young adults because he considers them  "less pretentious, more changeable, and more dramatic than adults." In his first book *Heartbeats and Other Stories*, from which "Being Alive" is taken, Sieruta has written stories he thinks he would have enjoyed reading as a teenager. "I want readers to find a character to whom they can relate," he says. "I also want them to gain a deeper understanding of people different from themselves."

Sieruta works in a library in his home town, Detroit. When he gets story ideas at work, he says, "I'll scribble down one or two lines, then stuff them in my pocket and put them all together at home." Sieruta says he often comes up with ideas for stories at night after going for a late walk.

Responding

1. **Personal Response** Do you think Nance should have run in Addie's place? Why or why not?

2. **Literary Analysis** This story begins and ends with the words "being alive." What does the *theme* of being alive mean in this story?

3. **Theme Connection** What do Addie, Nance, and Kenny each learn about themselves? How might their lives be different as a result?

Language Workshop

Characters and Dialogue The characters in "Being Alive" come to life through their *dialogue*, or conversation. For example, reread the conversation among Addie, Nance and Kenny on p. 113 about "outcasts." What does this conversation reveal about each character?

Choose one of the following situations and write a brief dialogue for the characters that helps bring them to life.

1. Two runners talk about an upcoming race both have entered. Each fears the other will win.

2. Three students who normally would not speak to each other plan a class report together.

3. Two students discuss whether or not a third student might have cheated on a test.

Writer's Portfolio

When Addie tells Nance she's worried about Kenny's health, Nance says she doesn't want to hear about it. She says, "I was always walking away from things I didn't want to hear." Do you think this is a good way to deal with problems? Write a letter to Nance and express your opinion.

Who Am I?

PROJECTS

Identify Yourself

How do the people around you view themselves? Write an "Identity Questionnaire" to be distributed to friends, family members, and other kids in your school. Brainstorm a list of questions that will help uncover your participants' true thoughts about who they are. Consider questions such as "What do you like about yourself?"; "What are your dreams for the future?"; "What worries you most?" Then tabulate the responses to find patterns of similarity and dissimilarity. How do the survey results compare with your own views? Report your findings to the class.

Mirror Image?

Take a close look at *Queen Isabo,* the abstract painting by Pablo Picasso on p. 68. What do you think the painting reveals about its subject? Now try an abstract of your own—but make yours a self-portrait. Use oils, pencils, crayons, or watercolors to create a picture that reflects how you see yourself. For more examples of abstract art, check the library for books with art by Jackson Pollock, Paul Klee, and Roy Lichtenstein, as well as Picasso.

Writing a Comparison

Which character from this unit seems most similar to you in personality? In what ways are you similar? In what ways are you different? Write a compare/contrast essay that describes how you are the same and how you are different from the character you've chosen. Find quotations from the text that illustrate your comparisons.

FURTHER READING

Sometimes it takes a difficult or even dangerous situation to discover who you really are. The characters in the following books find they have to take some risks as they search for an identity.

The Contender by Robert Lipsyte. Alfred Brooks escapes trouble on the streets by learning to box at a local gym. He hopes his new self-discipline and long hours of practice will help him become a contender in the ring and out of it.

Lord of the Flies by William Golding. If you were stranded on a deserted island, would it change the kind of person you are? This chilling novel describes what happens to a group of English schoolboys who face that very situation.

I Know Why the Caged Bird Sings by Maya Angelou. In this first volume of her autobiography, noted writer Maya Angelou describes her early life in Arkansas, St. Louis, and San Francisco. She reveals how, after a traumatic childhood experience forced her into years of silence, an understanding teacher helped her speak again.

The Miracle Worker by William Gibson. Teacher Annie Sullivan opens up new worlds of experience for her rebellious student, Helen Keller, in this riveting play.

The House on Mango Street by Sandra Cisneros. Growing up on the West Side of Chicago isn't easy. In the short chapters that make up this novel, a young girl named Esperanza describes the events happening around her and talks about her hopes, dreams, and fears.

UNIT 3

Facing the Enemy

Sooner or later we all have to square off with an enemy. Sometimes our enemies are real—a bully in the locker room, a fierce dog on the way home from school. Sometimes they're imagined—a wailing ghost in the attic, or a tour group from Mars in the backyard. In some cases the opponent we face is definitely real—a dreaded disease—but we can't see it, and there are no set rules on how to fight it.

The selections in Unit 3 all concern a confrontation with an enemy. You'll have to read these stories carefully—in some cases the enemy is distant, and hard to spot; in others, you may find the enemy uncomfortably close to home.

Priscilla and the Wimps

Listen, THERE WAS TIME WHEN YOU COULDN'T EVEN go to the *rest room* around this school without a pass. And I'm not talking about those little pink tickets made out by some teacher. I'm talking about a pass that could cost anywhere up to a buck, sold by Monk Klutter.

Not that Mighty Monk ever touched money, not in public. The gang he ran, which ran the school for him, was his collection agency. They were Klutter's Kobras, a name spelled out in nailheads on six well-known black plastic windbreakers.

Monk's threads were more . . . subtle. A pile-lined suede battle jacket with lizard-skin flaps over tailored Levis and a pair of ostrich-skin boots, brassed-toed and suitable for kicking people around. One of his Kobras did nothing all day but walk a half step behind Monk, carrying a fitted bag with Monk's gym shoes, a roll of rest-room passes, a cashbox, and a switchblade that Monk gave himself manicures with at lunch over at the Kobras' table.

Speaking of lunch, there were a few cases of advanced malnutrition among the newer kids. The ones who were a little slow in handing over a cut of their lunch money and were therefore barred from the cafeteria. Monk ran a tight ship.

I admit it. I'm five foot five, and when the Kobras slithered by, with or without Monk, I shrank. And I admit this, too: I paid up on a regular basis. And I might add: so would you.

This school was old Monk's Garden of Eden. Unfortunately for him, there was a serpent in it. The reason Monk didn't recognize trouble when it was staring him in the face is that the serpent in the Kobras' Eden was a girl.

Practically every guy in school could show you his scars. Fang marks from Kobras, you might say. And they were all highly visible in the shower room: lumps, lacerations, blue bruises, you name it. But girls usually got off with a warning.

Except there was this one girl named Priscilla Roseberry. Picture a girl named Priscilla Roseberry, and you'll be light years off. Priscilla was, hands down, the largest student in our particular institution of learning. I'm not talking fat. I'm talking big. Even beautiful, in a bionic way. Priscilla wasn't inclined toward organized crime. Otherwise, she could have put together a gang that would turn Klutter's Kobras into garter snakes.

Priscilla was basically a loner except she had one friend. A little guy named Melvin Detweiler. You talk about The Odd Couple. Melvin's one of the smallest guys above midget status ever seen. A really nice guy, but, you know—little. They even had lockers next to each other, in the same bank as mine. I don't know what they had going. I'm not saying this was a romance. After all, people deserve their privacy.

Priscilla was sort of above everything, if you'll pardon a pun. And very calm, as only the very big can be. If there was anybody who didn't notice Klutter's Kobras, it was Priscilla.

Until one winter day after school when we were all grabbing our coats out of our lockers. And hurrying, since Klutter's Kobras made sweeps of the halls for after-school shakedowns.

Anyway, up to Melvin's locker swaggers one of the Kobras. Never mind his name. Gang members don't need names. They've got group identity. He reaches down and grabs little Melvin by the neck and slams his head against his locker door. The sound of skull against steel rippled all the way down the locker row, speeding the crowds on their way.

> **Words to Know**
> **bionic** (p. 130) having both biological and electronic parts
> **shakedown** (p. 130) taking someone's money by force
> **hammerlock** (p. 131) a wrestling hold in which a person's arm is twisted and held behind the person's back

"Okay, let's see your pass," snarls the Kobra.

"A pass for what this time?" Melvin asks, probably still dazed.

"Let's call it a pass for very short people," says the Kobra, "a dwarf tax." He wheezes a little Kobra chuckle at his own wittiness. And already he's reaching for Melvin's wallet with the hand that isn't circling Melvin's windpipe. All this time, of course, Melvin and the Kobra are standing in Priscilla's big shadow.

She's taking her time shoving her books into her locker and pulling on a very large-size coat. Then, quicker than the eye, she brings the side of her enormous hand down in a chop that breaks the Kobra's hold on Melvin's throat. You could hear a pin drop in that hallway. Nobody'd ever laid a finger on a Kobra, let alone a hand the size of Priscilla's.

Then Priscilla, who hardly ever says anything to anybody except to Melvin, says to the Kobra, "Who's your leader, wimp?"

This practically blows the Kobra away. First he's chopped by a girl, and now she's acting like she doesn't know Monk Klutter, the Head Honcho of the World. He's so amazed, he tells her. "Monk Klutter."

"Never heard of him," Priscilla mentions. "Send him to see me." The Kobra just backs away from her like the whole situation is too big for him, which it is.

Pretty soon Monk himself slides up. He jerks his head once, and his Kobras slither off down the hall. He's going to handle this interesting case personally. "Who is it around here doesn't know Monk Klutter?"

He's standing inches from Priscilla, but since he'd have to look up at her, he doesn't. "Never heard of him," says Priscilla.

Monk's not happy with this answer, but by now he's spotted Melvin, who's grown smaller in spite of himself. Monk breaks his own rule by reaching for Melvin with his own hands. "Kid," he says, "you're going to have to educate your girl friend."

His hands never quite make it to Melvin. In a move of pure poetry Priscilla has Monk in a hammerlock. His neck's popping like gunfire, and his head's bowed under the immense weight of her forearm. His suede jacket's peeling back, showing pile.

Priscilla's behind him in another easy motion. And with a single mighty thrust forward, frog-marches Monk into her own locker. It's incredible. His ostrich-skin boots click once in the air. And suddenly he's gone, neatly wedged into the locker, a perfect fit. Priscilla bangs the door shut, twirls the lock and strolls out of school. Melvin goes with her, of course, trotting along below her shoulder. The last stragglers leave quietly.

Well, this is where fate, an even bigger force than Priscilla, steps in. It snows all that night, a blizzard. The whole town ices up. And school closes for a week.

About Richard Peck

Richard Peck is a former high school English teacher who decided he could help young adults more by writing books for them. Many of his stories and books involve teenagers who

experience painful situations. Peck believes that conformity and lack of communication, particularly among boys and men, are the most damaging problems that young adults face.

Although the characters in his books often experience difficult personal problems, Mr. Peck says he always tries to convey a sense of humor and a message of hope. His novels include *Father Figure* and *Are You in the House Alone?*

Responding

1. **Personal Response** What is your reaction to the ending of this story?

2. **Literary Analysis** An *allusion* is a reference to a person, place, event, or work of art. The narrator says, "This school was old Monk's Garden of Eden." What is the allusion in this sentence? What does it tell you about the situation at the school?

3. **Theme Connection** Would Priscilla's solution to the Monk Klutter problem be a good method to use in real life? Tell why or why not.

Language Workshop

Figurative Language *Figurative language* describes one thing by comparing it to something else. For example, the narrator in the story says, "Monk ran a tight ship." Monk is being compared to a strict captain on a ship.

Explain what the underlined figurative language means in each of the following quotations from the story:

1. "Picture a girl named Priscilla Roseberry, and <u>you'll be light years off.</u>"

2. "[Priscilla] could have put together a gang <u>that would turn Klutter's Kobras into garter snakes.</u>"

3. "[Priscilla] <u>frog-marches</u> Monk into her own locker."

Writer's Portfolio

Imagine that Monk somehow survives the week in Priscilla's locker. Will the experience change him? Write a scene that shows what Monk is like one year later.

B E R N A R D   E D E L M A N ,   E D I T O R

We Gotta Get Out of This Place

from *Dear America: Letters Home from Vietnam*

In a youth culture dominated by rock 'n' roll, "We Gotta Get Out of This Place," sung by a British group called The Animals, was one of the most popular songs for troops in Vietnam. Its title alone expressed what was on the mind of even the most ardent soldier. In a war in which each of us knew from the day we arrived in country the date on which we could expect to leave, getting out of Vietnam was what almost all of us longed for.

We looked forward to the day when we could consider ourselves "short," when we'd be "two-digit midgets"—have under a hundred days left in country—when we'd need, as we joked, a stepladder to get into bed and a parachute to get out.

Our time in Vietnam, though, was not without its diversions. Letters to and from those we loved were our lifeline to the World. Holidays were emotional anchors that we celebrated as best we could. R&R—five- or six-day jaunts to such places as Bangkok or Hong Kong or Hawaii—was anticipated eagerly. But getting home was our goal.

> ### Terms to Know
>
> **R&R** (p. 134) abbreviation for rest and relaxation, or time off from military duty
>
> **VC** (p.136) the Viet Cong, Vietnamese Communist guerrillas
>
> **post-traumatic stress disorder** (p. 136) a psychological condition resulting from undergoing an extremely difficult experience. Sufferers may experience flashbacks, feelings of extreme fear, or a variety of physical symptoms.
>
> **morale booster** (p. 139) something that helps improve one's attitude in terms of one's courage, confidence, or enthusiasm

Tuesday, Sept. 6, 1966

Dear Mom,

...You'll probably be hearing about us again. Yesterday my platoon had six injured and one killed. We had a fire fight that lasted nine hours. We killed a lot of VC on this operation we're on now, but we also have had a lot killed.

I wrote Sue and told her to give you back my ring. It's still a good ring although it doesn't work too good. I can always give it to some other chump, I mean girl.

Well, Mom, I don't have much time, and I just wanted you to know I'm all right.

When you go to church, I want you to give all the people you see this address and tell them to send anything they can, like old clothes and anything.

I went down to this orphanage the other day, and these little kids are pitiful. They sleep on plain floors and don't get hardly anything to eat.

The reason I want you to tell everyone to help them is because I feel I may have killed some of their parents and it makes me feel sick to know they have to go on with nothing. Address: Mang-Lang Orphanage, Le-Loi Street, Tuy Hoa, Vietnam.

Love, Your son,
Dan

PFC Daniel Bailey was assigned to A Troop, 2nd Battalion, 17th Cavalry, 101st Airborne Division, from May 1966 through June 1967, operating in II Corps. He is unemployed and receives disability compensation from the Veterans Administration for post-traumatic stress disorder. He lives in Clarington, Pennsylvania.

6 July 1967

My Darling Claudia,

It's raining outside. A damp smell in the air and the raindrops slamming onto the plasterboard roof. Sound of cricket and frog, and the rumble of distant bomb explosions shake the earth here many miles away. Lightning flashes bare the heavens for a brief glimpse at a troubled sky watching over a war-torn land. The area is flooded, and mud clings to boots with a slurp-sucking sound. Soaked uniform hanging on chair to dry and shriveling up into a wrinkled mass. A chilling air is coddled by two ceiling fans and swirled through my body. I miss you, my darling. The night is cold, and you are warm and loving and soft.

At times like this, my darling, I feel as if I would do anything if I could just be back again with you. Sometimes you have to pretend you're not really lonely or else you'd find yourself going out of your mind. But when the day is done, and you're lying alone with your thoughts, then there's no more fooling and that's when it really hurts. The days seem to go by quickly, but the weeks seem forever. Today I have been in Vietnam 73 days, 10½ weeks, a little over 2½ months. The guys who are over here now tell me, looking back, that the time flew by. But right now it seems so very long until you're in my arms again.

Darling, it's midnight, so please forgive the short letter but I'm very tired now. Be careful Dia.

I love you,
Michael

1Lt. Robert Michael Murray, who served with Company A, 5th Special Forces Group, based at Bien Hoa, from April 1967 to April 1968, wrote this to Claudia Johnston. They married in May 1968, two weeks after he returned from Vietnam. He is now an attorney, practicing in White Plains, New York.

I Must Go On

We fought together, six months today,
As I rolled over, there he lay.
His eyes were open, his hands clenched tight,
The look of death, a look of fright.

I knew right then that he was dead,
And wondered why, not me instead.
His life was short, not many years,
Full of hope yet full of fears.

We'd talked and laughed of times gone by,
And never thought that we might die,
But here he lay, no breath of life,
No thought of home, or his young wife.

I turned my head and looked away,
I fought the words I could not say.
HE'S DEAD, He's Dead and gone,
But I am here and must go on.

I must go on.

—Timothy F. Schlink

1Lt. Timothy Schlink was assigned to Company C, 2nd Battalion, 1st Infantry, 196th Light Infantry Brigade, Americal Division, based at Tay Ninh and Chu Lai, from September 1966 through June 1967. After his best friend was killed by a land mine, Lt. Schlink wrote this poem to his father while trying to find words to express his feelings to the new widow. Today he is financial manager for Pacific Bell in San Jose, California.

13 December '68

My Darling Mic,

    Today has been another long day at Moung Soui [Laos], but at least now it is ended and I'm that much closer to being with you and Robin once again. You know

I actually enjoy this tour as long as I am busy enough to keep my thoughts from wandering back to you—but that is never for very long. It is almost strange that the one who has always made me so happy can now make me sad—because I miss you so much, darling one.

I have been giving some serious thought lately to what else I could be happy doing. You know how much the Army means to me. But then I have only one love and that is for my little family. Mic, it has been so very difficult for me, especially the past few months, to be away from you. And I know that if I stay in, we will eventually be separated again. That thought causes me quite a lot of worry. Baby, for once in my life I just can't make a decision—what do you think?

Still no word on R&R. That is a bitter pill, I know, for we have both been longing so much for it. The only time that really looks hopeful is February—and even that isn't sure. Like you said, if there were anyone I could write to, I would. If I don't mention R&R, don't worry that I have forgotten—it will just be that I haven't heard. Love, I'm so sorry.

The pictures of you and Robin were real morale boosters. You two must be two of God's most precious specimens. Gosh, you both look so good—and that daughter of ours is going to grow up to be as pretty as her mother—almost! Mic, old Joseph still loves you. As you must already know and though the days grow longer, the time grows yet shorter until these lonely arms hold you tight once again.

> Your own,
> Joe

Capt. Joseph K. Bush, Jr., whose home was in Temple, Texas, never got his R&R. While serving as an adviser to Laotian forces at Moung Soui, he was killed during an attack by North Vietnamese commandos on 10 February 1969. He was 25 years old.

Dear Madeline,

Hello my dear sister.

Boy, I sure feel close to you. Since your last letter, I almost feel as if you are my sister. It's good to have someone to tell your troubles to. I can't tell them to my parents or Darlene because they worry too much, but I tell you truthfully I doubt if I'll come out of this alive.

In my original squad I'm the only one left unharmed. In my platoon there's only 13 of us. It seems every day another young guy 18 and 19 years old like myself is killed in action. Please help me, Mad. I don't know if I should stop writing my parents and Darlene or what.

I'm going on an operation next month where there is nothing but VC and VC sympathizers. The area is also very heavily mined. All of us are scared cause we know a lot of us won't make it. I would like to hear what you have to say about it, Madeline, before I make any decisions.

Oh, and one more favor. I'd like the truth now. Has Darlene been faithful to me? I know she's been dating guys, but does she still love me best? Thanks for understanding. See ya if it's God's will. I have to make it out of Vietnam though, cause I'm lucky. I hope. Ha ha.

Miss ya,

Love,
Ray

PFC Raymond C. Griffiths went to Vietnam just after Christmas in 1965 and was assigned to Company A, 1st Battalion, 9th Marines, 3rd Marine Division. He wrote this letter to Madeline Velasco, a friend from high school in San Francisco, California, in June 1966. He was killed a few weeks later, on the Fourth of July. He was 19 years old.

November 27 [1969]
Thursday

Hi Sweet Thing,

Yesterday I can say it was one of the happiest days in my life. Hearing about the baby. It is one of the best things a man over here can be told. I wish you could have seen the way me and my friends were acting after we heard about it. We were shooting our rifles and making all kinds of noise. The people in the village thought we were going crazy. It was really something to see. I wanted to be home so bad.

Denise, how has the baby been feeling? Is she getting used to being in the world? Does she seem to be happy? How are you feeling after having her? How many times do you have to see the doctor a month? What did the doctor say about your and her health?

Today is Thanksgiving, and I have a lot to be thankful for—a wonderful wife and being able to have a child of ours. I'm thankful to be a father.

> All my love,
> Bernie
> Father of one girl

PFC Bernard Robinson was assigned to the 3rd Marine Division's Civil Action Program 357 in I Corps between June 1969 and July 1970. He now owns a video-rental store in New York City.

About Bernard Edelman

During the Vietnam War, Bernard Edelman served in the United States Army as a broadcast specialist  and correspondent. To help reveal the personal thoughts and feelings of Americans who served in Vietnam, Bernard Edelman collected the letters included here and many others in his book *Dear America: Letters Home from Vietnam.* In the introduction, Edelman dedicates the book to all Vietnam veterans and their loved ones.

Born and raised in Brooklyn, Edelman still lives in New York City, where he has worked as an editor, photographer, reporter, and curator.

Responding

1. **Personal Response** Which of these letters affected you the most? Why?

2. **Literary Analysis** *Irony* occurs when there is a great contrast between what is expected and what actually happens. Joseph Bush says in his letter that he is trying to decide whether or not to stay in the Army. What is *ironic* about the letter?

3. **Theme Connection** How does fighting a war seem to affect these soldiers' ideas about what is most important in life? Support your statement with examples from the letters.

Language Workshop

Root Words Knowing root words can help you figure out meanings of words that belong to the same word family. For example, when you read the term *adviser* (p. 139), you can see that the first word contains the root word *advise*, meaning "to give advice to." From this clue and the context of the sentence, you can probably figure out that an *adviser* is someone who gives advice.

Figure out the root word for each of the following underlined words. Use what you know about the root word and context clues to write a brief definition of the underlined word.

1. During the battle the radio equipment was not <u>operational</u>.

2. The lieutenant wanted to <u>ensure</u> the safety of his soldiers.

3. The entire <u>battalion</u> was ordered to attack at dawn.

Writer's Portfolio

How would you respond if you received one of these letters? Write a letter back to one of these soldiers, or write a letter to another soldier you have known or read about. What do you want to tell him or her?

PETE SEEGER

Where Have All the Flowers Gone?

Where have all the flowers gone,
Long time passing?
Where have all the flowers gone,
Long time ago?
Where have all the flowers gone?
The girls have picked them every one.
Oh, when will you ever learn?
Oh, when will you ever learn?

Where have all the young girls gone,
Long time passing?
Where have all the young girls gone,
Long time ago?
Where have all the young girls gone?
They've taken husbands every one.
Oh, when will you ever learn?
Oh, when will you ever learn?

Where have all the young men gone,
Long time passing?
Where have all the young men gone,
Long time ago?
Where have all the young men gone?
They're all in uniform.
Oh, when will we ever learn?
Oh, when will we ever learn?

Where have all the soldiers gone,
Long time passing?
Where have all the soldiers gone,
Long time ago?
Where have all the soldiers gone?
They've gone to graveyards, every one.
Oh, when will they ever learn?
Oh, when will they ever learn?

Where have all the graveyards gone,
Long time passing?
Where have all the graveyards gone,
Long time ago?
Where have all the graveyards gone?
They're covered with flowers every one.
Oh, when will they ever learn?
Oh, when will they ever learn?

Where have all the flowers gone,
Long time passing?
Where have all the flowers gone,
Long time ago?
Where have all the flowers gone?
Young girls picked them every one.
Oh, when will they ever learn?
Oh, when will they ever learn?

from Anne Frank: The Diary of a Young Girl

In June of 1942, a young Jewish girl living in Holland received a diary for her thirteenth birthday. Anne Frank began to record her most intimate thoughts in the diary, writing letters to an imaginary friend named Kitty. Less than a month later, when Anne and her family went into hiding to escape from the Nazis, Anne's diary went with her.

For more than two years, the Franks and four other people shared cramped living quarters in a hidden space over a warehouse that became known as "The Secret Annex." Anne's diary was her refuge, the only place where she could freely describe the turbulent emotions and events of the years in hiding. This excerpt was written shortly before Anne Frank's fifteenth birthday.

Dit is een foto, zoals ik me zou wensen, altijd zo te zijn. Dan had ik nog wel een kans om naar Holywood te komen. Maar tegenwoordig zie ik er jammer genoeg meestal anders uit. Anne Frank. 10 Oct. 1942. Zondag.

[Wednesday, 3 May, 1944]

. . . As you can easily imagine we often ask ourselves here despairingly: "What, oh, what is the use of the war? Why can't people live peacefully together? Why all this destruction?"

The question is very understandable, but no one has found a satisfactory answer to it so far. Yes, why do they make still more gigantic planes, still heavier bombs and, at the same time, prefabricated houses for reconstruction? Why should millions be spent daily on the war and yet there's not a penny available for medical services, artists, or for poor people?

Why do some people have to starve, while there are surpluses rotting in other parts of the world? Oh, why are people so crazy?

I don't believe that the big men, the politicians and the capitalists alone, are guilty of the war. Oh no, the little man is just as guilty, otherwise the peoples of the world would have risen in revolt long ago! There's in people simply an urge to destroy, an urge to kill, to murder and rage, and until all mankind, without exception, undergoes a great change, wars will be waged, everything that has been built up, cultivated, and grown will be destroyed and disfigured, after which mankind will have to begin all over again.

I have often been downcast, but never in despair; I regard our hiding as a dangerous adventure, romantic and interesting at the same time. In my diary I treat all the privations as amusing. I have made up my mind now to lead a different life from other girls and, later on, different from ordinary housewives. My start has been so very full of interest, and that is the sole reason why I have to laugh at the humorous side of the most dangerous moments.

I am young and I possess many buried qualities; I am young and strong and am living a great adventure; I am still in the midst of it and can't grumble the whole day long. I have been given a lot, a happy nature, a great deal of cheerfulness and strength. Every day I feel that I am developing inwardly, that the liberation is drawing nearer and how beautiful nature is, how good the people are about me, how interesting this adventure is! Why, then, should I be in despair?

Three months after Anne Frank wrote this passage in her diary, the Nazis raided the "Secret Annex." Anne and the others were arrested and sent to German and Dutch concentration camps. In March of 1945, two months before Holland was liberated from the Germans, Anne died in the concentration camp at Bergen-Belsen.

About Pete Seeger

Pete Seeger is a writer, political organizer, and songwriter. He is perhaps best known as a  folksinger. Some of Seeger's most popular songs include "Turn, Turn, Turn," "If I Had a Hammer," and "Kisses Sweeter than Wine." As a young man, he toured the country singing to "common folks" in migrant laborer camps and union halls. More recently, Pete Seeger has been involved in the movement to preserve the environment.

About Anne Frank

Anne Frank was born in 1929 and died in 1945, one of the six million Jews who perished under  Hitler's regime. Though her life was brief, Anne filled it with spirit, humor, courage, and love.

When Otto Frank, Anne's father, was released from the Auschwitz concentration camp in 1945, he learned that Anne and the rest of his family had died in the camps. But friends had found Anne's diary in the Secret Annex and had saved it. Otto Frank decided to share his daughter's words with the rest of the world. In the years since the Holocaust, *Anne Frank: The Diary of a Young Girl* has affected and inspired millions of people.

Responding

1. **Personal Response** Can you relate to the feelings behind Pete Seeger's song and Anne Frank's diary entry? Explain.

2. **Literary Analysis** "Where Have All the Flowers Gone?" uses *repetition*. What effect do the repeating phrases create?

3. **Theme Connection** What do the poem and the diary entry each have to say about war?

Language Workshop

Visualizing When you *visualize* something, you picture what it looks like. What do you visualize when you read "Where Have All the Flowers Gone?" Draw a picture or write a description in your own words.

Writer's Portfolio

Write a song or a poem that expresses your feelings about war.

Future Tense

GARY COULDN'T WAIT FOR TENTH GRADE TO START so he could strut his sentences, parade his paragraphs, renew his reputation as the top creative writer in school. At the opening assembly, he felt on edge, psyched, like a boxer before the first-round bell. He leaned forward as Dr. Proctor, the principal, introduced two new staff members. He wasn't particularly interested in the new vice-principal, Ms. Jones; Gary never had discipline problems, he'd never even had to stay after school. But his head cocked alertly as Dr. Proctor introduced the new Honors English teacher, Mr. Smith. Here was the person he'd have to impress.

He studied Mr. Smith. The man was hard to describe. He looked as though he'd been manufactured to fit his name. Average height, brownish hair, pale white skin, medium build. Middle age. He was the sort of person you began to forget the minute you met him. Even his clothes had no particular style. They merely covered his body.

Mr. Smith was . . . just there.

Gary was studying Mr. Smith so intently that he didn't hear Dr. Proctor call him up to the stage to receive an award from last term. Jim Baggs jabbed an elbow into his ribs and said, "Let's get up there, Dude."

Dr. Proctor shook Gary's hand and gave him the County Medal for Best Composition. While Dr. Proctor was giving Jim Baggs the County Trophy for Best All-Round Athlete, Gary glanced over his shoulder to see if Mr. Smith looked impressed. But he couldn't find the new teacher. Gary wondered if Mr. Smith was so ordinary he was invisible when no one was talking about him.

On the way home, Dani Belzer, the prettiest poet in school, asked Gary, "What did you think of our new Mr. Wordsmith?"

"If he was a color he'd be beige," said Gary. "If he was a taste he'd be water. If he was a sound he'd be a low hum."

"Fancy, empty words," sneered Mike Chung, ace reporter on the school paper. "All you've told me is you've got nothing to tell me."

Dani quickly stepped between them. "What did you think of the first assignment?"

"Describe a Typical Day at School," said Gary, trying unsuccessfully to mimic Mr. Smith's bland voice. "That's about as exciting as tofu."

"A real artist," said Dani, "accepts the commonplace as a challenge."

That night, hunched over his humming electric typewriter, Gary wrote a description of a typical day at school from the viewpoint of a new teacher who was seeing everything for the very first time, who took nothing for granted. He described the shredded edges of the limp flag outside the dented front door, the worn flooring where generations of kids had nervously paced outside the principal's office, the nauseatingly sweet pipe-smoke seeping out of the teachers' lounge.

And then, in the last line, he gave the composition that extra twist, the little kicker on which his reputation rested. He wrote:

```
The new teacher's beady little eyes
missed nothing, for they were the optical
recorders of an alien creature who had come
to Earth to gather information.
```

The next morning, when Mr. Smith asked for a volunteer to read aloud, Gary was on his feet and moving toward the front of the classroom before Mike Chung got his hand out of his pocket.

The class loved Gary's composition. They laughed and stamped their feet. Chung shrugged, which meant he couldn't think of any criticism, and Dani flashed thumbs up.

> ### Words to Know
> **optical recorder** (p. 154) a machine that records visual images, for example, a camera
>
> **extraterrestrial** (p. 155) outside the earth, from outer space
>
> **iota** (p. 155) a tiny part or amount
>
> **minutiae** (p. 155) very small matters

Best of all, Jim Baggs shouldered Gary against the blackboard after class and said, "Awesome tale, Dude."

Gary felt good until he got the composition back. Along one margin, in a perfect script, Mr. Smith had written:

You can do better.

"How would he know?" Gary complained on the way home.

"You should be grateful," said Dani. "He's pushing you to the farthest limits of your talent."

"Which may be nearer than you think," snickered Mike.

Gary rewrote his composition, expanded it, complicated it, thickened it. Not only was this new teacher an alien, he was part of an extraterrestrial conspiracy to take over Earth. Gary's final sentence was:

```
Every iota of information, fragment of
fact, morsel of minutiae sucked up by those
vacuuming eyes was beamed directly into
a computer circling the planet. The data
would eventually become a program that
would control the mind of every school kid
on Earth.
```

Gary showed the new draft to Dani before class. He stood on tiptoes so he could read over her shoulder. Sometimes he wished she were shorter, but mostly he wished he were taller.

"What do you think?"

"The assignment was to describe a typical day," said Dani. "This is off the wall."

He snatched the papers back. "Creative writing means creating." He walked away, hurt and angry. He thought: *If she doesn't like my compositions, how can I ever get her to like me?*

That morning, Mike Chung read his own composition aloud to the class. He described a typical day through the eyes of a student in a wheelchair. Everything most students take for granted was an obstacle: the bathroom door too heavy to open, the gym steps too steep to climb, the light switch too high on the wall. The class applauded and Mr. Smith nodded approvingly. Even Gary had to admit it was really good—if you considered plain-fact journalism as creative writing, that is.

Gary's rewrite came back the next day marked:

Improving. Try again.

Saturday he locked himself in his room after breakfast and rewrote the rewrite. He carefully selected his nouns and verbs and adjectives. He polished and arranged them in sentences like a jeweler strings pearls. He felt good as he wrote, as the electric typewriter hummed and buzzed and sometimes coughed. He thought: *Every champion knows that as hard as it is to get to the top, it's even harder to stay up there.*

His mother knocked on his door around noon. When he let her in, she said, "It's a beautiful day."

"Big project," he mumbled. He wanted to avoid a distracting conversation.

She smiled. "If you spend too much time in your room, you'll turn into a mushroom."

He wasn't listening. "Thanks. Anything's okay. Don't forget the mayonnaise."

Gary wrote:

    The alien's probes trembled as he read
    the student's composition. Could that skinny,
    bespectacled earthling really suspect its
    extraterrestrial identity? Or was his
    composition merely the result of a creative
    thunderstorm in a brilliant young mind?

Before Gary turned in his composition on Monday morning, he showed it to Mike Chung. He should have known better.

"You're trying too hard," chortled Chung. "Truth is stronger than fiction."

Gary flinched at that. It hurt. It might be true. But he couldn't let his competition know he had scored. "You journalists are stuck in the present and the past," growled Gary. "Imagination prepares us for what's going to happen."

Dani read her composition aloud to the class. It described a typical day from the perspective of a louse choosing a head of hair to nest in. The louse moved from the thicket of a varsity crew-cut to the matted jungle of a sagging perm to a straight, sleek blond cascade.

The class cheered and Mr. Smith smiled. Gary felt a twinge of jealousy. Dani and Mike were coming on. There wasn't room for more than one at the top.

In the hallway, he said to Dani, "And you called my composition off the wall?"

Mike jumped in. "There's a big difference between poetical metaphor and hack science fiction."

Gary felt choked by a lump in his throat. He hurried away.

Mr. Smith handed back Gary's composition the next day marked:

See me after school.

Gary was nervous all day. What was there to talk about? Maybe Mr. Smith hated science fiction. One of those traditional English teachers. Didn't understand that science fiction could be literature. *Maybe I can educate him,* thought Gary.

When Gary arrived at the English office, Mr. Smith seemed nervous too. He kept folding and unfolding Gary's composition. "Where do you get such ideas?" he asked in his monotone voice.

Gary shrugged. "They just come to me."

"Alien teachers. Taking over the minds of schoolchildren." Mr. Smith's empty eyes were blinking. "What made you think of that?"

"I've always had this vivid imagination."

"If you're sure it's just your imagination." Mr. Smith looked relieved. "I guess everything will work out." He handed back Gary's composition. "No more fantasy, Gary. Reality. That's your assignment. Write only about what you know."

Outside school, Gary ran into Jim Baggs, who looked surprised to see him. "Don't tell me you had to stay after, Dude."

"I had to see Mr. Smith about my composition. He didn't like it. Told me to stick to reality."

"Don't listen." Jim Baggs body-checked Gary into the schoolyard fence. "Dude, you got to be yourself."

Gary ran all the way home and locked himself into his room. He felt feverish with creativity. Dude, you got to be yourself, Dude. It doesn't matter what your so-called friends say, or your English teacher. You've got to play your own kind of game, write your own kind of stories.

The words flowed out of Gary's mind and through his fingers and out of the machine and onto sheets of paper. He wrote and rewrote until he felt the words were exactly right:

> With great effort, the alien shut down the electrical panic impulses coursing through its system and turned on Logical Overdrive. There were two possibilities:
>
> 1. This high school boy was exactly what he seemed to be, a brilliant, imaginative, apprentice best-selling author and screen-writer, or,
>
> 2. He had somehow stumbled onto the secret plan and he would have to be either enlisted into the conspiracy or erased off the face of the planet.

First thing in the morning, Gary turned in his new rewrite to Mr. Smith. A half hour later, Mr. Smith called Gary out of Spanish. There was no expression on his regular features. He said, "I'm going to need some help with you."

Cold sweat covered Gary's body as Mr. Smith grabbed his arm and led him to the new vice-principal. She read the composition while they waited. Gary got a good look at her for the first time. Ms. Jones was . . . just there. She looked as though she'd been manufactured to fit her name. Average. Standard. Typical. The cold sweat turned into goose pimples.

How could he have missed the clues? Smith and Jones were aliens! He had stumbled on their secret and now they'd have to deal with him.

He blurted, "Are you going to enlist me or erase me?"

Ms. Jones ignored him. "In my opinion, Mr. Smith, you are overreacting. This sort of nonsense"—she waved Gary's composition—"is the typical response of an overstimulated adolescent to the mixture of reality and fantasy in an environment dominated by manipulative music, television, and films. Nothing for us to worry about."

"If you're sure, Ms. Jones," said Mr. Smith. He didn't sound sure.

The vice-principal looked at Gary for the first time. There was no expression in her eyes. Her voice was flat. "You'd better get off this science fiction kick," she said. "If you know what's good for you."

"I'll never tell another human being, I swear," he babbled.

"What are you talking about?" asked Ms. Jones.

"Your secret is safe with me," he lied. He thought, *If I can just get away from them. Alert the authorities. Save the planet.*

"You see," said Ms. Jones, "you're writing yourself into a crazed state."

"You're beginning to believe your own fantasies," said Mr. Smith.

"I'm not going to do anything this time," said Ms. Jones, "but you must promise to write only about what you know."

"Or I'll have to fail you," said Mr. Smith.

"For your own good," said Ms. Jones. "Writing can be very dangerous."

"Especially for writers," said Mr. Smith, "who write about things they shouldn't."

"Absolutely," said Gary, "positively, no question about it. Only what I know." He backed out the door, nodding his head, thinking, *Just a few more steps and I'm okay. I hope these aliens can't read minds.*

Jim Baggs was practicing head fakes in the hallway. He slammed Gary into the wall with a hip block. "How's it going, Dude?" he asked, helping Gary up.

"Aliens," gasped Gary. "Told me no more science fiction."

"They can't treat a star writer like that," said Jim. "See what the head honcho's got to say." He grabbed Gary's wrist and dragged him to the principal's office.

"What can I do for you, boys?" boomed Dr. Proctor.

"They're messing with his moves, Doc," said Jim Baggs. "You got to let the aces run their races."

"Thank you, James." Dr. Proctor popped his forefinger at the door. "I'll handle this."

"You're home free, Dude," said Jim, whacking Gary across the shoulder blades as he left.

"From the beginning," ordered Dr. Proctor. He nodded sympathetically as Gary told the entire story, from the opening assembly to the meeting with Mr. Smith and Ms. Jones. When Gary was finished, Dr. Proctor took the papers from Gary's hand. He shook his head as he read Gary's latest rewrite.

"You really have a way with words, Gary. I should have sensed you were on to something."

Gary's stomach flipped. "You really think there could be aliens trying to take over Earth?"

"Certainly," said Dr. Proctor, matter-of-factly. "Earth is the ripest plum in the universe."

Gary wasn't sure if he should feel relieved that

he wasn't crazy or be scared out of his mind. He took a deep breath to control the quaver in his voice, and said: "I spotted Smith and Jones right away. They look like they were manufactured to fit their names. Obviously humanoids. Panicked as soon as they knew I was on to them."

Dr. Proctor chuckled and shook his head. "No self-respecting civilization would send those two stiffs to Earth."

"They're not aliens?" He felt relieved and disappointed at the same time.

"I checked them out myself," said Dr. Proctor. "Just two average, standard, typical human beings, with no imagination, no creativity."

"So why'd you hire them?"

Dr. Proctor laughed. "Because they'd never spot an alien. No creative imagination. That's why I got rid of the last vice-principal and the last Honors English teacher. They were giving me odd little glances when they thought I wasn't looking. After ten years on your planet, I've learned to smell trouble."

Gary's spine turned to ice and dripped down the backs of his legs. "You're an alien!"

"Great composition," said Dr. Proctor, waving Gary's papers. "Grammatical, vividly written, and totally accurate."

"It's just a composition," babbled Gary, "made the whole thing up, imagination, you know."

Dr. Proctor removed the face of his wristwatch and began tapping tiny buttons. "Always liked writers. I majored in your planet's literature. Writers are the keepers of the past and the hope of the future. Too bad they cause so much trouble in the present."

"I won't tell anyone," cried Gary. "Your secret's safe with me." He began to back slowly toward the door.

Dr. Proctor shook his head. "How can writers keep secrets, Gary? It's their natures to share their creations with the world." He tapped three times and froze Gary in place, one foot raised to step out the door.

"But it was only a composition," screamed Gary as his body disappeared before his eyes.

"And I can't wait to hear what the folks back home say when you read it to them," said Dr. Proctor.

"I made it all up." Gary had the sensation of rocketing upward. "I made up the whole . . ."

About Robert Lipsyte

Robert Lipsyte grew up in New York City and spent summers in upstate New York: "I hid out, reading and writing and daydreaming. It was a perfect childhood for a writer." He was very overweight until the age of fourteen, when he  slimmed down after mowing lawns for a summer. Lipsyte writes about being heavy and losing weight in his novel *One Fat Summer*.

Lipsyte, who has had a long career as a sportswriter and TV sports talk show host, often uses his knowledge of sports when writing for young adults. His book *The Contender*, for example, is about the struggle of a poor teenager in Harlem to become a professional boxer.

Responding

1. Personal Response Did Gary get what he deserved? Explain.

2. Literary Analysis Explain the *humor* behind the title of this story.

3. Theme Connection What mistakes did Gary make in "facing the enemy"? Give him some advice.

Language Workshop

Capitalizing Proper Nouns and Adjectives *Proper nouns* name a particular person, place, or thing. *Proper adjectives* are formed from proper nouns. When you write, proper nouns and proper adjectives should be capitalized. Look at these examples from "Future Tense."

> Gary   Ms. Jones   English teacher

For each of the following, capitalize the proper nouns and proper adjectives.

1. It sounds like dr. proctor is not really a doctor.

2. Poor gary may be on his way to pluto.

3. According to jim, we have a martian in our french class.

Writer's Portfolio

What do you think will happen when Gary reaches Dr. Proctor's planet? Be Gary and write a letter to Dr. Proctor from your new home. Try to persuade him to let you return to Earth.

LOIS LOWRY

The Harringtons' Daughter

THEY SAID THE YOUNG WOMAN NEXT DOOR WAS MAD. THE Harringtons' daughter—they called her that, as if she had no name of her own—was mad. They meant crazy.

That was all they said: that she was quite, quite mad, and I was to pay no attention. The shades on the south side of my grandparents' house, the side that faced the Harringtons, were drawn during the day, so that the vast living room was dim. Grandmother said the shades were to be kept drawn so that the summer sunlight, glaring in this rainless August, wouldn't fade the oriental rugs. But I knew better. The rugs had been faded all my life, and probably for a hundred years before that. They were the kind of rugs whose reds and blues were supposed to be muted by time and the tread of generations.

The reason the shades were drawn was so that we would not be forced to glimpse the Harringtons' daughter, who was quite, quite mad.

"What happened to her?" I asked Grandmother.

By her quick frown, I knew I shouldn't have asked. "She had an unfortunate experience, and completely lost her mind," Grandmother murmured. She adjusted her glasses and took up her knitting from the basket beside her chair. "Frederick, may we have some music?"

Grandfather turned to the radio and played with the dial until the sound of a solo violin throbbed into the room.

"Brahms," he said with satisfaction, and picked up the evening newspaper.

I stared into the room, wondering what Grandmother had meant by an "unfortunate experience." Only this evening the maid, serving dinner, had spilled some gravy on the linen tablecloth. That was an unfortunate experience, judging by Grandmother's sharp look and the maid's intake of breath.

My train had been late in arriving the day before: another unfortunate experience, no doubt, causing Grandmother to wait an extra twenty minutes at the sweltering, litter-strewn station.

My mother, their only daughter, was very ill. One more unfortunate experience, and why I was here unexpectedly. It had happened so quickly: a routine doctor's appointment; some tests; some bad news; surgery. "Don't worry," Mother had said. "I'll be home in a week." But something had not gone well. There were specialists now, and consultants; it had turned into two weeks, and then three. No visitors allowed, only my father. And he had sent me away, to this silent house where the shades were drawn and a madwoman lived next door.

I leafed through a magazine, with a glum look. I had overheard my grandparents describe me to each other: "sullen" they said, with distaste. And I suppose it was true. I was seventeen and had not intended that my summer would be like this. I had intended that the summer between my high school graduation and my entrance into college would be one of friends and merriment, parties and pranks: the kind of summer my classmates were having back home, without me.

It occurred to me suddenly that I, too, was quite, quite mad. Angry.

"Excuse me," I said to my grandparents, probably sullenly, and left the room.

The kitchen through which I walked was spotless and empty, not at all like other people's kitchens, like my own family's kitchen back home, where a bowl of apples was always on the table, where checkered dishtowels dangled from the oven doorhandle, and hastily scribbled notes and reminders were magnetically attached to the refrigerator by tiny metallic ladybugs and bananas.

My grandparents' kitchen was unblemished white, like an operating room. Now that the maid was finished for the evening, there was no visible food, no visible punctuation of color anywhere, only the dull black handles and gleaming metal blades of knives attached to a wall rack. The dull, churning hum of the dishwasher marred the silence.

I unlocked the screen door that led to the back lawn and went outside. Grandmother's carefully tended flower gardens still bloomed, though they had suffered in the drought; tall, pink hollyhocks stood crowded against the wall of the house, beside rigidly staked white glads, and at their feet, masses of pale dahlias drooped, needing rain. The usually immaculate grass was brown in spots. There was a ban on watering, Grandmother had explained this morning,

Names of Flowers

hollyhock (p. 166) a tall plant with a stiff, leafy stem and large flowers

glads (p. 166) short for gladiolas; plants with sword-shaped leaves and spikes of large flowers in various colors

dahlia (p. 166) a tall plant with large, bright flowers

astilbe (p. 167) an herb with clusters of small white, yellow, or reddish flowers

honeysuckle (p. 167) a climbing shrub or vine with fragrant white, yellow, or red flowers

aster (p. 167) a flower with white, pink, red, blue, or purple daisylike petals around a yellow center

her voice taut with controlled dismay. "The astilbe has died," she had said, pointing to dry brown fronds of what had been flowers in the shaded corner by the porch.

Now, in the twilight, all color was flattened to gray. There was no breeze.

"Hello."

The voice startled me, and I turned to the fence, mounded with honeysuckle vines, to see the Harringtons' daughter looking at me.

I had never seen her before, though I had met her parents, previous summers. They were older than mine, with no children left at home. But their daughter—the madwoman who was staring at me now, above the honeysuckle—was quite young. Twenty-five, perhaps? It was hard to tell. Her hair was in a long braid and she was dressed in a cotton robe, loose around her. She was thin and tall, not pretty, but attractive, with big dark eyes.

"Hello," I replied, and went to the fence so that we faced each other.

"What's your name?" she asked. Her voice was little more than a whisper.

"Nina. I'm visiting my grandparents. What's your name?"

She laughed, a low breathy chuckle. "Secret," she said.

Did she mean that Secret was, actually, her name? Or that her name was a secret? I didn't feel that I could ask.

"It's hot, isn't it?" I said instead.

"Is it?" She looked around, as if I had called her attention to something that she had missed. "I don't feel."

Then she turned away. I saw, suddenly, that her hands were filled with flowers. The Harringtons' yard was not manicured, like Grandmother's, not carefully tended; but there were flowers there, thick and tangled with weeds. While I watched, she went to a clump of asters and wrenched some blossoms loose.

"It might have been here," I heard her say. "This might have been the place."

A door opened, and a rectangle of golden light appeared on the Harringtons' darkening lawn. I saw Mrs. Harrington appear in the doorway, peering into the yard, and I heard her call to her daughter.

"Come in now. We didn't know where you were. You mustn't run off like that. Daddy was worried."

It was as if she spoke to a child. Like a child, the young woman went obediently up the steps to her mother. "I had to get flowers," I heard her say. "I need flowers, still. I can't find—"

"No more, now," her mother told her before she closed the door behind them. "No more flowers."

I went back into the house, where Brahms still played, my grandmother still knit, and my grandfather had finished his paper and turned to a book. Later, my father called, as he did each night, to say there was no change.

My grandmother introduced me, dutifully, to people my age: great-nieces of friends, the son of the Episcopal minister. I spent an interminable evening with a girl who talked endlessly of horse shows, and went to the movies one night with the minister's son, who was younger than I and idiotically proud of having been expelled from prep school.

I played the piano in my grandparents' high-ceilinged music room. I read. I wrote letters. I took walks.

One night, late, as I was preparing for bed, there were screams from the house next door. I stood, stricken, my hands frozen where they had been buttoning my nightgown, and listened through the open, curtained window. They were not screams of terror, but of grief: terrible, anguished cries that rose again and again, finally subsiding in sobs.

No one mentioned it at breakfast. Yet surely my grandparents had heard.

Finally I said, "The Harringtons' daughter was screaming last night; did you hear her?"

Grandmother shifted uncomfortably in her chair while she stirred her tea. She nodded. I thought, for a moment, that she would speak of the weather: of the relentless heat, of the lack of rain, of the disastrous effect on her dahlias.

"Her parents called to apologize early this morning," she said.

"They *what?*" I asked, shocked. "*Apologized?* Did I hear you correctly?"

"It's very embarrassing for them," Grandmother replied.

"Tragic," she added, finally.

"What happened to her?" I asked. The question, though I asked in a normal voice, seemed loud in the silent dining room, against the thin clink of silver spoons.

"She lost her child."

For a moment I pictured a small child misplaced, somehow, its mother searching the house and yard, calling its name. But I knew, of course, it was not what Grandmother had meant.

Grandfather folded his newspaper and set it aside. "It was a terrible accident," he said. "On a boat." He stood, preparing to leave for his office. His briefcase waited on the mahogany table in the hall.

"I'm not sure I'm following this," I said loudly. "The woman's child died, and her parents are *embarrassed?* Is that what you're saying?"

Grandfather looked at me. "Embarrassed was the wrong word," he said slowly. "They are helpless. You'll understand that better when you're older."

He went to the dining room doorway and then turned back. "The paper says there is a chance of rain soon," he said, before he left the room.

That evening, thunder rumbled in the distance and the air was oppressively still. I wandered again into the dark yard and saw that the woman I had come to think of as

Secret was standing alone, on the other side of the fence. Her hands were empty.

Almost without thinking, I went to Grandmother's garden and began to pull the few remaining blossoms from the plants there. The wilting pink hollyhocks, the limp glads, the dahlias with browning buds that would never open: all of them I gathered in my arms. Then I opened the gate at the end of the fence and took the flowers to her.

"These are for you," I told her. "I wish there was something more I could give you."

She remembered my name. "You're Nina," she said. "Thank you, Nina."

I nodded.

"Do you have a baby?" she asked in her low whisper.

"No. I'm only seventeen."

"Someday you will." Her face had no expression.

"I hope so."

"Mine is named John. He'll be two soon."

I didn't say anything. She stroked the flowers that she held, and touched them to her face.

She turned away from me, and I thought she was going back to the house. But she stood still, and began to talk in a low voice. "He's such a bright little boy, Johnny. But I didn't know he could unbuckle the strap." She looked back at me, and noticed the belt around the waist of my dress. "Just like yours, a little buckle just like that.

"Unbuckle it," she commanded me in a fierce whisper.

I obeyed her and undid my belt. It slid loose, and I held it in my hands. I looked at her.

She laughed oddly. "But you don't disappear," she said.

"Would you like me to take you inside?" I asked in confusion.

She moved away from me fearfully. "Oh, no," she said. "I can't go in. I can't go back. I have to keep looking." She glanced around her feet, at the withered grass. "But it all looks alike, the water. I think it was *there*—" and she dropped a spray of flowers to the ground. "But it looks the same here." And she dropped another, in another spot.

For a moment, she wandered around the yard, murmuring and dropping flowers. In my mind, for a moment, I saw what she was seeing: the relentless water that had closed in an instant over her child.

Then she looked back at me, suddenly. "Can you help me?" she asked.

"No," I whispered. "I'm sorry. I'm so sorry."

"Why are you here? I thought I was alone. I was sure I was all alone out here."

"I'm visiting my gra—" I began, and then stopped. I went to where she stood.

"I'm here because I'm losing someone, too," I told her. "And I know you can't help me, either. But I don't want to be all alone."

THAT NIGHT, WHEN MY FATHER CALLED MY GRAND-parents' house and said once more that there was no change, I told him I was coming home. It was raining, at last, when, disapproving, they took me to the train station the next day: not a downpour that would revitalize the earth and the ruined landscape, but a steady drizzle that cooled us, that softened the dry, set lines in my grandmother's face and was better than nothing at all.

My mother did not die, not then. And I did not go to college, not that September. Instead I stayed at home with my mother as she gradually grew stronger. Together we read aloud, and laughed, and she sat, watching, while I painted our kitchen bright blue. Then she hemmed by hand the new curtains I made from a fabric as vibrantly colored as rainbows.

The Harringtons' daughter killed herself. "Took her own life" is the way Grandmother put it in a letter, and she enclosed a newspaper clipping that used the same phrase. I don't know how, and I am just as glad not to know. Not knowing, I can imagine that she found a place that looked—that *felt*—like the place where all she had lost had gone, and that she slid into it, cool and welcome and unalone.

Her name was Sigrid Harrington. I had mistaken the sound for Secret. And as she had predicted, I did eventually have children of my own. In years to come, I would encounter other secrets and would grow to understand the wish to draw the shades against them. Sometimes the memory of the Harringtons' daughter kept me from doing so. I wish I could thank her for that gift, the way she thanked me for my small and helpless offering of flowers.

About Lois Lowry

Lois Lowry knew at a young age that she wanted to be a writer. The middle child of three, she describes herself as a solitary child "who lived in the world of books and my own imagination." Because her father was a career military officer, Lowry grew up in various parts of the world, including Hawaii, New York City, Tokyo, and Maine.

Lowry says that she feels a great urgency "to do what I can to convey the knowledge that we live intertwined on this planet and that our future as human beings depends upon our caring more, and doing more, for one another." Her books include *Number the Stars*, *A Summer to Die*, *Anastasia on Her Own*, and *The Giver*.

Responding

1. **Personal Response** What would you like to say to either Sigrid Harrington or the narrator?

2. **Literary Analysis** On page 167, the narrator contrasts the Harringtons' rather messy yard with her grandmother's very neat one. How is each yard a *symbol* of each family? How do the differences between the two yards *symbolize* the differences between the two families?

3. **Theme Connection** Who or what is the "enemy" in this story? Who faces this enemy and what happens as a result?

Language Workshop

Homonyms *Homonyms* are words that sound alike but have different meanings and sometimes different spellings. Sometimes a word may be confused with one of its homonyms. In "The Harringtons' Daughter," for example, the narrator describes her grandmother's voice as being "taut with dismay." *Taut* (meaning "tight") and *taught* (meaning "instructed") are homonyms, and should not be confused.

Choose the correct word in each of the following sentences.

1. The girl took a (flour/flower) from the garden.

2. Her grandmother did not want her to (waist/waste) her time.

3. (Their/There) was no reason for the girl to stay any longer.

Writer's Portfolio

Write a comparison of Sigrid Harrington and the narrator. What did they have in common? How were they different from each other? What, if anything, did each girl learn from the other?

Facing the Enemy

PROJECTS

How I See It

In each of the selections you've just read the central character is forced to face an enemy. Retell one of these confrontations with a piece of original art. You may want to do a pencil sketch, a watercolor, or even a montage of images that you've cut from magazines and newspapers. Keep the tone of the selection in mind as you plan your art; if, for example, the tone is lighthearted, you may want to draw a caricature or a comic strip.

Scenes from Real Life

Think back to the different types of confrontation you read about in "Facing the Enemy." Now check recent newspapers for a story about a real-life confrontation. Clip the article and bring it into class. In small groups, discuss the event. What kind of confrontation does the article describe? What was the result? Does the article remind you of one of the selections in this unit?

Writing About a Confrontation

The characters in this unit must face some difficult situations. How do people you know handle confrontations? Choose someone to interview about an "enemy" he or she has faced. Let them know that this enemy could be another person, an inner problem, or even an imaginary opponent. Use the notes you take during the interview to write an article for your class that describes the situation and tells how the person handled the confrontation.

FURTHER READING

Whether a confrontation happens on the battlefield or in your backyard, facing up to it is a challenge. In each of these books, the characters must decide how to handle that challenge.

The Outsiders by S. E. Hinton. The author was seventeen when she wrote this compelling novel about Ponyboy Curtis, a sensitive teenager caught in the war between the greasers and the Socs.

The Red Badge of Courage by Stephen Crane. In his first battle, a young soldier in the Civil War confronts the horrors of war.

Fallen Angels by Walter Dean Myers. A mistake in Army paperwork sends Richie Perry to the Vietnam War. Richie doesn't know if he'll have the skills or the luck to ever see home again.

Anne Frank: The Diary of a Young Girl by Anne Frank. This young Jewish girl's diary reveals her secret hopes and fears for the two years her family hid from the Nazis during World War II, before they were discovered and sent to concentration camps.

To Kill a Mockingbird by Harper Lee. A small Southern town in the 1930s threatens to explode with violence when a white lawyer defends a black man falsely accused of rape.

All Quiet on the Western Front by Erich Maria Remarque. This moving novel describes the experiences of four young German soldiers during World War I.

UNIT 4

Matters of the Heart

What makes opposites attract? What can begin with a look and last a lifetime? What *is* that crazy thing called love?

The selections in Unit 4 are all about love, and how the course it runs is rarely smooth, but always worth the effort. As you read, consider each character's definition of love. Consider also how each character chooses to show love. Is there something in one of these stories that reminds you of a love you've known?

CYNTHIA RYLANT

$\mathcal{C}$heckouts

$\mathcal{H}$ER PARENTS HAD MOVED HER TO Cincinnati, to a large house with beveled glass windows and several porches and the *history* her mother liked to emphasize. You'll love the house, they said. You'll be lonely at first, they admitted, but you're so nice you'll make friends fast. And as an impulse tore at her to lie on the floor, to hold to their ankles and tell them she felt she was dying, to offer anything, anything at all, so they might allow her to finish growing up in the town of her childhood, they firmed their mouths and spoke from their chests and they said, It's decided.

They moved her to Cincinnati, where for a month she spent the greater part of every day in a room full of beveled glass windows, sifting through photographs of the life she'd lived and left behind. But it is difficult work, suffering, and in its own way a kind of art, and finally she didn't have the energy for it anymore, so she emerged from the beautiful house and fell in love with a bag boy at the supermarket. Of course, this didn't happen all at once, just like that, but in the sequence of things that's exactly the way it happened.

She liked to grocery shop. She loved it in the way some people love to drive long country roads, because doing it she could think and relax and wander. Her parents wrote up the list and handed it to her and off she went without complaint to perform what they regarded as a great sacrifice of her time and a sign that she was indeed a very nice girl. She had never told them how much she loved grocery shopping, only that she was "willing" to do it. She had an intuition which told her that her parents were not safe for sharing such strong, important facts about herself. Let them think they knew her.

Words to Know

reverie (p. 180) dreamy thoughts

shard (p. 180) broken piece or fragment

harried (p. 181) worried; having lots of problems

bland (p. 181) smoothly agreeable and polite; dull

brazen (p. 181) bold, shameless

Once inside the supermarket, her hands firmly around the handle of the cart, she would lapse into a kind of reverie and wheel toward the produce. Like a Tibetan monk in solitary meditation, she calmed to a point of deep, deep happiness; this feeling came to her, reliably, if strangely, only in the supermarket.

Then one day the bag boy dropped her jar of mayonnaise and that is how she fell in love.

He was nervous—first day on the job—and along had come this fascinating girl, standing in the checkout line with the unfocused stare one often sees in young children, her face turned enough away that he might take several full looks at her as he packed sturdy bags full of food and the goods of modern life. She interested him because her hair was red and thick, and in it she had placed a huge orange bow, nearly the size of a small hat. That was enough to distract him, and when finally it was her groceries he was packing, she looked at him and smiled and he could respond only by busting her jar of mayonnaise on the floor, shards of glass and oozing cream decorating the area around his feet.

She loved him at exactly that moment, and if he'd known this perhaps he wouldn't have fallen into the brown depression he fell into, which lasted the rest of his shift. He believed he must have looked the jackass in her eyes, and he envied the sureness of everyone around him: the cocky cashier at the register, the grim and harried store manager, the bland butcher, and the brazen bag boys who smoked in the warehouse on their breaks. He wanted a second chance. Another chance to be confident and say witty things to her as he threw tin cans into her bags, persuading her to allow him to help her to her car so he might learn just a little about her, check out the floor of the car for signs of hobbies or fetishes and the bumpers for clues as to beliefs and loyalties.

But he busted her jar of mayonnaise and nothing else worked out for the rest of the day.

Strange, how attractive clumsiness can be. She left the supermarket with stars in her eyes, for she had loved the way his long nervous fingers moved from the conveyor belt to the bags, how deftly (until the mayonnaise) they had picked up her items and placed them into her bags. She had loved the way the hair kept falling into his eyes as he leaned over to grab a box or a tin. And the tattered brown shoes he wore with no socks. And the left side of his collar turned in rather than out.

The bag boy seemed a wonderful contrast to the perfectly beautiful house she had been forced to accept as her home, to the *history* she hated, to the loneliness she had become used to, and she couldn't wait to come back for more of his awkwardness and dishevelment.

Incredibly, it was another four weeks before they saw each other again. As fate would have it, her visits to the supermarket never coincided with his schedule to bag. Each time she went to the store, her eyes scanned the checkouts at once, her heart in her mouth. And each hour he worked, the bag boy kept one eye on the door, watching for the red-haired girl with the big orange bow.

Yet in their disappointment these weeks there was a kind of ecstasy. It is reason enough to be alive, the hope you may see again some face which has meant something to you. The anticipation of meeting the bag boy eased the girl's painful transition into her new and jarring life in Cincinnati. It provided for her an anchor amid all that was impersonal and unfamiliar, and she spent less time on thoughts of what she had left behind as she concentrated on what might lie ahead. And for the boy, the long and often tedious hours at the supermarket which provided no challenge other than that of showing up the following workday . . . these hours became possibilities of mystery and romance for him as he watched the electric doors for the girl in the orange bow.

And when finally they did meet up again, neither offered a clue to the other that he, or she, had been the object of obsessive thought for weeks. She spotted him as soon as she came into the store, but she kept her eyes strictly in front of her as she pulled out a cart and wheeled it toward the produce. And he, too, knew the instant she came through the door—though the orange bow was gone, replaced by a small but bright yellow flower instead—and he never once turned his head in her direction but watched her from the corner of his vision as he tried to swallow back the fear in his throat.

It is odd how we sometimes deny ourselves the very pleasure we have longed for and which is finally within our reach. For some perverse reason she would not have been able to articulate, the girl did not bring her cart up to the bag boy's checkout when her shopping was done. And the bag boy let her leave the store, pretending no notice of her.

Words to Know

perverse (p. 182) contrary and willful

articulate (p. 182) put one's thoughts into words

This is often the way of children, when they truly want a thing, to pretend that they don't. And then they grow angry when no one tries harder to give them this thing they so casually rejected, and they soon find themselves in a rage simply because they cannot say yes when they mean yes. Humans are very complicated. (And perhaps cats, who have been known to react in the same way, though the resulting rage can only be guessed at.)

The girl hated herself for not checking out at the boy's line, and the boy hated himself for not catching her eye and saying hello, and they most sincerely hated each other without having ever exchanged even two minutes of conversation.

Eventually—in fact, within the week—a kind and intelligent boy who lived very near her beautiful house asked the girl to a movie and she gave up her fancy for the bag boy at the supermarket. And the bag boy himself grew so bored with his job that he made a desperate search for something better and ended up in a bookstore where scores of fascinating girls lingered like honeybees about a hive. Some months later the bag boy and the girl with the orange bow again crossed paths, standing in line with their dates at a movie theater, and, glancing toward the other, each smiled slightly, then looked away, as strangers on public buses often do, when one is moving off the bus and the other is moving on.

About Cynthia Rylant

Cynthia Rylant grew up in the Appalachian mountains of West Virginia. She lived with her grandparents in a four-room house with no running water or indoor plumbing, and later with her mother in town.

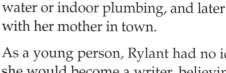

As a young person, Rylant had no idea she would become a writer, believing her life was too limited and dull to write about. She now realizes that her unique experiences growing up gave her a rich supply of material to use in her books: "I come from people who worked very, very hard and whose lives were never simple nor easy. In my books I try to touch on how hard life can be sometimes, but always, always show that for everything that we lose, we will get something back."

Rylant's other books for young adults include *A Blue-Eyed Daisy, A Fine White Dust, A Kindness,* and *Missing May.*

Responding

1. **Personal Response** Has something like the situation in "Checkouts" ever happened to you or someone you know? Tell about it.

2. **Literary Analysis** A story is *ironic* when events lead to an unexpected result. Tell what is *ironic* in this story and explain why.

3. **Theme Connection** Describe the relationship that the boy and the girl have. How is each of them affected by this relationship?

Language Workshop

Using Dashes A *dash* is used to show a sudden change of thought or to set off words that interrupt the main thought of a sentence. Cynthia Rylant uses dashes in "Checkouts":

He was nervous—first day on the job—and along had come this fascinating girl. . . .

In the following sentences, insert dashes where they belong.

1. The girl we never know her name was not happy that her family moved.

2. At the supermarket her favorite place to be she noticed the bag boy.

3. A long time went by four whole weeks before she saw him again.

Writer's Portfolio

What if the girl had gone back to the boy's checkout line? What if the boy had said hello to her? Describe what you think would have happened if either (or both) of those things had taken place.

ROBERT CORMIER

Protestants Cry, Too

To BEGIN WITH, MY BROTHER ARMAND FELL IN LOVE eleven times between Easter Sunday and Thanksgiving Day of 1938, and so it was no surprise, to me at least, when he announced at supper one night three years later that he wanted my parents' permission to marry.

After all, marriage seemed to be the inevitable destination of love, and I marvelled that he had not married long before.

My father took the news without expression, his doorway-wide shoulders hunched over the table as he chewed the blood sausage slowly and deliberately, but my mother flushed deeply, paled, looked at my father in horror and back at Armand in disbelief. My other brothers and sisters immediately set up a chorus of hoots and whistles, like a fleet of ships docking at Boston Harbor.

"But you're only nineteen," my mother protested, automatically passing the bowl of mashed potatoes to Esther. Her appetite shamed my mother but was a thing of pride to my father, who believed that an enormous quantity of food was as important to children as an enormous quantity of beer was to men.

"Well, if I'm old enough to work, I'm old enough to get married," Armand answered, addressing my mother defiantly while his eyes were sliding apprehensively to my father. Armand seldom looked uncertain. Hundreds of times I had seen him spear a line drive with finesse and send it arrowing to first base. He held the record for home

runs with the Frenchtown Tigers and had broken more windows by his feats with the bat than any other boy in the neighborhood. In high school, Armand had been—of all things—the star of the Debating Team (*Resolved:* That the government should assume control of the nation's railroads) and he had also played basketball. And somehow he always found time for love.

"That's what makes the world go round, Jerry-boy," he'd tell me as I watched him combing his hair prior to a date.

I was much younger than Armand and had my private thoughts about love: foolish and unnecessarily troublesome, involving going to terrible dances and wearing Sunday clothes on, say, a Wednesday night and taking baths two or three times a week. Yet, I had to admit that if Armand pursued love so faithfully, certainly there must be some good in it.

At the supper table that night, however, I did not envy him and I suddenly realized that he had gradually changed in the past few months. He had been vague about the nature of his dates and he had been alternately happy and morose. Sometimes, he sat on the piazza steps in the evening, staring at nothing in particular and would dismiss me with a curt shake of his head when I asked him if he wanted to toss the baseball around for a while or bat me a few balls.

Words to Know

morose (p. 188) gloomy

piazza (p. 188) a large porch

maudlin (p. 188) sentimental in a weak, silly way

"How much are you making at the shop?" my father asked, reaching for another slice of bread.

"Fifty cents an hour and I'm due for a raise next month," Armand answered.

"How much have you saved?"

"Two hundred and ten dollars. And she's got almost as much. She's a secretary uptown and says she doesn't mind working to help us get settled."

"She . . . she," my mother said, exasperated. "Who is this *she?*"

"Yes, which one?" Esther asked. Her appetite apparently had been dealt a fatal blow by the announcement because she had put down her fork although her plate was still half full. "Is it Yolande or Theresa or Marie-Rose or Jeanne?"

My mother silenced her with a look.

"I thought you said there was safety in numbers, Ma," Paul offered. Paul was the smart one, a high honor student with a memory so acute that he got on your nerves.

"Enough," my father commanded like an umpire calling strike three. He turned to Armand. "My son, you're no longer a boy. You've been working more than a year since your graduation from high school. You've found out what it means to earn a living. And I admit that a man needs love and marriage and children."

My mother snorted with disgust. She always claimed that my father was incurably romantic, and she dreaded wedding receptions and anniversary parties at St. Jean's Hall because he always got sentimental and maudlin and drank too much beer and insisted on proposing innumerable toasts to the glories of love or singing old Canadian ballads about people dying of broken hearts.

"Would it be too much to tell us the name of this girl who is coming into the family?" my mother asked.

Armand scratched his head and tugged at his ear: a bad sign.

"Jessica Stone," he said.

"Jessica?" Esther asked. "What kind of name is that?"

"Stone . . . Stone," my mother mused.

"A Protestant," Paul exclaimed, his voice like a door slamming shut.

My mother made the sign of the cross, and in the awesome silence that followed we turned our eyes to my father. His head was bowed and his huge shoulders sagged in defeat. His knuckles were white where his hands gripped the table. I too clutched the table, tensing myself for the explosion to come. But when my father raised his head at last, there was no violence in his manner, although his voice filled me with fear because it was terrible in its quietness.

"All right," he said wearily. "You don't want a good Canadian girl, fine. Maybe you don't like pea soup. And an Irisher, fine, maybe you don't like corn beef and cabbage. And, an Eye-talian, that, too, is all right if you don't like spaghetti." Fury gathered in his eyes. "But a Protestant? Are you crazy, my boy? Is that what we sent you to the good Catholic schools for? Is this what you were an altar boy for? To marry a Protestant?"

Ethnic Stereotypes

Armand's father describes French Canadians, the Irish, and Italians in terms of stereotypes about what each ethnic group likes to eat. Notice that he seems willing to accept a daughter-in-law from any of these ethnic groups, which traditionally were Catholic.

"I love her," Armand said, leaping to his feet. "This isn't Canada, Pa. This is the United States of America, 1941. . . ."

"Armand, Armand," my mother whispered, a pleading in her voice.

"Hey, Armand," Paul said, bright and interested.

"What kind of Protestant?"

"What do you mean—what kind?" my father roared.

"Congregational," Armand said. "She sings in the choir at the Congregational Church. She's a good girl. She believes in God . . ."

Excitement danced in my veins. I had never known a Protestant. My family had come late from Canada and we had settled in a neighborhood far removed from the world of Protestants and Yankees. Although my father had become a fierce patriot, a staunch supporter of Franklin D. Roosevelt and a loyal Democrat, he seldom ventured outside of Frenchtown. As a result, I knew little of Protestants. They were people who lived on the other side of town, people who did not have to go to church on Sunday morning if they felt like staying in bed and whose churches closed up in the summer for vacations. Sister Angela assured us that Protestants could get to heaven, but she implied that this was allowed by the Catholic Church out of the goodness of its heart. Suddenly, my excitement fled by a sudden sense that the world was crumbling at my feet. My loyalty moved toward my father and mother, although I still ached for Armand, who stood at the table like some lonely hero who finds his deeds stricken from the rolls of honor.

My father suddenly relaxed. He shrugged and smiled. "Well, why should we get excited?" he asked my mother. "This week a Protestant and next week maybe a . . . a Hindu. And the week after that . . ."

"Next week and next year and forever, it will still be Jessica," Armand cried. "This isn't puppy love, Pa. I've been going out with her for seven months."

For Armand, of course, this was some sort of record.

"Seven months?" my father asked, astounded. "You've been going around with a Protestant for seven months behind my back?"

"Not behind your back," Armand said. "Have I ever

brought any girl home here? No. Because I wanted to wait until I met the right one. And Jessica's the right one . . ."

"Well, don't plan on bringing *her* here," my father said. "I don't want her name mentioned again under this roof." He banged his fist on the table and a dish fell to the floor. My mother jumped up in alarm, and Armand turned on his heel and left the house, slamming the door behind him.

So began what my brother Paul described as the Six-month War of the Renault family, and the war usually was fought at the supper table. My father was not a man for stiff rules, but he had always insisted that the entire family be home for supper, to break bread together at least once a day. Even Armand in his rebellion dared not break that law. Otherwise, however, he became a silent and brooding figure, spending little time at home. He worked all day in the comb shop and went off to meet his Jessica every evening. He didn't whistle off-key anymore as he dressed for his dates, and he acted as though we had all become invisible to him.

Words to Know

brooding (p. 191) thinking anxiously or gloomily about, worrying

pointer (p. 191) a hint or suggestion

I had been pressed into service as a pitcher for the Tigers because Roger Lussier broke his arm, and I lost three games in a row. Armand agreed to give me some pointers, but he was not much help because he seemed like someone split in half, part of him murmuring to me, "Fine, fine," even when I threw a bad pitch, and another part of him far away, deep in thought. Paul said that a kind of doom hung over our house. He was melodramatic and often used words like *doom* and *holocaust* (Edgar Allan Poe was his favorite writer), and yet I had to admit that Armand's troubles had cast a shadow over us all.

Supper time became exercises in agony.

"I see in the paper where a fellow who left his religion got killed in a car crash in Boston," my father would offer to no one in particular.

"I'm not leaving my religion," Armand would reply, addressing the picture of the St. Lawrence River on the wall. "She's willing to take religious instruction, to go halfway . . ."

"Pass the gravy," my father would say.

And my mother would pass the gravy to my father while she looked with stricken eyes at Armand.

Or, my father would announce:

"I understand that the Blanchemaisons are going to lose their house. To the bank. A big-shot Protestant there is signing the papers tomorrow."

"Mister Blanchemaison has been drunk for six months and his family's on relief. It's the city that's making the bank take the house," Armand explained, looking at me as if I had brought up the question.

"And who's the mayor of the city? A Protestant, that's who," my father announced triumphantly to Esther, who looked at him in perplexity.

Or, with a quiet air of victory, he would ask my mother, "You know Theophile LeBlanc, the caterer? Well, he was putting on a feed at a fancy Protestant wedding last Saturday. He said that it was disgusting. Nobody sang any songs, nobody danced and nobody even got drunk. They stood around and ate sandwiches made with crackers. People who don't sing and dance at a wedding: they don't have hearts . . ."

One day I burst into the house after finally winning a ball game (although I almost spoiled the victory by giving up four home runs in the ninth inning) and found the rooms unusually quiet, all the kids gone off somewhere, and my father at work. I heard voices in the parlor and was about to enter when I halted in my tracks, held back by the intimate quality of the voices.

"I know, I know, Armand," my mother was saying. "I agree that she's a nice girl. Polite and charming. But going behind your father's back to meet her is one thing—inviting her here without warning him, is another . . ."

"But don't you see, Ma," Armand said, "that he thinks all Protestants are some kind of monsters because he's never really known one? I'll bet he's never spoken more than five minutes with a Protestant. You met Jessica. You say she's a fine girl. I think Pa will, too, if he has a chance to meet her . . ."

"I still get the shivers wondering what he'll say when he learns that I've met her, that we sat in a drugstore together and had a college ice . . ."

"Please, Ma," Armand pleaded. "His bark is worse than his bite. You always said he's a sentimental man."

"I don't know, Armand, I don't know," she said, her voice tender and troubled.

I drew back in horror, appalled at the conspiracy, my mother's treachery, her disloyalty to my father. I ran up the street to meet him; and as I saw him stalking home from work, I became aware for the first time of my father as a *person*, not simply a big man who either roared with anger or boomed with laughter, who consumed incredible amounts of beer and whose word was law. Knowing that he could be betrayed gave him a sudden, human countenance. I studied the deep lines on his face, the network of wrinkles near his eyes that had always fascinated me because of their resemblance to spider webs, and I realized that they were the result of long hard days at work and the problems of bringing up a family. And instead of bursting out my information, I remained silent and carried his empty lunchpail, shy with him suddenly and warm and itchy all over my body.

The following Sunday afternoon, I cried out in astonishment as I glanced out the parlor window and saw Armand coming along the sidewalk with a girl. He held her elbow tenderly, as if she were fragile and precious beyond price. He didn't look where he was going but gazed at her raptly. I had to admit that I did not blame him for staring at her: she was slender and blond and lovely, dressed in something pink and white, and the colors blended with the soft tones of her delicate face. The autumn wind rose suddenly and she lifted her hand to hold a tiny pink hat, the gesture filled with grace. I myself would have gladly run a mile to chase that hat for her if the wind chanced to blow it off.

My mother stood beside me, her cheeks flushed, her eyes wide with concern. She looked like the guilty party who is unmasked in the last chapter of the serials at the Globe Theater on Saturday afternoons.

"God help us," she whispered breathlessly. Straightening her shoulders and sighing, she called to my father: "Louis, company's coming up the street . . ."

My father, who was in the kitchen listening to the Red Sox baseball game on the radio, groaned loudly. "Company? Who comes to disturb a man after dinner on Sunday?" My father pretended that he wanted only privacy on weekends or in the evenings, but when company did arrive he played the role of the perfect host to the hilt, keeping the beer flowing and my mother busy serving food. People usually found it hard to leave because my father always insisted on one more drink, one more joke, one more argument.

My mother greeted Armand and Jessica at the front door as my father entered the living room, yawning and straightening his tie. Armand's entrance caught him with his mouth wide open. My father jerked his tie, his mouth closed in surprise and he stood rigidly in the doorway.

The scent of a subtle perfume filled the air as the girl entered. Her eyes were blue, and for the first time I realized that blue was the most beautiful color in the world.

"This is Jessica Stone," Armand announced, his hand

still at her elbow but protectively now. "Jessica, this is my father and mother." I had to suppress a giggle at his formality. "And my brother Jerry," he added, pointing to me. "The other kids are out somewhere, playing around."

Jessica smiled hesitantly and I saw her hand tremble at her side. Armand guided her to the davenport. I wondered whether her cheeks gave her pain: that smile seemed to be hurting her. And no wonder, I thought, as I looked at my father, who stood like a figure of wrath at the doorway.

My mother seemed to be everywhere at once, adjusting the curtain, flicking an invisible speck of dust from the end table, touching Armand's shoulder and pushing me from the room. I heard the big leather chair squeak menacingly as my father lowered himself into it.

Shamelessly, I stood near the door, straining to catch every sound and nuance of the conversation. My mother and Armand carried on a strange wandering conversation about the weather, talking at length of tumbling leaves and the great amount of rain that had fallen during the week and the way nights were becoming chilly. I was impatient for the foolish conversation to end. Finally, a huge silence settled in the room.

Roger Lussier called to me from the outside steps, and I remembered in dismay that we were supposed to go to the movies. I didn't answer, hoping he would go away.

After a while, my father cleared his throat. "I was listening to the ball game," he said. "Do you follow baseball?"

I peeked into the room and saw Jessica sitting stiffly beside Armand. "I play tennis," she said.

"Tennis," my father said, as if that were the most ridiculous sport in the world.

"She's very good," Armand offered. "She won a trophy last year."

Silence again except for Roger's voice, sounding

impatient and shrill now.

"Your father. Where does he work?" my father asked.

"In the Savings Bank," she answered.

"A banker?" my father inquired, giving the word the same contempt that he used for Republican.

"He's a teller," she amended.

"But he works in a bank," my father declared, with a kind of triumph.

"Yes," she answered, her voice strained.

Roger was setting up such a howl outside that I went to the back door. Actually, I was somewhat relieved to end my eavesdropping because I shared the pain and embarrassment of Jessica Stone. Roger was worried that we would be late for the movie, but my mind was still in the parlor.

> ### Words to Know
>
> **eavesdropping** (p. 196) listening to a conversation that one is not supposed to hear
>
> **inquisition** (p. 196) a thorough investigation or questioning
>
> **exude** (p. 196) display in an obvious way

"All right," I told him. "Let's go. But wait just one minute more . . ." I reentered the house and stood by the parlor doorway again.

"Franklin D. Roosevelt is the greatest president the country ever had," my father was saying. "The greatest man in the world."

"Abraham Lincoln was a great president, too," Jessica answered, a hint of defiance in her voice.

I couldn't bear to listen any further and was happy to join Roger on the back steps. I was in a hurry to get to the Globe Theater, or any place that was far away from the inquisition going on in the parlor.

When I arrived home at supper time, my father was sitting in the kitchen, exuding an air of victory. His shoes were off and his feet extended luxuriously out on the floor. My mother busied herself at the stove: there was always something cooking there, morning, noon and night, that needed her attention.

"And did you see her sitting there so prim and proper?" my father was asking. "What kind of girl is that? I tell you, it's like Theophile LeBlanc said. Protestants have no juices. Did you see the girl smile? No. Did she laugh? No. And anyone who thinks that Abraham Lincoln is greater than Franklin D. Roosevelt . . ." He shook his head in disbelief.

"Louis . . . Louis," my mother said. "She's a nice girl, a fine girl, and she loves your son. Does it matter what she thinks of Roosevelt or Lincoln? Does it matter what church she goes to?" A bit of anger crept into her voice. "And how could you act so rude to a guest in your house?"

"But don't you see?" he asked. "I wanted to show Armand that the girl is not for him, that she would not fit into his life, into our life. She plays tennis. She doesn't follow the Red Sox. She sings in a Protestant choir. And it's plain to see she's a Republican . . ."

"But she's hardly old enough to vote," my mother said.

"Well, maybe we'll see a change in Armand now," my father said, settling back, wriggling his feet, "now that I've"—he groped for the word and pinned it down exultantly—"*exposed* her."

My father's exposure of Jessica Stone did not affect Armand's love for her. In fact, he announced a few nights later that he was planning to give her an engagement ring for Christmas. My father closed his eyes when he heard the news and his lips moved in what I hoped was a silent prayer but feared was an oath too terrible for us to hear. I looked at my father and Armand and my mother and did some praying of my own. I felt allegiance to my father whose oldest son was defying him, who was ready to turn his back on his family and who no longer was interested in such things as baseball for the sake of a girl. Yet, I also sympathized with Armand because I agreed that Jessica Stone was more beautiful than any girl in Frenchtown.

And my heart also had room for my mother, torn between her husband and her son. When I saw the sorrow in her face as she looked at one and then the other, I easily forgave her for going behind my father's back to help Armand. And yet . . . yet, I was tired of the situation because it seemed to me that there were more important things in the world than love, and every time I brought up one of these things—for instance, the frustrating December weather that had not turned cold enough for ice skating—someone would tell me to go out and play or Paul would accuse me of having no appreciation of drama. I wanted to tell him that if drama was something that made your chest ache with strangeness, then I wanted no part of it.

We were all involved in a large drama, however, when the voice of the announcer on the radio one Sunday afternoon stunned us with the news that the Japanese had attacked a place called Pearl Harbor.

My father jumped from his chair in alarm and excitement, indignant to learn that someone had dared challenge the nation led by Franklin D. Roosevelt.

"Paul," he bellowed. "Paul . . ."

My brother came running from the bedroom where he had been reading a book as usual.

"Where is Pearl Harbor?" my father asked him.

"In Hawaii," Paul answered promptly.

We learned more about Pearl Harbor and the vast world of the Pacific Ocean in the weeks to come, and my father spent many hours at the radio, shaking his head at the news, perpetually angry. He seemed to take it as a personal insult that American boys were being wounded and dying.

One supper time when my father, after the usual prayer of grace, added another prayer for the good

American boys who were in battle, Armand said: "A good many of those boys are Protestants . . ."

My father paused, deep in thought. "And a good many are Catholic, too," he answered after a while, the belligerency gone from his voice.

"Well, here's one Catholic you can add to the roll. I'm going to enlist."

A sharp cry came from my mother, but somehow I had eyes only for my father. For the first time in months, he looked at Armand directly.

"No," my father protested. "You're just a boy . . ."

"I'm an American," Armand said.

"I thought you were going to get married in the spring," Paul interjected.

"Jessica and I talked it over," Armand said. "How can we get married when there's a war going on? She said she's willing to wait . . ." He looked at my father. "Pa, I want your permission to enlist. Me and Jessica, that's something else. I know you don't approve of us, but I'll tell you this much: as soon as I come back, we're going to be married."

"But why volunteer?" my father asked. "There are a lot of others who can go."

His question surprised me because it was obvious that Armand's enlistment would solve the problem of his romance. I pondered again the mysterious ways of grown-ups. For myself, I had no fear for Armand's safety. In my eyes, he had been born to become a hero, whether on a baseball field or in battle, and I was sure of his indestructibility.

"Every man has his duty to perform," Armand said, and his words were quiet and somehow sad and gallant.

Incredibly, tears formed in the corners of my father's eyes. At first, I thought he must be sick because I had never seen him cry before. He sniffed and blew his nose and cleared his throat.

"Hey, Pa," Paul said. "You're crying."

"Who's crying?" my father bellowed, his wet eyes finding my mother, who sat stunned and grief-stricken across from him, her face cruelly bleak as if winter had blown across her features. "It's the onions in the soup," my father said. "Onions always bring tears to a man's eyes . . ."

THE CLOCK IN THE STEEPLE OF THE CONGREGATIONAL Church in the square stroked the hour of nine and we listened to its echoes in the crisp morning air. The army bus stood at the corner and I was fascinated by its color, the olive drab giving an air of emergency to the gathering of people on the sidewalk. The fellows who were leaving for military service were not yet in uniform, but already there was a hint of the military in their bearing. A soldier in uniform paced the sidewalk impatiently near the bus.

My father and I stood with Armand in front of King's Shoe Store. My mother had remained at home, having kissed Armand goodbye without allowing tears to fall, and unwilling to take the chance of breaking down as he got on the bus. The other children were in school, but my father had allowed me to see Armand off.

"I hope they send us down South for basic training," Armand said. "At least, it'll be warm there." His voice seemed unnaturally thin and high-pitched, and his eyes searched the square, looking for Jessica. I saw her first, the blond hair vivid in the drabness of the morning. She walked swiftly toward us, opening her arms to Armand as she approached, but she arrested the gesture when she saw my father. They had not met since that terrible Sunday in the parlor.

My father shifted on one foot and then another. Finally, he looked down at me. "Come, Jerry, let's go find that soldier and ask him when the bus is leaving . . ."

"Thanks, Pa," Armand said.

As we approached the soldier, he placed a silver whistle in his mouth and blew it fiercely. He called out:

"Okay, you guys, fall in. On the double. On the double . . ."
He would have made a fine cheerleader.

My father and I returned to Armand and Jessica, who were holding hands, huddled together as if the day had suddenly turned too cold to bear.

"It's time," my father said, touching Armand's shoulder.

Armand drew back his shoulders and shook hands with my father. He punched me lightly on the arm. He turned to Jessica and kissed her gently on the cheek and then gathered her in his arms, holding her closely. He pulled away from her abruptly and looked at us all for a long moment, his face pale and his chin trembling a little. And then he walked quickly toward the bus and was lost in the crowd of fellows who were leaving with him.

Jessica turned away from us. She kept her face averted as the bus gradually filled, as the soldier took one final look around the square, as the motor roared into life.

Words to Know

avert (p. 201) turn away

disperse (p. 201) scatter, go off in different directions

audible (p. 202) loud enough to be heard

Armand waved to us from inside the bus, but there was little comfort in that last glimpse.

The bus turned the corner and was gone. The people began to disperse and my father, Jessica, and I seemed to be alone as if we were standing on a small invisible island there in the square. She still did not look at us, although I could see the reflection of her face in a store window. Clutching her coat at the neck, she left us abruptly, walking away without warning.

My father watched her go, shrugging his shoulders.

"Pa," I said, "you were wrong."

"What do you mean, wrong?" he asked gruffly, pulling his handkerchief out of his pocket.

"You said Protestants have no heart, that they don't laugh or cry. Jessica was crying. I saw her face and she was crying just like you cried the other night at supper."

He looked at her retreating figure. He blew his nose

feebly and the sound was not as magnificent as usual, barely audible above the traffic. He lifted his arms and let them drop at his sides.

"There's no fool like an old fool," he said, mysteriously. Then: "Come, Jerry, let's go find her before she's too far away . . . "

I had to run to keep pace with him as we threaded our way through the crowd. We finally caught up to her near the drinking fountain on the other side of the square. My father touched her arm, and suddenly she was folded in his embrace and never before had I seen people look so happy while they were crying.

About Robert Cormier

As a teenager, Robert Cormier knew he wanted to be a writer. He worked for thirty years as a newspaper reporter and columnist, and says,

"During the evenings and often late into the night, I did my *real* writing—stories, first, and later, novels."

When asked why many of his stories involve tragedy, Mr. Cormier explains, "The fact is that teenagers do not live in a peppermint world of fun and frolic. Their world is vividly real, perhaps harsher and more tragedy-prone than the everyday world their mothers and fathers inhabit."

Cormier enjoys the letters and telephone calls he gets from his young adult readers. His award-winning books for young adults include *The Chocolate War, I Am the Cheese,* and *Fade.*

Responding

1. **Personal Response** What questions do you want to ask after reading this story? Jot them down and share them with others. Try answering a few of the questions.

2. **Literary Analysis** A *stereotype* is a fixed, narrow view of what a person or a certain group of persons is like. What stereotypes about Protestants does Jerry's father have? How do they affect his attitude toward Jessica?

3. **Theme Connection** Some say "love conquers all." Do you think that's true in this story? Explain.

Language Workshop

Prefixes The prefixes *in-* and *un-* often mean *not*, as in these words from the story:

invisible not visible   *uncertain* not certain

Knowing the meaning of these prefixes can help you figure out the meaning of the words in which they appear. Find at least six more words in the selection in which the prefix *in-* or *un-* means *not*. Write a definition for each of these words.

Writer's Portfolio

Will Armand survive the war? Will the Renault family accept Jessica Stone? Write down your version of what happens next in this story. If you like, write it as a scene from a play.

King of the Roller Rink

He was one of the handsomest boys I'd ever seen. Somebody said he was part Indian, and with his powerful, dark good looks and eyes blue and brooding as thunderclouds, I thought of him as some kind of bird god in disguise. He had money, or at least his family did. On those cool summer evenings in that resort town on the only mountain (or what prairie people like to call a mountain) within a thousand miles, he wore white sweaters that looked like they cost the earth and he didn't rent those metal skates the skinny key boys would fit, then clamp, to your runners. He wore his own boot skates made of richly glowing leather, and he was king of the roller rink.

We skated around the edges of the outdoor rink with the sunken concrete floor and the floodlights and, above, the black pine-scented sky that seemed somehow less real than the loud speakers that blared "Wake Up, Little Suzie" and "Teen Angel" as we clung to each other and shrieked with desperate laughter, hoping Karl the King would notice us.

But he skated every number with Sheila-Rae in her shorts and tight-fitting orlon sweaters. Every night she rented expensive white boot skates to complement his brown ones. He seemed extraordinarily pleased with her prettiness, her blondness, as he spun her easily around the floor with a cool hawklike arrogance that took my breath away.

I was fourteen, underdeveloped, and wore my hair over my eyes as much to hide as to look mysterious. Sheila-Rae was everything I wasn't; her hair and makeup and body seemed flawless. But if I squinted my eyes to block out the other skaters, I could almost imagine it was me holding hands with Karl the King around and around the small crowded floor as everyone scattered to keep from being mowed down by our beautiful, quick, steadily pumping feet.

After each number, Karl and Sheila-Rae floated back to the front of the rink. Kids who weren't skating milled around there on the rough wood platform, or rolled and stumbled back to the booth near the ticket stand, where they bought drinks and cellophane bags of Cheezies.

Karl and Sheila-Rae never seemed to eat or drink. They just skated as if that's all they were made for. When the music started up again, with two or three kicks they were off, and you got the feeling from the way she looked up and smiled into his face that she would have given her soul to make that summer last forever.

Lizzie Keyes and I had purchased identical five-year diaries at the Log Cabin Gift Shop, where fat ladies on vacation hunted down teacups, hand-painted with Mounties or maple leaves. And each night under hissing street lamps we sighed, rolling our eyes, before we separated to be alone with Karl on the crisply lined pink paper. Next day, as we lazed back in her sweaty pine-log room with a picture of King George over the bed, Lizzie would read, "Last night, when Karl skated by? I swear, he looked over and smiled right at me. It was right between 'Deep Purple' and 'Party Doll.' Please, God, make this be a sign!"

In the white heat of day, along the beaches or in the little stores open only during tourist season, we never spied Karl or Sheila-Rae. It was as if, mothlike, they hid their gorgeous flight, appearing only when the music and the floodlights and the dark, cool, rusty-red painted floor of the roller rink lured them out to skate again.

The first time I saw Sheila-Rae up close, she wore shorts and a powder-blue sweater. A white stretchy headband drew her medium-length hair off her forehead and she glowed and chatted animatedly with three fascinated boys who kept a slight distance from her. Karl had just taken off for an unaccustomed round by himself. He skated backwards, hands in his pockets. His hair was so short and perfectly groomed, it barely moved in the little breeze he made. It was then I noticed Sheila-Rae had a small ketchup stain on the front of her sweater, a sweater that closely resembled one I had seen for sale at Woolworth's. She shivered. The sweater was thin. She hadn't skated enough yet to work up much heat.

Over one of the many white sweaters he owned, Karl wore a silky jacket that bore the letters of a university I didn't recognize. Lizzie, who wasn't especially bright, kept saying that those weren't his initials. A short, sweaty boy who had been tagging after her all night informed us that Karl's parents sent him to a university in the States. Karl, he said, was nineteen years old!

At that moment he seemed as unattainable to me as the boot skates I longed to own but knew my parents would never consent to buy for me.

Sheila-Rae stood talking to the boys, who playfully shoved one another and grinned like maniacs into her open smiling mouth. Karl, cruising the rink with hooded eyes, suddenly swooped into the crowded sidelines and appeared seconds later with a girl who wasn't much older than me. Her teeth were unbearably white against her summer tan. Her straight, slim legs flashed above rented boot skates. She flirted with Karl as if she'd been doing it all her life. They sailed past Sheila-Rae. Karl waved. The girl smiled her triumph, then gave a little squeal and clutched at him, having temporarily lost her balance.

Sheila-Rae said goodbye to the boys. They gawked after her as she slowly rolled back onto the rink and skated out the rest of "Heartbreak Hotel" on her own.

Karl skated three more songs with the legs-and-teeth girl, and Sheila-Rae swirled and dove through the crowds, passing them several times, each time with increasing vigor and power and what looked to be sheer joy.

On the fourth song Karl dumped his new partner, who went off the rink and sulked on a bench. She made a show of removing one boot as if it were causing her great pain. She snapped at one of the key boys to bring her another and he, pimply, Brylcreem-slicked, in a gaping unbuttoned shirt, snarled back to get it herself.

Karl whisked around the rink after Sheila-Rae. She executed a graceful arabesque just before he caught up, then she quickly spun around, laughing, to face him. She skated backwards, her hips swaying slightly with the movement. Karl reached out and placed his hands on her waist. They skated together right off the floor. Minutes later they disappeared into the night.

For the next two nights they didn't show. We'd leave early and saunter down the street to the café crowd at the Totem Pole—a log-style barn of a building that sold the best fries in town and played the hottest music. But Karl and Sheila-Rae weren't in either place. They'd vanished like a dream, leaving us vaguely frustrated and unsatisfied.

On the third evening, Karl showed up late at the roller rink in the company of a boy whose silk jacket bore the identical letters to his. The two sleek girls with them wore shorts and heavy Nordic ski sweaters. Close up, their skin, with makeup softly defined, was the color of scrubbed peaches. One collided with then pushed past me. Her soft sweater grazed my sweaty, bare arm. I turned to say "Sorry," or something stupid like that, but she was laughing attractively at nothing in particular, so I didn't bother. I noticed her citrus-smelling perfume; she was the type who would dab it on her sweater. The whole effect of her made me miserable with longing for a skiing holiday in Banff, a place I'd only ever heard about.

Karl had rented boot skates for his friends. I struggled with a heavy clamp-on skate that had suddenly left my runner during "Stupid Cupid." Then I whizzed back to the floor so I could be there to watch them come on.

Just as I thought, these girls didn't know how to skate. Instead, they flapped and fluttered around like land-marooned swans, gold bangle bracelets shimmering on their slender wrists beneath the false lights of the rink. They laughed, clinging to Karl and his friend. The friend skated well but with no heart-stopping style.

Sheila-Rae appeared half an hour later, her hair done up in a tight blond bun. I skated away from Lizzie, mumbling some excuse, and went to the newly arrived skaters at the benches. I plunked down near a key boy who was in the middle of trying to explain to a drunk why the clamp-ons he rented wouldn't fit on the shoes he was wearing. Loose-lipped, the drunk listened for a while, then insisted that he *always* skated in cowboy boots. Across from us, Sheila-Rae came and seated herself and frowned over the laces of her rented boot skates. Her makeup base was too dark, too orangey; a little bit had rubbed off onto her white turtleneck sweater. The drunk cowboy leered at her legs and asked where she'd got those nice boots. I wanted to tell her to go into the washroom and scrub and scrub until she glowed like the night I'd seen her up close in the pale blue sweater with the ketchup stain. I wanted to warn her about those untouchable girls who were not like us, but then Sheila-Rae got to her feet, swept grandly past, and headed out to the manic activity on the roller-rink floor.

The girl with the citrus-smelling perfume skated with Karl. They looked like models who'd just stepped from between the pages of a magazine. She had released his arm and he now had a friendly grip on her hand. All of the passion and arrogance had gone from his skating. It briefly occurred to me that maybe she was his sister or a cousin, but Sheila-Rae rolled slowly past and the girl looked after her, then quickly up into the mask Karl had made of his face. She made him let go of her hand so she could cling to his arm again.

But the strangest sight of all was Sheila-Rae as she skated around and around that rink not looking up, not noticing Karl. Between songs, when everyone else stopped skating, she kept right on like she didn't have a care in the world. And from far away, under those lights, when you didn't know her makeup was wrong and had made a stain on her thin white sweater, she looked and skated like a queen.

About Martha Brooks

Martha Brooks grew up in Manitoba, Canada, near a hospital and tuberculosis sanitarium where her father worked as a doctor and her mother worked as a nurse. She believes that her early experiences with death and illness made her a "keen observer of human behavior." She says, "I learned very early that failure, adversity, and unfairness are all part of living, and because of this I was able to deal quite well with disappointment while at the same time not giving up hope."

Ms. Brooks enjoys writing for young adults and often relies on her daughter's advice when working on a story. She has written short stories and a novel for young adults called *Only a Paper Moon*.

Responding

1. **Personal Response** If you had to choose, would you rather be friends with Karl or Sheila-Rae? Give the reasons for your choice.

2. **Literary Analysis** The *setting* of this story is an outdoor roller skating rink in a Canadian resort town. Why is the setting important in this story? What do you learn about the characters that you might not have learned if they were in a different setting?

3. **Theme Connection** What brings Karl and Sheila-Rae together? What pulls them apart? Have you known anyone who had a relationship like theirs?

Language Workshop

Using Imagery At the beginning of the story, the narrator says she thought of Karl "as some kind of bird god in disguise." Look at these other examples of bird *imagery* in the story. Tell what these images reveal about the characters.

1. ". . . [Karl] spun her easily around the floor with a cool hawklike arrogance that took my breath away." (p. 204)

2. ". . . Karl, cruising the rink with hooded eyes, suddenly swooped into the crowded sidelines and appeared seconds later with a girl who wasn't much older than me." (p. 207)

3. ". . . [These girls] flapped and fluttered around like land-marooned swans, gold bangle bracelets shimmering on their slender wrists beneath the false lights of the rink." (p. 208)

Writer's Portfolio

At the end of the story, the narrator says Sheila-Rae skated "like she didn't have a care in the world." How do *you* think Sheila-Rae was feeling? Write down her thoughts as she skated alone around the roller rink.

So Close

ℳY GRANDMOTHER WAS VERY FOND OF COOKIES made of banana, egg, and coconut, so my mother and I always stopped at Mrs. Hong's house to buy these cookies for her on our way back from the marketplace. My mother also liked to see Mrs. Hong because they had been very good friends since grade-school days. While my mother talked with her friend, I talked with Mrs. Hong's daughter, Lan. Most of the time Lan asked me about my older sister, who was married to a teacher and lived in a nearby town. Lan, too, was going to get married—to a young man living next door, Trung.

Trung and Lan had been inseparable playmates until the day tradition did not allow them to be alone together anymore. Besides, I think they felt a little shy with each other after realizing that they were man and woman.

Lan was a lively, pretty girl who attracted the attention of all the young men of our hamlet. Trung was a skillful fisherman who successfully plied his trade on the river in front of their houses. Whenever Lan's mother found a big fish on her kitchen windowsill she would smile to herself. Finally she decided that Trung was a fine young man and would make a good husband for her daughter.

Trung's mother did not like the idea of her son giving good fish away, but she liked the cookies Lan brought her from time to time. Besides, the girl was very helpful; whenever she was not busy at her house Lan would come over in the evening and help Trung's mother repair her son's fishing net.

Trung was happiest when Lan was helping his mother. They did not talk to each other, but they could look at each other when his mother was busy with her work. Each time Lan went home Trung looked at the chair Lan had just left and secretly wished that nobody would move it.

One day when Trung's mother heard her son call Lan's name in his sleep, she decided it was time to speak to the girl's mother about marriage. Lan's mother agreed they should be married and even waived the custom whereby the bridegroom had to give the bride's family a fat hog, six chickens, six ducks, three bottles of wine, and thirty kilos of fine rice, for the two families had known each other for a long time and were good neighbors.

The two widowed mothers quickly set the dates for the engagement announcement and for the wedding ceremony. Since their decision was immediately made known to relatives and friends, Trung and Lan could now see each other often.

One day as Trung helped Lan to plant a mango tree behind her house, he asked her: "Have you ever looked at those dainty town boys who pass by your house all the time?" Instead of answering Trung, Lan poked a hard finger at his ribs and laughed. Then she said: "You are not bad looking at all; so don't bother about them. Besides, my mother said that in darkness everything, everybody looks the same!" To a shy young man like Trung the remark was quite bold, but he was very pleased and happy.

At last it was the day of their wedding. Friends and relatives arrived early in the morning to help them celebrate. They brought gifts of ducks, chickens, baskets filled with fruits, rice wine, and colorful fabrics. Even though the two houses were next to each other, the two mothers observed all the proper wedding day traditions.

First Trung and his friends and relatives came to Lan's house. Lan and he prayed at her ancestors' altars and asked for their blessing. Then they joined everyone for a luncheon.

After lunch there was a farewell ceremony for the bride. Lan stepped out of her house and joined the greeting party that was to accompany her to Trung's home. Tradition called for her to cry and to express her sorrow at leaving her parents behind and forever becoming the daughter of her husband's family. In some villages the bride was even supposed to cling so tightly to her mother that it would take several friends to pull her away from her home. But instead of crying, Lan smiled. She asked herself, why should she cry? The two houses were separated by only a garden; she could run home and see her mother any time she wanted to. So Lan willingly followed Trung and prayed at his ancestors' altars before joining everyone in the big welcome dinner at Trung's house that ended the day's celebrations.

Later in the evening of the wedding night Lan went to the river to take a bath. Because crocodiles infested the river, people of our hamlet who lived along the riverbank chopped down trees and put them in the river to form barriers and protect places where they washed their clothes, did their dishes, or took a bath. This evening, a wily crocodile had avoided the barrier by crawling up the riverbank and sneaked up behind Lan. The crocodile grabbed her and went back to the river by the same route that it had come.

Trung became worried when Lan did not return. He went to the place where she was supposed to bathe, only to find that her clothes were there but she had disappeared. Panic-stricken, he yelled for his relatives. They all rushed to the riverbank with lighted torches. In the flickering light they found traces of water and crocodile claw prints on the wet soil. Now they knew that a crocodile had grabbed the young bride and dragged her into the river.

Since no one could do anything for the girl, all of Trung's relatives returned to the house, urging the bridegroom to do the same. But the young man refused to leave the place; he just stood there, crying and staring at the clothes of his bride.

Suddenly the wind brought him the sound of Lan calling his name. He was very frightened, for according to an old belief a crocodile's victim must lure a new victim to his master; if not, the first victim's soul must stay with the beast forever.

Trung rushed back to the house and woke all his relatives. Nobody doubted he thought he had heard her call, but they all believed that he was the victim of a hallucination. Everyone pleaded with him and tried to convince him that nobody could survive when snapped up by a crocodile and dragged into the river to be drowned and eaten by the animal.

The young man brushed aside all their arguments and rushed back to the river. Once again, he heard the voice of his bride in the wind, calling his name. Again he rushed back and woke his relatives. Again they tried to persuade him that it was a hallucination, although some of the old folks suggested that maybe the ghost of the young girl was having to dance and sing to placate the angry crocodile because she failed to bring it a new victim.

No one could persuade Trung to stay inside. His friends wanted to go back to the river with him, but he said no. He resented them for not believing him that there were desperate cries in the wind.

Words to Know

placate (p. 216) soothe or satisfy the anger of

avenge (p. 216) take revenge, get back at

incoherently (p. 216) with no logical connection of ideas

Trung stood in front of the deep river alone in the darkness. He listened to the sound of the wind and clutched the clothes Lan had left behind. The wind became stronger and stronger and often changed direction as the night progressed, but he did not hear any more calls. Still he had no doubt that the voice he had heard earlier was absolutely real. Then at dawn, when the wind died down, he again heard, very clearly, Lan call him for help.

Her voice came from an island about six hundred meters away. Trung wept and prayed: "You were a good girl when you were still alive, now be a good soul. Please protect me so that I can find a way to kill the beast in order to free you from its spell and avenge your tragic death." Suddenly, while wiping away his tears, he saw a little tree moving on the island. The tree was jumping up and down. He squinted to see better. The tree had two hands that were waving at him. And it was calling his name.

Trung became hysterical and yelled for help. He woke all his relatives and they all rushed to his side again. At first they thought that Trung had become stark mad. They tried to lead him back to his house, but he fiercely resisted their attempt. He talked to them incoherently and pointed his finger at the strange tree on the island. Finally his relatives saw the waving tree. They quickly put a small boat into the river and Trung got into the boat along with two other men. They paddled to the island and discovered that the moving tree was, in fact, Lan. She had covered herself with leaves because she had no clothes on.

At first nobody knew what had really happened because Lan clung to Trung and cried and cried. Finally, when Lan could talk they pieced together her story.

Lan had fainted when the crocodile snapped her up. Had she not fainted, the crocodile surely would have drowned her before carrying her off to the island. Lan did not know how many times the crocodile had tossed her into the air and smashed her against the ground, but at one point, while being tossed in the air and falling back onto the crocodile's jaw, she regained consciousness. The crocodile smashed her against the ground a few more times, but Lan played dead. Luckily the crocodile became thirsty and returned to the river to drink. At that moment Lan got up and ran to a nearby tree and climbed up it. The tree was very small. Lan stayed very still for fear that the snorting, angry crocodile, roaming around trying to catch her again, would find her and shake her out of the tree. Lan stayed in this frozen position for a long time until the crocodile gave up searching for her and went back to the river. Then she started calling Trung to come rescue her.

Lan's body was covered with bruises, for crocodiles soften up big prey before swallowing it. They will smash it against the ground or against a tree, or keep tossing it into the air. But fortunately Lan had no broken bones or serious cuts. It was possible that this crocodile was very old and had lost most of its teeth. Nevertheless, the older the crocodile, the more intelligent it usually was. That was how it knew to avoid the log barrier in the river and to snap up the girl from behind.

Trung carried his exhausted bride into the boat and paddled home. Lan slept for hours and hours. At times she would sit up with a start and cry out for help, but within three days she was almost completely recovered.

Lan's mother and Trung's mother decided to celebrate their children's wedding a second time, because Lan had come back from the dead. All their friends came and sang to the happy couple. At midnight, at the end of the last serenade, "The Wedding Night," the bride and bridegroom were supposed to open the windows of their room to thank the minstrels. But Lan and Trung kept the window closed. Perhaps they were too tired or too busy to open it. The serenade party left good-humoredly, saying one could do well only one thing at a time!

About Huynh Quang Nhuong

Huynh Quang Nhuong was born in 1946 and grew up in a small village on a riverbank in central Vietnam. During the rainy season he helped his

parents cultivate the rice fields and during the dry season he helped his father hunt in the jungle.

Like his father, Huynh left the village to go to college. Afterward, he was drafted into the South Vietnamese army. While fighting in the Vietnam War, Huynh was shot and permanently paralyzed. He has lived in the United States since 1969. "So Close" is taken from his book of memoirs, *The Land I Lost: Adventures of a Boy in Vietnam.*

Responding

1. **Personal Response** What different feelings did you have as you read this selection? Would you have enjoyed life in the village? Explain.

2. **Literary Analysis** When the author describes the incident with Lan and the crocodile, what does he do to create a feeling of *suspense?*

3. **Theme Connection** How might Lan's narrow escape affect her relationship with Trung?

Language Workshop

Who **and** *Whom*   The pronouns *who* and *whom* are often confused. Use *who* when the word is the *subject* of the sentence or clause. Use *whom* when the word acts as the *object*. For example, look at the following:

Lan was a pretty girl <u>who</u> attracted much attention.

Who is correct because it is the subject of a clause. But look at this sentence:

Lan was the girl <u>whom</u> the crocodile attacked.

In this case, *whom* is correct because it is the object. The subject of the clause is *crocodile*. One more example:

Trung brought fish to Lan, with <u>whom</u> he had fallen in love.

Whom is correct because it is the object of the preposition *with*. After a preposition, always use *whom*.

Choose the correct pronoun in each sentence below.

1. Trung, (who/whom) was a fisherman, wanted to marry Lan.

2. Lan often helped her future mother-in-law, (who/whom) she would visit in the evenings.

3. To (who/whom) did Lan call when the crocodile carried her away?

Writer's Portfolio

Compare the marriage customs described in "So Close" with the marriage customs that are familiar to you. What are the advantages and disadvantages of each set of customs? Which customs would you prefer?

ELLEN CONFORD

I Hate You, Wallace B. Pokras

$\mathcal{I}$ HATE YOU, WALLACE B. POKRAS.

After all we've meant to each other, how could you do this to me?

Maybe I was wrong. Maybe we haven't meant that much to each other. Maybe you were just hanging around with me till Ms. Right came along.

Using me, that's what you were doing. Just using me as a convenient date: someone to go to dances with, someone to take to team parties, someone handy for social occasions.

Handy. Like a pocket calculator. And you *did* have me in the palm of your hand, didn't you? What a dope I was.

I mean, I really thought those kisses meant something to you. I thought they were sincere kisses. I would never kiss someone I didn't love—or at the very least, like a whole lot.

But they lied, Wallace, you worm. Those kisses lied. You have lying lips. They go perfectly with your cheating heart.

A regular Benedict Arnold, that's what you are. A traitor, a fink, a creep, a . . .

You think I didn't see you. I'll bet you thought you could get away with it. How were you to know I'd be at the movies last night? And how were you to know that at the last minute I'd decided to go with Pam and Becky because you told me you'd be busy?

Busy. Boy, you were busy all right. Busy as a little beaver.

Well, you've got a surprise coming, Wallace. You didn't get away with it. I saw you. I saw you with that blonde— that refugee from a jeans commercial. It was dark and the movie had already started, but I saw you walk down the aisle with her looking for seats in the front. You're not hard to spot, you know, you big hunk. *I mean hulk!* Hulk is what

I meant. Even with the lights down, your hair still looks like it's on fire. Even when you slouch, you're still practically six feet tall.

You looked ridiculous with her, you know. She was barely five feet tall. You look like Mutt and Jeff together. I never did get to see her face. I was so humiliated I dragged Pam and Becky out of the movies while the final credits were still rolling. So all I saw were your backs as you walked toward some empty seats. I don't know how she managed to sit down at all in those jeans. They looked like they were painted on with a spray can.

Yes, you have a real surprise coming, Wallace Benedict Arnold Pokras. Because I'm just going to sit here by the phone, waiting for you to call.

Oh, you'll call. Eventually. You'll have to. Either to try and pretend nothing ever happened, while you're planning to keep both of us on the string at the same time, or to make some lame excuse about why we can't go to Jerry's party next Saturday.

So I'm just going to sit here by the phone and wait.

And when you call, you're going to get it right between the eyes.

They hanged Benedict Arnold, you know. (Or did they shoot him? I'm not sure.) Whichever, it's too good for you. Too quick. Too easy.

You're going to suffer, Wallace, like you're making me suffer. A long, slow, agonizing revenge, that's what I'm going to give you.

Ever read "The Pit and the Pendulum," Wallace?

We had to read it for English this year. Which means you had to read it last year but probably didn't. You'd be failing again right now if it weren't for me, Wallace. You ungrateful rat!

Or is that why you started going with me? Because I'm good in English? You really *are* using me! You have to pass English to stay on the team.

Words to Know

conniving (p. 222) secretly doing something wrong

vindictive (p. 223) wanting to take revenge

ogle (p. 224) look at with desire, stare at

And the minute football season is over, you're going to drop me like an old shoe.

Oh, Wallace, you calculating, scheming, conniving, lying . . .

Well, there are still three weeks left in the football season. Let's see you pull through your English midterm without me. Because if you think you can expect any help from me, you've got another think coming.

And after I gave you the best months of my life.

What I don't understand is why you spent the whole summer with me. You didn't need me then. You didn't even have to go to summer school after I tutored you for two weeks before finals, and got you through English 11 by the skin of your teeth.

Was it gratitude?

Hah! You haven't got a grateful bone in your oversized body. If you had, you wouldn't be sneaking around darkened movie theaters with that bargain basement Brooke Shields.

Letting you fail English and watching you get kicked off the team is a start; a good start, true, but just a start. You're going to have to suffer a lot more than that before justice is done.

I'm not a vindictive person, Wallace. Not normally. I'm not mean or spiteful. Even when Pam grabbed the very last suede fringed vest on sale at Zohlmann's for a ridiculously low price right out from under my nose, I didn't bear a grudge. She got it first; her hand was faster, and even though it was *me* who said, "Oh, look at that fantastic vest!" I was a good sport about it. Even though it was too big for her and would have been absolutely *perfect* for me, I didn't brood over it.

Fair's fair, she grabbed it first, though there'll probably *never* be a sale like that again, and that vest was *exactly* the thing I needed to wear with my new antelope cords, and the one time I asked to borrow it she *said* it was at the cleaners.

I'm just not the type to harp on something like that.

But love is not a suede vest, Wallace, you louse.

Or what I thought was love. What you let me believe was love. Or what you led me to believe was love. Or at the very least, like. With demonstrations of affection. Holding my hand at the shopping mall; dunking me in the pool; hugging me when I beat you three times in a row at

PacMan; kissing me under the porch light, not caring that Jerry and Becky were sitting in the car ogling us.

Being betrayed by someone with whom you thought you had a deep and meaningful relationship brings out the dark, ugly side of a person's nature, Wallace. It leads a person to think—and do—things she would never ever consider under ordinary circumstances, particularly if she is of such a calm, understanding, unspiteful nature as I am.

Things like slipping rat poison into your Gatorade. (How appropriate, Wallace. Rat poison for a rat.) Or driving a stake through your heart. Or telling your new little playmate that you're deranged, and while you look like a normal person, every time there's a full moon you develop an unholy craving for chicken hearts.

But those are all too easy, Wallace, you crumb. (Except for that last one, which isn't bad.) No, whatever my revenge is, it has to be slow, drawn-out: fitting punishment for your betrayal.

Something like this: On the day of the big game with Northside, the game that decides the Section II Championship, you "accidentally" fall down the stairs and sprain your ankle. Nothing big and serious, you understand. Just a dumb old sprained ankle. It's such a stupid, careless injury. But you won't be able to put any weight on your foot, so you'll sit on the bench the whole time and watch as Northside wipes the field with us, because you're not in there to stop them on defense.

And you'll watch as the first quarter goes by, then the second and the third, and Northside will be rolling up points, because you're the star defensive back and everyone depends on you.

And the fourth quarter will drag by and everyone will know that if it weren't for you and your stupid ankle, Jefferson would have won the game, the section championship, and gone on to the county finals.

And when the game is over and you feel lower than a

worm (which is what you are, anyway) and everyone's trying not to hate you—or at least, trying not to show that they hate you—I'll come up to you and say, "Oh, Wallace, what a shame. I guess you didn't know there was a scout from Ohio State here to watch you today . . ."

Mean? Rotten? Nasty? Sadistic?

You bet. But only what you deserve, Wallace. How do you think *I* feel right now? Right this minute? Sitting here by the phone, waiting for you to call, but dreading it at the same time. Wanting you to be able to explain everything but knowing you can't, knowing it's over, that what we once had is forever shattered, like a mirror broken into a hundred unlucky pieces.

I remember the first day we met. The guidance office told me they had someone who needed tutoring in English, and there you were, your hair looking like it was on fire, this great, big hunk—I mean *hulk!* Hulk is what I mean—looking like a nursery-school kid who'd flunked fingerpainting.

"I feel kind of stupid having a tutor who's younger than me," you said. You looked down at your great, big feet, hoping, I suppose, that I wouldn't notice your face turning the same color as your hair.

"Barbara is an honor student," Mrs. Rizzo had said. "She can give you help in the basics, which is really what you need."

"Barbie," you said. "Like the doll."

"Hardly," I said coolly, thinking, Boy, this one's a real nerd.

But you didn't turn out to be a nerd, Wallace.

A rat, a louse, a fink, a creep, a crumb, a Benedict Arnold, yes. But not a nerd.

I thought you were nice.

Gentle.

Honest.

Decent.

Even though I thought at first you were illiterate, you liked it when I read poetry to you. You said it was so romantic.

That's a great gimmick, Wallace. Go all misty-eyed when your tutor reads "How do I love thee?" Take her hand and whisper, "I'd like to learn that one by heart so I could say it to you." And blush. That was a really nice touch, that shy, embarrassed blush.

And it was all an act? Are you that good an actor? Were you stringing me along right from the beginning? Were you telling all the guys, "She really fell for me. She's going to put her heart and soul into *this* tutoring job. Don't worry about my eligibility next year."

How could you be so sly, so devious, so dishonest? How could you toss my heart around like a football, trifle with my affections, trample my dreams into shreds with your cleats?

Maybe two can playact at this game, Wallace, you con man.

Maybe when you do call, I won't let on that I saw you with that bleached blonde in her sprayed-on jeans. Oh, I could tell her hair was bleached, even though it was dark in the theater and I could only see her from the back, so I couldn't really check for black roots. No one is born with hair the color of Kraft Vanilla Caramels. That's probably not the only phony thing about her either. I'll bet that man-eating little shrimp is 99 and 44/100 percent artificial ingredients.

But maybe I won't say a word about her. Maybe I'll just act as if absolutely nothing has happened. Everything's fine. Everything's just dandy. I'll pretend that nothing has changed between us. We'll go on just as before.

And then I'll start tutoring you for your English midterm.

And I'll teach you all the wrong answers.

I'll tell you that Charles Dickens wrote *Catcher in the Rye* to expose the evils of the bread industry in Victorian England. I'll tell you that the past tense of sneak is snuck. I'll tell you that alliteration means the art of writing letters. I'll tell you that *The Rubaiyat of Omar Khayyam* is a poem about a rich guy with a yacht entirely encrusted with rubies.

And then, when you flunk your English midterm and get kicked off the team, you'll come to me and say, "But I wrote the answers you gave me! You *told* me that poem was about a guy with a red boat."

And I'll say, "And you told me you loved me." (Practically.) "Betrayal for betrayal, Wallace. Let the punishment fit the crime. By the way, in case anyone asks you, that's from a song by Stephen Foster. How does it feel, Wallace, to be betrayed by someone you trusted?"

And then he'd realize that I'd known all along. That I'd been acting, just as he'd been acting, that I hadn't been fooled.

"Time to pay the piper, Wallace. As in *The Pied Piper of Hamelin*, by Edna St. Vincent Millay. How does it feel?"

Sweet revenge. Mean, rotten, nasty, sadistic, devious . . .

But I'll never pull it off.

I hate you, Wallace B. Pokras. And I'll never be able to hide it for three weeks while I pretend to still love you. I don't even know if I'll be able to speak to you and sound normal when that phone rings, let alone deceive you for three weeks the way you've deceived me all these months.

It's just not like me, Wallace. Spitefulness, meanness of spirit, vindictive acts of violence simply aren't in my nature. That's why it's so hard for me to think up exactly the right mean, rotten, nasty, sadistic thing to do to you.

But give me time. I'll overcome my basic decency and think of something that will make you sorry you were ever—

The phone.

My hand is shaking.

"Hello?" My voice is shaking, too. I hope he doesn't notice. If it's him.

It's him.

"Your cousin Ginger from Baltimore? To the Empire State Building? . . . That's where you were all day? Oh, Wallace! . . . Crying? No, of course not. I think I'm getting a little cold, that's all. . . . Tonight? You mean, with Ginger and your aunt and uncle? . . . Oh, yes! I mean, I'd love to. . . . No, I'm sure my brother would just love to meet Ginger. . . . She's *twelve?* . . . Yeah, perfect. . . . Last night? . . . You *were?* . . . Isn't that the funniest coincidence. So was I! For goodness sake, you must have walked right by me and I never saw you. . . . "

About Ellen Conford

Ellen Conford's books for young adults are known for their humorous characters and lively dialogue. Conford, who began writing in third grade, says

her characters are not duplicates of real people, but their "personalities, mannerisms, and characteristics" resemble those of kids and adults she has known.

Conford's hobbies include "reading, playing Scrabble, doing crossword puzzles, collecting old cookbooks, watching movies, and *eating*." Her many books for young adults include *Dear Lovey Hart, I Am Desperate; Why Me?;* and *A Royal Pain.*

Responding

1. **Personal Response** If you had a similar experience, would you react the same way the narrator does? Explain.

2. **Literary Analysis** How would you describe the overall atmosphere or *mood* in this story? How does author Ellen Conford create and sustain this mood?

3. **Theme Connection** What advice would you have for Wallace or the narrator about their relationship?

Language Workshop

Summarizing When you *summarize* something you have read, you retell the most important events or ideas in a few sentences. Write a brief summary of the story.

Writer's Portfolio

Would a boy react in the same way as the female narrator of "I Hate You, Wallace B. Pokras"? Write a similar story in which the narrator is a male.

CLAIRE BARLIANT

What to Reply When
Someone Wonders

What's wrong?
he asks offhandedly
as I walk by
my teeth locked together tightly
an enameled barricade
restraining a river
of angry answers.
I'll tell you what's wrong.
It's the sun, that traitor, for months
deserting me
for some lonely cloud.
It's the browngreen color
which washes over everything
cats grass people bicycles me
and seeps into the soul.
It's seeing you with
her
and knowing
that if only you were with me,
everything would be
right.

A R N O L D   A D O F F

𝔐ixed 𝔖ingles

She tosses the tennis ball high

                    into   the   air.

Her

racket comes down harder than I   e v e r

                           k n e w

a

racket could hit.

It

is a serve into the inside corner,

that I barely see: kicking   chalk

as

it flies away, untouched   by   me

I know this will be love.

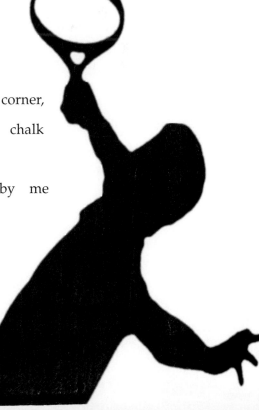

NIKKI GIOVANNI

Kidnap Poem

ever been kidnapped
by a poet
if i were a poet
i'd kidnap you

put you in my phrases
and meter you to jones beach
or maybe coney island
or maybe just to my house

lyric you in lilacs
dash you in the rain
alliterate the beach
to complement my sea

play the lyre for you
ode you with my love song
anything to win you
wrap you in the red Black green
show you off to mama

yeah if i were
a poet i'd kid
nap you

About Claire Barliant

Claire Barliant has been writing poetry since kindergarten. She says, "I never decide 'I'm going to write a poem now.' I see something or feel something, and I know it will be a poem eventually." Barliant recently graduated from high school in Chicago and is a student at Smith College.

About Arnold Adoff

Arnold Adoff grew up in New York City reading, listening to jazz, and having lively discussions with his family. In addition to writing poetry, he has edited several poetry anthologies for young adults. He says poems "should be read three times: for meaning; for rhythm; for technical tricks. My poems demand active participation."

About Nikki Giovanni

Nikki Giovanni teaches college and has written numerous books of poetry. She says she enjoys writing for young readers: "I hope my poetry reaches both the heart and the mind of a child who is a child and the adult who still nurtures the child within."

Responding

1. **Personal Response** What are your favorite lines in these poems? Why do you like them?

2. **Literary Analysis** *Free verse* is poetry without a regular rhyme scheme. Why do you think these poets chose to write in free verse instead of rhyme?

3. **Theme Connection** What does each of these poems have to say about being in love?

Language Workshop

Punctuation in Poetry Poets don't always follow standard rules for capitalization and punctuation in their poems. For example, in "Kidnap Poem," Nikki Giovanni doesn't use any periods or commas, and only uses one capital letter. In "Mixed Singles," Arnold Adoff uses extra spaces between words and even letters. What effect does this have on the poems?

Compare how the three poets use punctuation and capitalization in their poems. Then choose another poem (it could be one of your own) and show at least two different ways of using punctuation and capitalization to make the poem more interesting or effective.

Writer's Portfolio

These three poems express different messages about falling in love. Create a poem, song, or cartoon that conveys your ideas about love.

ꟿatters of the ꟼeart

PROJECTS

Love Poems

"What to Reply When Someone Wonders," "Mixed Singles," and "Kidnap Poem" are all examples of modern non-traditional love poems. Choose one of these poems and compare it to a more traditional love poem, perhaps one by Shakespeare, Elizabeth Barrett Browning, or Lord Byron. Begin your comparison by discussing the different styles of the two poems you've chosen, and then consider which poem you think is more effective at expressing the complexities of love. Finish by presenting your analysis to the class.

Say It with Music

In small groups, vote on a favorite selection from "Matters of the Heart." Then work together to choose a piece of music that best reflects that selection. As a group, jot down your reasons for choosing the music you did. Present your music to the class, along with a dramatic reading of a passage or two from the book. End your presentation by explaining how your group feels the song fits the story.

Writing from the Heart

How many great works of literature have been inspired by love? Can you add one to the number? Write a short story about a matter of the heart. If you like, use a selection in this unit as a writing model. Remember to keep your story simple and focused: it's a lot more effective to write in detail about a single experience than to try and cover someone's entire life in just two or three pages. Keep your audience in mind as you write, offering vivid details that will capture your reader's interest.

FURTHER READING

Will you know true love when you find it? Each of the following selections answers that question in a different way.

The Pigman by Paul Zindel. High school students John and Lorraine befriend a gentle old man whose attitude toward life at first amuses and then impresses them. But when Mr. Pignati dies, John and Lorraine must acknowledge their role in his death.

Romeo and Juliet by William Shakespeare. Though this play is hundreds of years old, the tragic story of these two famous lovers still moves us today.

Pygmalion by George Bernard Shaw. The arrogant Professor Higgins bets a friend that he will be able to instill proper manners in Eliza Doolittle, a strong-willed, poorly educated young woman. This play was the basis for the musical *My Fair Lady*.

Children of the River by Linda Crew. Not all of Sundara's family could escape from Cambodia. Now that the survivors have found a home in Oregon, they cling to their Cambodian traditions. Sundara wants to be obedient, but her feelings for Jonathan, a popular white student at her high school, complicate her life.

Ethan Frome by Edith Wharton. Ethan Frome, his wife Zeena, and Zeena's beautiful young cousin Mattie are caught in a love triangle that changes the rest of their lives.

Acts of Love by Maureen Daly. Retta Caldwell's family is unhappy when she and Dallas Dobson, son of troubled Danny Dobson, fall in love. What will happen to the young couple when Retta's family moves to California?

UNIT 5

Right or Wrong

What's the right thing to do? What's the wrong thing to do? Sometimes the answer seems to be a balancing act between your idea of what's right and someone else's—or between what you know you want and what you know is right.

The stories you're about to read each concern a decision about what's right and what's wrong. You may not agree with or approve of these decisions. If that's the case, what would you have done differently?

LAURENCE YEP

Waters of Gold

MANY YEARS AGO, THERE LIVED A WOMAN everyone called Auntie Lily. She was Auntie by blood to half the county and Auntie to the other half by friendship. As she liked to say, "There's a bit of Heaven in each of us." As a result, she was always helping people out.

Because of her many kind acts, she knew so many people that she couldn't go ten steps without meeting someone who wanted to chat. So it would take her half the day to go to the village well and back to her home.

Eventually, though, she helped so many people that she had no more money. She had to sell her fields and even her house to her neighbor, a rich old woman. "If you'd helped yourself instead of others, you wouldn't have to do this," the neighbor said smugly. "Where are all those other people when you need them?"

"That isn't why I helped them," Auntie Lily said firmly. She wound up having to pay rent for the house she had once owned. She supported herself by her embroidery; but since her eyes were going bad, she could not do very much.

One day an old beggar entered the village. He was a ragbag of a man—a trash heap, a walking pig wallow. It was impossible to tell what color or what shape his clothes had once been, and his hair was as muddy and matted as a bird's nest. As he shuffled through the village gates, he called out, "Water for my feet. Please, water for my feet.

> ### Words to Know
> **pig wallow** (p. 240) a mudhole that a pig lies in
> **cleaver** (p. 241) a cutting tool with a large, heavy blade and a short handle
> **shamble** (p. 242) walk awkwardly or unsteadily

One little bowl of water—that's all I ask."

Everyone ignored him, pretending to concentrate on their chores instead. One man went on replacing the shaft of his hoe. A woman swept her courtyard. Another woman fed her hens.

The beggar went to each in turn, but they all showed their backs to him.

After calling out a little while longer, the beggar went to the nearest home, which happened to belong to the rich old woman. When he banged at her door, he left the dirty outline of his knuckles on the clean wood. And when the rich woman opened her door, his smell nearly took her breath away.

Now it so happened that she had been chopping vegetables when the beggar had knocked. When the beggar repeated his request, she raised her cleaver menacingly. "What good would one bowl of water be? You'd need a whole river to wash you clean. Go away."

"A thousand pardons," the old beggar said, and shambled on to the next house.

Though Auntie Lily had to hold her nose, she asked politely, "Yes?"

"I'd like a bowl of water to wash my feet." And the beggar pointed one grimy finger toward them.

Her rich neighbor had stayed in her doorway to watch the beggar. She scolded Auntie Lily now. "It's all your fault those beggars come into the village. They know they can count on a free meal."

It was an old debate between them, so Auntie Lily simply said, "Any of us can have bad luck."

"Garbage," the rich old woman declared, "is garbage. They must have done something bad, or Heaven wouldn't have let them become beggars."

Auntie Lily turned to the beggar. "I may be joining you on the road someday. Wait here."

Much to the neighbor's distress, Auntie Lily went inside and poured water from a large jar in her kitchen into a bucket. Carrying it in both hands, she brought it outside to the beggar and set it down.

The beggar stood on one leg, just like a crane, while he washed one callused, leathery sole over the bucket. "You can put mud on any other part of me, but if my feet are clean, then I feel clean."

As he fussily continued to cleanse his feet, Auntie Lily asked kindly, "Are you hungry? I don't have much, but what I have I'm willing to share."

The beggar shook his head. "I've stayed longer in this village than I have in any other. Heaven is my roof, and the whole world my house."

Auntie Lily stared at him, wondering what she would look like after a few years on the road. "Are you very tired? Have you been on the road for very long?"

"No, the road is on me," the beggar said, and held up

his hands from his dirty sides. "But thank you. You're the first person to ask. And you're the first person to give me some water. So place the bucket of water by your bed tonight and do not look into it till tomorrow morning."

As the beggar shuffled out of the village again, Auntie Lily stared down doubtfully at the bucket of what was now muddy water. Then, even though she felt foolish, she picked it up again.

"You're not really going to take that scummy water inside?" laughed the rich neighbor. "It'll probably breed mosquitoes."

"It seemed important to him," she answered. "I'll humor him."

"Humoring people," snapped the neighbor, "has got you one step from begging yourself."

However, Auntie Lily carried the bucket inside anyway. Setting it down near her sleeping mat, she covered the mouth of the bucket with an old, cracked plate so she wouldn't peek into it by mistake, and then she got so caught up in embroidering a pair of slippers that she forgot all about the beggar and his bucket of water.

She sewed until twilight, when it was too dark to use her needle. Then, because she had no money for oil or candles, she went to sleep.

The next morning Auntie Lily rose and stretched the aches out of her back. She sighed. "The older I get, the harder it is to get up in the morning."

She was always saying something like that, but she had never stayed on her sleeping mat—even when she was sick. Thinking of all that day's chores, she decided to water the herbs she had growing on one side of her house.

Her eyes fell upon the beggar's bucket with its covering plate. "No sense using fresh water when that will do as well. After all, dirt's dirt to a plant."

Squatting down, she picked up the bucket and was surprised at how heavy it was. "I must have filled it fuller than I thought," she grunted.

She staggered out of the house and over to the side where rows of little green herbs grew. "Here you go," she said to her plants. "Drink deep."

Taking off the plate, she upended the bucket; but instead of muddy brown water, there was a flash of reflected light and a clinking sound as gold coins rained down upon her plants.

Auntie Lily set the bucket down hastily and crouched, not trusting her weak eyes. However, where some of her herbs had been, there was now a small mound of gold coins. She squinted in disbelief and rubbed her aching eyes and stared again; but the gold was still there.

She turned to the bucket. There was even more gold inside. Scooping up coins by the handful, she freed her little plants and made sure that the stalks weren't too bent.

Then she sat gazing at her bucket full of gold until a farmer walked by. "Tell me I'm not dreaming," she called to him.

The farmer yawned and came over with his hoe over his shoulder. "I wish I were dreaming, because that would mean I'm still in bed instead of having to go off to work."

Auntie Lily gathered up a handful of gold coins and let it fall in a tinkling, golden shower back into the bucket. "And this is real?"

The farmer's jaw dropped. He picked up one coin with his free hand and bit into it. He flipped it back in with the other coins. "It's as real as me, Auntie. But where did you ever get that?"

So Auntie Lily told him. And as others woke up and stepped outside, Auntie told them as well, for she still could not believe her luck and wanted them to confirm that the gold was truly gold. In no time at all, there was a small crowd around her.

If the bucket had been filled with ordinary copper cash, that would have been more money than any of them had ever seen. In their wildest dreams, they had never expected to see that much gold. Auntie Lily stared at the bucket uncomfortably. "I keep thinking it's going to disappear the next moment."

The farmer, who had been standing there all this time, shook his head. "If it hasn't disappeared by now, I don't think it will. What are you going to do with it, Auntie?"

Auntie Lily stared at the bucket, and suddenly she came to a decision. Stretching out a hand, she picked up a gold coin. "I'm going to buy back my house, and I'm going to get back my land."

The farmer knew the fields. "Those old things? You could buy a valley full of prime land with half that bucket. And a palace with the other half."

"I want what I sweated for." Asking the farmer to guard her bucket, Auntie Lily closed her hand around the gold coin. Then, as the crowd parted before her, she made her way over to her neighbor.

Now the rich old woman liked to sleep late; but all the noise had woken her up, so she was just getting dressed when Auntie knocked. The old woman yanked her door open as she buttoned the last button of her coat. "Who started the riot? Can't a person get a good night's sleep?"

With some satisfaction, Auntie Lily held up the gold coin. "Will this buy back my house and land?"

"Where did you get that?" the old woman demanded.

"Will it buy them back?" Auntie Lily repeated.

The rich old woman snatched the coin out of Auntie Lily's hand and bit into it just as the farmer had. "It's real," the old woman said in astonishment.

"Will it?" Auntie asked again.

"Yes, yes, yes," the old woman said crabbily. "But where did you ever get that much gold?"

When Auntie Lily told her the story and showed her the bucket of gold, the rich old woman stood moving her mouth like a fish out of water. Clasping her hands together, she shut her eyes and moaned in genuine pain. "And I sent him away. What a fool I am. What a fool." And the old woman beat her head with her fists.

That very afternoon, the beggar—the ragbag, the trash heap, the walking pig wallow—shuffled once more through the village gates with feet as dirty as before. As he went, he croaked, "Water for my feet. Please, water for my feet. One little bowl of water—that's all I ask."

This time, people dropped whatever they were doing when they heard his plea. Hoes, brooms, and pots were flung down, hens and pigs were kicked out of the way as everyone hurried to fill a bucket with water. There was a small riot by the village well as everyone fought to get water at the same time. Still others rushed out with buckets filled from the jars in their houses.

"Here, use my water," one man shouted, holding up a tub.

A woman shoved in front of him with a bucket in her arms. "No, no, use mine. It's purer."

They surrounded the old beggar, pleading with him to use their water, and in the process of jostling one another, they splashed a good deal of water on one another and came perilously close to drowning the beggar. The rich old woman, Auntie Lily's neighbor, charged to the rescue.

"Out of the way, you vultures," the rich old woman roared. "You're going to trample him." Using her elbows, her feet, and in one case even her teeth, the old woman fought her way through the mob.

No longer caring if she soiled her hands, the old woman seized the beggar by the arm. "This way, you poor, misunderstood creature."

Fighting off her neighbors with one hand and keeping her grip on the beggar with the other, the old woman hauled him inside her house. Barring the door against the rest of the village, she ignored all the fists and feet thumping on her door and all the shouts.

"I really wasn't myself yesterday, because I had been up the night before tending a sick friend. This is what I meant to do." She fetched a fresh new towel and an even newer bucket and forced the beggar to wash his feet.

When he was done, he handed her the now filthy towel. "Dirt's dirt, and garbage is garbage," he said.

However, the greedy old woman didn't recognize her own words. She was too busy trying to remember what else Auntie Lily had done. "Won't you have something to eat? Have you traveled very far? Are you tired?" she asked, all in the same breath.

The old beggar went to the door and waited patiently while she unbarred it. As he shuffled outside, he instructed her to leave the bucket of water by her bed but not to look into it until the morning.

That night, the greedy old woman couldn't sleep as she imagined the heap of shiny gold that would be waiting for her tomorrow. She waited impatiently for the sun to rise and got up as soon as she heard the first rooster crow.

Hurrying to the bucket, she plunged her hands inside expecting to bring up handfuls of gold. Instead, she gave a cry as dozens of little things bit her, for the bucket was filled not with gold but with snakes, lizards, and ants.

The greedy old woman fell sick—some said from her bites, some claimed from sheer frustration. Auntie Lily came herself to nurse her neighbor. "Take this to heart: Kindness comes with no price."

The old woman was so ashamed that she did, indeed, take the lesson to heart. Though she remained sick, she was kind to whoever came to her door.

One day, a leper came into the village. Everyone hid for fear of the terrible disease. Doors slammed and shutters banged down over the windows, and soon the village seemed deserted.

Only Auntie Lily and her neighbor stepped out of their houses. "Are you hungry?" Auntie Lily asked.

"Are you thirsty?" the neighbor asked. "I'll make you a cup of tea."

The leper thanked Auntie Lily and then turned to the neighbor as if to express his gratitude as well; but he stopped and studied her. "You're looking poorly, my dear woman. Can I help?"

With a tired smile, the rich old woman explained what had happened. When she was finished, the leper stood thoughtfully for a moment. "You're not the same woman as before: You're as kind as Auntie Lily, and you aren't greedy anymore. So take this humble gift from my brother, the old beggar."

With that, the leper limped out of the village; and as he left, the illness fell away from the old woman like an old, discarded cloak. But though the old woman was healthy again, she stayed as kind as Auntie Lily and used her own money as well and wisely as Auntie Lily used the waters of gold.

About Laurence Yep

As an American of Chinese heritage, Laurence Yep says he grew up feeling like an outsider. Because he looked Chinese, his American peers treated him as if he were a foreigner. Even among many of his

Chinese American friends, he felt different because he did not speak Chinese.

Laurence Yep enjoys writing for a young adult audience. He believes that his books are popular with teenagers because he writes about "the theme of being an outsider—an alien—and many teenagers feel they're aliens." His award-winning books include *Dragonwings, Child of the Owl, Sea Glass, Dragon Steel,* and *The Rainbow People.*

Responding

1. **Personal Response** How do you think you would have treated the beggar and the leper? Why would you have treated them that way?

2. **Literary Analysis** Folk tales like "Waters of Gold" usually have a *moral*. What moral, or lesson, do you learn from this story?

3. **Theme Connection** Auntie Lily tells the rich woman "Kindness has no price." What does she mean?

Language Workshop

Creating a Vivid Setting Laurence Yep weaves details about life in Auntie Lily's village throughout the story. For example, on p. 241 he describes what the villagers do while ignoring the beggar. One fixes his hoe, another sweeps her courtyard, and yet another feeds her hens. What do these details tell you about village life? Find at least five other descriptive details in the story that make the setting come to life.

Writer's Portfolio

How might this story be different if it were set in *your* neighborhood? Write a modern-day version of "Waters of Gold."

I, Hungry Hannah Cassandra Glen...

WHEN MR. AUGUSTUS FRANCHER'S HEART BURST, I told Crow we were going to the service at Bascind's Funeral Home because, afterward, at Mrs. Francher's house, there would be food.

"How are we supposed to get in? Nobody asked us," he said.

"They will. First we go to the service—to show respect, you know. Mrs. Francher sees us there and she says, 'You two fine young people must come over to my house after the funeral and have some delicious food.'"

"Safety Pin Francher says that? Wake up, Hannah dreamer."

"Maybe she won't say it exactly that way," I admitted.

"Maybe she won't," Crow mocked. "Forget it. I don't want to go." He scraped his Adidas on the curb.

"You never want to go anywhere." Just because of his face. He had to go to school, he couldn't get out of that, but he didn't like to go anyplace else where there were a lot of people.

"You go," he said.

"Not without you." We went everywhere together. We had been friends since we were four years old. "Just think of all that food," I urged Crow. "I bet there'll be those little tiny fancy hot dogs with toothpicks stuck in them. You know how good they smell? And a baked ham stuck all over with cloves and slices of pineapple on top. There's got to be a cake—maybe a three-layer chocolate cake with chocolate icing—and ice cream and tons of cookies. She's got the whole store to choose from."

I talked about food until Crow couldn't stand it. "I'll go, I'll go, since you want to do it so much."

"Just for me. Big-hearted you."

Crow was always hungry. His elbows stuck out like sticks. His stepfather, Willie, was on half time at the Buffalo Chemical Works, but even when he was on full time and they had more money, Crow was hungry.

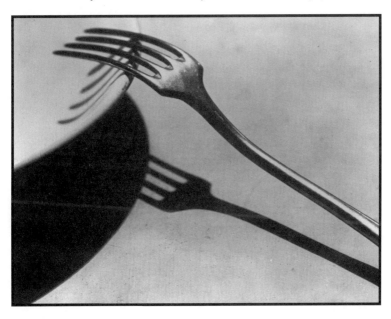

Willie said workingmen had to get fed first. (That was Willie.) Then, said Willie, came the littlest kids, Jay, Mike, Chris, and Kelly. After that came the women—Crow's mother and Willie's two daughters, Lisa and Janet. After that, said Willie, came older boys. That was Crow. His mom always saved him something, but he never got enough to eat.

In the funeral parlor, we signed our names in the guest book. David James Alpern. Hannah C. Glen. We followed two men into the chapel and Crow sat down in the last row. If there'd been a darkest corner, he would have chosen that. I sat down next to him.

In the front row, Mrs. Francher sniffled loudly. She was tall and shaped like a summer squash, skinny on top and swelling out on the bottom. In the store she always wore a dark green smock held together with safety pins. Today she had on a black dress and black hat, no safety pins anywhere in sight.

Crow's stomach rumbled and then mine did, like a two-piece band. "What'd you have for breakfast?" I whispered. He shrugged. I had had two grape jelly sandwiches and a glass of instant milk. After she got laid off at the paper-bag factory, my mother began buying powdered milk instead of whole milk. She said it was cheaper and just as good for us. Every day she went out looking for work. As soon as she found a job, we'd have real milk again and plenty of eggs. At night, instead of macaroni and cheese, we'd have hamburgers that sizzled delicious-smelling fat all over the stove and vegetables cooked with hunks of margarine. And for dessert we'd have cookies and freestone peaches in thick syrup.

A man wearing a peppermint-striped tie passed us and then came back. I thought he was going to say something about Crow. Once, on a bus, a man said in a loud voice to the woman with him that Crow's parents should do something about his face. Mostly, people just stared.

"You, young lady," Peppermint Tie said, "shouldn't be chewing gum in here."

I spit the gum out into my hand. As soon as Peppermint Tie went by I put it up under my upper lip to save for later. Crow said it made him hungrier to chew gum. It was just the opposite for me.

Sometimes I thought that if Crow didn't have that stuff on his face he would be prettier than a girl. He had high cheekbones and his eyes were dark and shining, but it was hard to notice because his face looked as if it had been splashed with gobs of rusty paint. A splash like a map of

Tennessee covered half his forehead, wandered down over his left eye, and dribbled out onto his cheek. Another splash around his mouth and chin looked like a mushy baked apple, and a splash on his neck looked like a four-legged spider.

A minister came into the chapel from a side door and stood near the open coffin. He cleared his throat. "Good afternoon, friends." He began talking about Mr. Francher. "Augustus Francher has left us. He was a fine, upstanding man."

No, I thought, that's wrong. He was a fine man, but he didn't stand up any more than he had to. Mr. Francher was fat, his face was round and yellow as a lemon pie, and he wheezed when he talked. If he and Mrs. Francher were both in the store, she waited on the customers and Mr. Francher sat on a high stool in front of the cash register. He always wore big soft shoes, a white shirt with a little bow tie, and baggy black pants.

"He lived a good life," the minister said. "He had charity in his heart and we are saddened that he has been struck down in his prime." Mrs. Francher sniffled loudly and called out, "Oh, Augustus, Augustus."

Mr. and Mrs. Francher's grocery store was in the front of their house. Dried salamis hung in the window over dusty stacks of Campbell's baked beans and Diet Pepsi. Lots of mornings when Crow and I walked past on the way to school, Mr. Francher's round yellow face would be in the window, between the salamis, and he would wink at me.

At the end of the month when my mom was short of money, she'd send me to Francher's Groceteria for half a pound of bologna and a can of spaghetti for supper. "Tell Francher to put it on the bill, Hanny," she'd say.

And I'd go off, hoping and hoping that it would be Mr. Francher in the store. If it was Mrs. Francher, she'd finger a safety pin on her smock, click her tongue, and look up what we owed in her account book. "Twenty-five dollars and seventy-six cents. You'd better pay something on that." And she'd hold out her hand as if I had money in my pocket. I would try not to look at the tub of creamy-looking potato salad in the case or the round of cheese on the counter with the sharp cheese knife lying next to it. "Go home and see what your mother wants to pay on account," she'd order.

But if it was Mr. Francher, he'd put his hand on my shoulder, look right at me with his brown eyes that were bright as a chipmunk's, and say, "Now, daughter, just tell your mother not to forget she should pay up soon." And he'd pull the can of spaghetti down from the shelf. Once he'd told me that long ago he'd had a little sister who died, and her name, too, was Hannah. "A nice old-fashioned name," he said. He was shorter than his wife and, sitting on his stool, he would munch on cream-filled doughnuts, then wash them down with long sips from a bottle of soda. My mother said he was his own best customer.

The minister was through talking about Mr. Francher and everybody stood up to walk around the coffin where he lay, wearing a dark suit and tie, his hands folded together over his big round stomach. I stopped in surprise. He looked like a baby in a crib, a huge baby who would, at any moment, open his eyes and chuckle. His cheeks were puffed out and shining.

Mrs. Francher stood off to one side with another woman, also in black. They were holding hands. I walked slowly past the coffin, looking back at Mr. Francher over my shoulder. Was he really gone? Was it true that when I went to Francher's the next time, there would be no Mr. Francher to say, "Now, daughter . . . "? No Mr. Francher anymore to wink at me through the salamis? My eyes filled. Just then I understood that he was dead and what it meant.

Behind me, Crow jabbed his finger into my back, reminding me why we were there. "Mrs. Francher," I said.

Her eyes were dark and puffy. She looked at me, through me. I didn't think she recognized me.

It was the other woman who answered. "Yes?" She was not as tall as Mrs. Francher, but she was shaped the same: summer squash. "What is it, dear?" she said. "What do you want?"

"I—can we—I'm sorry about Mr. Francher," I said. "I wish—I'm *sorry*."

Mrs. Francher's eyes focused. "You're the Glen girl." She reached up to the neck of her dress and a glimmer of surprise (that there was no safety pin there?) seemed to cross her face. I thought she was going to ask when my mother would pay up.

And fast, not so brave now that I was face-to-face with her, I said, "Can we, can Crow and—can David and I come after the funeral to your house?"

She grabbed my arm and bent close to me. "You came to the service. I didn't know you loved him so much."

I nodded dumbly. She smelled of chocolate mints and mothballs.

"And him?" Flapping her hand in Crow's direction, she looked away from him, but the other woman stared.

A man reached past me and pressed Mrs. Francher's shoulder. "My sympathies, Berenice."

"Thank you, Jack. Do you know my sister? This is my sister, Celia. Come to the house," she said. "You're coming to the house after, aren't you?"

"We'll be there," he said. "Jane made a meat pie."

"Move on, dear, move on," Mrs. Francher's sister said. She was all in black, too. "People are waiting. Move, children."

My mouth watered. A meat pie! "Thank you, we'll come to your house," I said, sort of low and fast, as we walked by Mrs. Francher and her sister.

Outside, cars with headlights on were lined up for the drive to the cemetery. Mrs. Francher and her sister got into Bascind's long black limousine. A chauffeur with a black peaked cap drove.

"I'm not going to die the way old Francher did," Crow said as we walked down the street. "I'm not going to wait around for it to come get me. When I'm ready, I'm going to do it myself."

"You mean kill yourself?"

He nodded. "I've thought about it a lot. I might do it soon."

"Soon? Now that is truly dumb. I never heard anything so magnifico dumb."

"Give me one good reason."

"I'll give you ten good reasons. You're too young. You don't know what you're saying. You get these ideas in your head and you think they mean something. Sometimes you make me so mad!"

"Now there's a good reason."

"Besides," I said coldly, "it's against the law."

"Oh, dear, dear, dear. I forgot that. After I stick my head in the oven some night, they're going to arrest my corpse and send it to jail for life."

"Would you please knock it off! I don't want you dead. So just forget it."

"Even if I leave you my track shoes?" He held up a foot temptingly.

"Oh, your brothers would get them."

"I'll make a will," he said. "I'll leave them to you in my will."

We sat on the stoop in front of my house where we could watch down the block to see when Mrs. Francher arrived back from the cemetery.

"Go get us some paper and pencils," Crow said.

"You want to play tic-tac-toe? Again?" It was his favorite game and no wonder, he always won.

"I'm going to write my will. You can do yours, too. Everybody should have a will."

"Not kids."

"Who says? Putting my track shoes in my will makes it

official. You get them, nobody else."

"I don't want your track shoes, and I don't want to make a will. I'm not going to die."

"Well, not right away," he agreed. "But you never know. I bet Mr. Francher didn't think he was going to drop dead. Give me your key. I'll go in and get the stuff if you're too lazy."

"You are one magnifico pest." I went into the apartment, tore paper out of my notebook, and grabbed two pencil stubs from the coffee tin in the kitchen. I didn't want to use up my ball-point pen.

"Make sure you leave me something good," Crow said when I sat down next to him again. He smoothed out his piece of paper on his knee.

"This is dumb," I said. Crow was already scribbling away. "I don't even know how to start."

"Don't be difficult, Hanny." He held up his paper and read out, "'I, David James Alpern, being of exceptionally sound mind and not so good body, do hereby make my last will and testament.' That's the way you begin. That's all there is to it. Then 'I leave to etcetera, etcetera.'"

After a while, I wrote. "I, the hungry Hannah Cassandra Glen, being of possibly sound mind and passably sound body, do hereby make my last will. I leave—"

But I couldn't think of anything I had that anyone would want. No, that was a lie. I didn't want to give my things away. I fingered the string of blue coral around my neck and thought of the green and white afghan on my bed, which my grandmother had made years before for my mother. It always somehow made me think of a spring day. I had never told anyone that, not even Crow. Then there were the six little glass chicks that my father had sent me when I was five, the last thing he ever sent me. The chicks sometimes marched across the top of my bureau, bumping into the jam jar in which I kept barrettes, shoelaces, and rubber bands, and sometimes made a magic circle on the floor at the side of my bed where I could see them as soon as I woke.

I peered over Crow's shoulder. He had just left an extra toilet plunger to his stepfather. I thought about putting down that I left a terrifico job making magnifico money (maybe as a private secretary to a very important person) to my mother. "Aren't you done yet?" I asked.

"In a minute." He kept writing and crossing out and writing.

My stomach rumbled. What if Mrs. Francher and her sister wouldn't let us in? *No way, you kids, all you want is food, you don't care about poor Mr. Francher being dead.*

I cleaned my fingernails and cuffed up the bottom of my Levis. They were my best pair. My mother had found them in a church rummage sale. "Not even worn at the knees, Hanny."

Crow turned over his paper to write on the other side. "Anyone would think you're serious about this," I said.

"I am." He covered his paper with his arm. "No peeking. I'll read it to you when I'm done."

I wrote down that I left Crow my afghan, but I crossed it out. How could I give that up? I was ashamed of my greediness and willed him my glass chicks. He probably wouldn't even like them.

Finally he stopped writing. "Okay. *Fini.*"

Terms to Know
Fini (p. 258) Latin for "finished"
aka (p. 258) also known as

"What now?" I said. "You get out there in traffic and let a car run over you so I can get your track shoes?"

"I wouldn't do it that way. It's not sure enough. Let me tell you, when I do it, I'm not botching it up."

"Read me your will or shut up."

"I, David James Alpern (aka Crow)," he read, "being of exceptionally sound mind and not so good body, leave to my best friend, Hannah Glen, my mighty brain, including all the words she doesn't know—"

"Thanks a lot."

"—a lifetime supply of Tootie Frooty gum—"

"Gimme a break!"

He stopped reading. "Are you going to listen?"

"I'll listen, I'll listen."

"—lifetime supply of Tootie Frooty gum and my track shoes. To my mother, *M*A*S*H* reruns forever and a quiet day. An extra toilet plunger to my stepfather, Willie. To my brothers, Jay and Mike, snot-free noses—shut up please so people can sleep!—birthdays at Burger King, and a snow shovel so you can make some money in the winter. To my sisters, Kelly and Chris, all the tangerines y'all want, a box full of chocolate chip cookies that never goes empty, and Wonder Woman tee shirts, red for Kelly, green for Chris. To Lisa and Janet, getting out of the house safe, thanks for the sandwich under the door, and winning all their volleyball games. And finally to all those others, teachers, acquaintances, enemies, and strangers, good good goodby, y'all, I'm not sorry to leave."

He glanced at me, the way he does, quick and sideways, so you don't get a good look at his face. "Like it? Think it was funny?"

I had to admit leaving a toilet plunger to his stepfather was fairly hilarious. "That's humor."

"Also there was some serious stuff in there," he said. "Like thanking Lisa and Janet. I thought that was important because when I die they might not know that I really like them. Read me yours."

"Nothing to read." I was hungry and that always made me feel mean.

"Didn't you leave me anything?"

"No." I tore up the paper and stuffed the scraps in my pocket. "Why aren't they back yet?" I said and I had a terrible thought. What if Mrs. Francher and her sister were going to have the food part of the funeral someplace else, not in their apartment behind the store? I thought about eating bread and jelly again for lunch and crackers and pasty milk for supper.

Just then the long black funeral car passed us. It stopped in front of Francher's Groceteria and Mrs. Francher and her sister got out. Other cars pulled up, one after the other. People spilled out, a whole crowd, all of them going into Mrs. Francher's house.

I spit on my fingers and scrubbed at my cheeks. "Do I look okay? Is my face clean? You better pull up your pants so you don't step on them."

"Maybe we shouldn't go, Hanny," Crow said all of a sudden.

"What? Now you say it? After all this? I know you, you're getting cold feet just because there's going to be a bunch of people there. Who cares, Crow? There's going to be *food*. Don't be gutless."

"If you're so brave, go yourself."

"I will," I shouted, "but you can just forget about eating any of that food, because I'm not bringing any back for you, Mr. Crow David Gutless."

"Shut up, Hanny, you have a big fat mouth!"

We went down the street, not speaking. The cars were gone. The store was locked and dark. In the window a sign said CLOSED ON ACCOUNT OF A DEATH IN THE FAMILY. Were they eating up all the food, the meat pies and the baked ham and the cookies and cakes? I led the way around the side and knocked on the door.

Nobody came. I knocked again. There was a white lace curtain on the window of the door. "You and your ideas. They're not going to let us in," Crow said, and the door swung open.

"We're here," I said to Mrs. Francher. She was in her stocking feet. She looked at me, then at Crow, as if she expected people, all right, but not us two. "We came to—" I almost said *eat*. I put my hand over my mouth and said, "We came to pay our respects."

"What?"

"Pay our respects." Behind me, I sensed Crow moving away, disappearing down the path.

Mrs. Francher's sister appeared and they stood in the doorway, side by side. They seemed to me like two swollen black balloons. From the room behind them, wonderful smells of meat and cooked fruit drifted toward me. I wanted to cry. "We're here," I said again.

Mrs. Francher looked at her sister. "Oh...You take care of it, Celia." She walked away, a funny duck-footed walk in her stocking feet.

"Well...well..." Mrs. Francher's sister said. "Just you?"

"No, me and my friend. Cr—David," I yelled to him. My mouth was full of saliva and I smiled hard and said, "We were both friends of Mr. Francher's. We were always friends."

Mrs. Francher's sister sighed and looked over her shoulder and finally said, "I suppose you can come in, then."

The living room was warm and crowded. People stood around in little clumps with glasses in their hands, talking. The curtains were drawn and there were pictures and little statues everywhere, on tables, on top of the TV, and on little hanging shelves above the couch.

A long table, loaded with food, took up almost the whole dining room. I squeezed Crow's hand. Our quarrel was forgotten. In the center of the table were two crystal bowls, one filled with apples, pears, grapes, and bananas, the other brimming with a fizzing red punch. There were platters of roast beef, ham, turkey, and salami, little fluted cups filled with butter, a wooden board with a cutting knife, and different kinds of cheeses. There was applesauce and fruit salad, baked potatoes wrapped in silver paper, tomatoes and cucumbers, bread and rolls and cakes and all kinds of hot casseroles.

"What should we do?" Crow whispered.

"Eat," I said, but first I slipped an apple and a pear and slices of ham and roast beef into my pockets. How surprised my mother would be tonight when she came home and found the refrigerator full. "Oh, Hanny," she'd say, "you shouldn't have done that, that's not nice." But she'd eat a slice of roast beef (her favorite) and then polish an apple on her shirt and cut it in half to share with me.

Crow and I filled plates with food. We found a place near a window away from people and began eating as fast as possible. We ate everything on our plates and went back to the table for more. People talked and laughed and no one bothered with us.

Crow's cheeks and lips were shiny with grease. We ate without stopping until neither of us could eat any more.

When we left, I was wonderfully full. Crow rubbed his bulging stomach and whispered, "Well, guess I'll go on living a little longer." And hearing that, I thought without shame how glad I was that Mr. Francher had died and left us this feast. I imagined him looking like a great baby in his coffin, winking at me and saying in his wheezy voice, which had always sounded to me like dark rough honey, "Now, daughter, now, daughter. . . . "

About Norma Fox Mazer

As a teenager, Norma Fox Mazer was a people-watcher with an active imagination. Today, she is a popular writer for young adults. Her success probably stems from her unusual understanding of

the emotions and problems of teenagers. She says, "I write and my readers read to find out the answers to questions, secrets, problems, to be drawn into the deepest mystery of all—someone else's life."

Mazer has written numerous novels and two collections of short stories, *Dear Bill, Remember Me? and Other Stories* and *Summer Girls, Love Boys, and Other Short Stories.*

Responding

1. **Personal Response** Do you like Hannah? Tell why or why not.

2. **Literary Analysis** Hannah says that Crow's elbows "stuck out like sticks." What does this *simile*, or comparison, tell you about Crow's elbows? Find three more similes in this story and explain what they mean.

3. **Theme Connection** Do any characters in this story do something wrong? Explain your answer.

Language Workshop

Using Commas With Direct Address In these sentences from the story, one character addresses, or speaks to, another by name.

"Who cares, Crow?"

"Shut up, Hanny, you have a big fat mouth!"

When someone is addressed by name or title, commas are used to separate the person's name from the rest of the sentence. Insert commas where needed in the following.

1. "Mr. Francher could I have some spaghetti on credit?" Hannah would ask.

2. "Here it is daughter and I hope you enjoy it."

3. "You give everything away Augustus!" Mrs. Francher would complain.

Writer's Portfolio

Hannah knows how to get what she wants. Imagine that she is entering an essay contest to win a scholarship to a summer camp. Be Hannah and write her essay. Keep in character as you state the reasons why you should receive the scholarship to camp.

CAROL FARLEY

Lose Now, Pay Later

I THINK MY LITTLE BROTHER IS CRAZY. AT LEAST I hope he is. Because if his loony idea is right, then all of us are being used like a flock of sheep, and that's a pretty gruesome thought. Humans just can't be that stupid. My brother has a dumb idea, that's all. It's just a dumb idea.

This whole situation started about eight months ago. That's when I first knew anything about it, I mean. My best friend, Trinja, and I were shopping when we noticed a new store where an old insurance office used to be. It was a cubbyhole, really, at the far end of the mall where hardly anybody ever goes. We were there because we'd used that entrance as we came home from school.

"Swoodies!" Trinja said, pointing at the letters written across the display window. "What do you think they are, Deb?"

I stared through the glass. The place had always looked dim and dingy before, full of desks, half-dead plants, and bored-looking people; but now it was as bright and glaring as a Health Brigade Corp office. There weren't any people inside at all, but there were five or six gold-colored machines lining the walls. Signs were hung everywhere.

SWEETS PLUS GOODIES = SWOODIES, one said. Flavors were posted by each machine; peanut-butter-fudge-crunch . . . butter-rum-pecan . . . chocolate-nut-mint . . . Things like that. The biggest sign of all simply said FREE.

I have to admit that the place gave me the creeps that first time I saw it. I don't know why. It just looked so bare and bright, so empty and lean, without any people or movement. The glare almost hurt my eyes. And I guess I was suspicious about anything that was completely free. Still, though, there was a terrific aroma drifting out of there—sort of a combination of all those flavors that were listed on the signs.

"Let's go in," Trinja said, grabbing my arm. I could see that the smell was getting to her too. She's always on a diet, so she thinks about food a lot.

"But it's so empty in there," I said, drawing away.

"They've just opened, that's all," she told me, yanking my arm again. "Besides, machines and robots run lots of the

stores. Let's go inside and see what's in there."

Do you know that wonderful spurt of air that rushes out when you first open an expensive box of candy? The inside of that store smelled just like the inside of one of those boxes. For a few seconds we just stood there sniffing and grinning. My salivary glands started swimming.

Trinja turned toward the nearest machine. "Coconut-almond-marshmallow." She was almost drooling. "I've got to try one, Deb." She pressed the button, and a chocolate cone dropped down, like a coffee cup from a kitcho machine. Then a mixture, similar to the look of soft ice cream, filled it. "Want to try it with me?" she asked, reaching for the cone. We both took a taste.

It was absolutely the neatest sensation I've had in my whole life. Swoodies aren't cold like ice cream or warm liked cooked pudding, but they're a blending of both in temperature and texture. The flavor melts instantly, and your whole mouth and brain are flooded with tastes and impressions. Like that first swoodie I tried, coconut-almond-marshmallow; suddenly, as my mouth separated the individual tastes, my brain burst into memories associated with each flavor. I felt as if I were lying on a warm beach, all covered with coconut suntan oil—then I heard myself giggling and singing as a group of us roasted marshmallows around a campfire—then I relived the long-ago moments of biting into the special Christmas cookies my grandmother made with almonds when I was little.

"Wow!" Trinja looked at me, and I could see that she had just experienced the same kind of reactions. We scarfed up the rest of that swoodie in just a few more bites, and we moved on to another flavor. With each one it was the same. I felt a combination of marvelous tastes and joyous thoughts. We tried every flavor before we finally staggered out into the mall again.

"I'll have to diet for a whole year now," Trinja said, patting her stomach.

"I feel like a blimp myself," I told her, but neither one of us cared. We both felt terrific. "Go ahead in there," I called to some grade-school kids who were looking at the store. "You'll love those swoodies."

"It's a publicity stunt, we think," Trinja told them. "Everything is free in there."

In no time at all the news about the swoodie shop had spread all over town. But days passed, and still everything was absolutely free. Nobody knew who the new owners were or why they were giving away their product. Nobody cared. The mall directors said a check arrived to pay for the rent, and that was all they were concerned about. The Health Brigade Corp said swoodies were absolutely safe for human consumption.

Swoodies were still being offered free a month later, but the shop owners had still not appeared. By then nobody cared. There were always long lines of people in front of the place, but the swoodies tasted so good nobody minded waiting for them. And the supply was endless. Soon more shops like the first one began opening in other places around the city, with machines running in the same quiet, efficient way. And everything was still absolutely free.

Soon all of us were gaining weight like crazy.

"It's those darn swoodies," Trinja told me as we left the mall after our daily binge. "I can't leave them alone. Each one must have a thousand calories, but I still pig out on them."

I sighed as I walked out into the sunshine. "Me too. If only there was some easy way to eat all the swoodies we want and still not gain any weight!"

The words were hardly out of my mouth when I noticed a new feature in the mall parking lot. Among all the usual heliobiles there was a tall white plastic box, sort of like those big telephone booths you see in old pictures. A flashing sign near the booth said THE SLIMMER. A short, thin woman was standing beside it. She was deeply tanned and her head was covered with a green turban almost the same color as the jumpsuit she was wearing.

Trinja looked at the sign, then glanced at the woman. "What's that mean?"

"It means that this machine can make you slimmer," the woman answered. She had a deep, strange-sounding voice. "Just step inside and you'll lose unwanted fat."

She seemed so serious and confident that I was startled. In the old days people thought they could lose weight in a hurry, but those of us who live in 2041 aren't that gullible. No pills or packs or wraps or special twenty-four-hour diets can work. There isn't any easy way to get rid of fat, and that's all there is to it. I knew this booth was a scam or a joke of some kind, but the woman acted as if it were a perfectly respectable thing. Her seriousness sort of unnerved me. I looked into the booth half expecting someone to jump out laughing. But it was empty, stark white, and, except for some overhead grill work, it was completely smooth and bare.

"How can a thing like this make you slimmer?" I asked.

The woman shrugged. "A new process. Do you care to try? Twenty-five yen to lose one pound of body fat."

Trinja and I both burst into laughter. "And how long is it before the pound disappears?" she asked.

The woman never even cracked a smile. "Instantly. Body fat is gone instantly." She gestured to a small lever on the side nearest to her. "I regulate the power flow according to your payment."

My mouth dropped open. "But that's impossible! No exercise? No chemicals? No starving on a retreat week?"

"No." The woman folded her arms and leaned against the smooth white sides of her cubicle, as if she didn't much care whether we tried her new process or not. Trinja and I stared at each other. I was wondering if the woman had tried her machine herself—she didn't have an ounce of fat.

"You got any money?" I asked Trinja. As she was

shaking her head, I was rummaging through my pack. "I've got a hundred and thirty yen."

"Five pounds then," the woman said, taking my money with one hand and setting her lever with the other. She literally pushed me into the booth and the door slammed behind me.

At first I wanted to scream because I was so scared. The whole thing had happened too fast. I wanted to prove that the woman and her slimmer were a big joke, but suddenly I was trapped in a coffinlike structure as bare and as bright as an old microwave oven. My heart was hammering and the hair on the back of my neck stood up straight. I opened my mouth, but before I could scream there was a loud humming sound and instantly the door flew open again. I saw Trinja's frightened face peering in at me.

"Are you all right, Deb? Are you okay? I guess she decided not to do anything after all. You ought to get your money back."

"Five pounds are gone," the woman said in her strange voice.

Trinja pulled me away. "I'll just bet!" she shouted back at the woman. "Somebody ought to report you and that phony machine! We might even call the Health Brigade Corp!" She leaned closer to me. "Are you really okay, Deb?"

I took a deep breath. "My jeans feel loose."

Frowning, Trinja shook her head. "It's just your imagination, that's all. What a fake! I think that woman was wacko, Debbie, really weird. The only thing slimmer after a treatment like that is your bank account. Nobody but nobody can lose weight that easily. We'll go to my house and you can weigh yourself. You haven't lost an ounce."

But Trinja was wrong. I really *was* five pounds lighter. I know it sounds impossible, but Trinja's calshow is never wrong. The two of us hopped and howled with joy. Then we ravaged her bedroom trying to find some more money.

We ran all the way back to the mall, worrying all the way that the woman and her miracle machine might have disappeared. But the slimmer was still there. Within minutes Trinja had used up her three hundred yen, and she looked terrific.

"I can't believe it! I just can't believe it!" she kept saying as she notched her belt tighter. "Twelve pounds gone in seconds!"

"For safety's sake I'll have to prick your wrist, my dear," the woman said. "For every ten pounds you lose we give a tiny little mark. Nobody will ever notice it."

"It didn't even hurt," Trinja said as we walked home. And neither of us could see the tiny blue pinprick unless we looked closely. We were both so happy about the weight loss that we almost floated. All our worries and problems about calories and fat and diets were over forever.

In no time at all the slimmers were all over the city, near all the swoodie stores. They've been a real blessing. Everybody says so. Now there's hardly a fat person left on the streets. A few people have so many blue marks on their wrists that you can see them, but most have just four or five pinpricks.

Nobody really understands how these slimmers work. The attendants, all just as strange-sounding as the woman in our mall, get so technical in their explanations that none of us can follow the principles they're talking about, so we don't much worry about it. The process has something to do with invisible waves that can change fat cells into energy, which then radiates away from the body.

"I don't care how the slimmers work," Trinja says happily. "Now I can eat swoodies all day long if I want, and I never gain an ounce. That's all I care about."

Everybody feels that way, I guess. We're too happy to want to upset anything by asking questions. Maybe that's why you don't hear about the swoodies or slimmers on the fax or the bodivision or read about them anywhere.

Nobody understands them well enough to sound very intelligent about them. But people all over Earth are beginning to use them. My cousin in Tokyo faxed to say that they have them in her area now and people there are just as happy as we are.

Except for my brother, Trevor. He's not the least bit happy, he says. Of course, few ten-year-olds worry about weight, so he doesn't know the joy of being able to eat everything in sight and still stay thin.

"Suppose the swoodies and the slimmers are run by aliens from outer space," he says. "From lots farther than we've been able to go. Maybe they have big starships posted around Earth, and they're gathering up the energy from human fat that's sent up from the slimmers. Maybe the swoodies are here so people will get fat quicker so that there'll be more to harvest through the slimmer machines. Then they'll take the fat back to their planet and use it as fuel."

"That's the dumbest thing I ever heard of!" Trinja has told him. "Why don't we hear about the spaceships, then? Why doesn't the Health Brigade Corp tell us to stop doing this if it isn't good for us?"

Trevor thinks he has the answers. He says the spaceships are invisible to human detection, and he says the aliens have hypnotized our leaders into being as calm and placid as we all are. The blue marks on our wrists play a big role. He says maybe after each of us has had so many blue marks, we'll be culled from the flock because our fat content won't be as good any more.

He's crazy, isn't he? He must think we all have the brains of sheep. Ten-year-old brothers can be a real pain. He simply doesn't know people yet, that's all. Humans would never sacrifice their freedom and dignity just so they could eat and still be thin. Even aliens ought to know that.

I could quit eating swoodies and using those slimmers any time I want to.

But all those little blue marks Trinja and I have are beginning to look like delicate tattooed bracelets, and we both think they look really neat on our wrists.

About Carol Farley

Carol Farley has lived in many different places and has had many different jobs. Married to a former officer in the U. S. Army, she has lived in Germany, Korea, and all over the United States. She has taught school, picked fruit, worked in an office, sold women's clothing, and worked in a library.

Farley says, "When writing, I'm trying to reach out to others in hope that together we can make sense out of the emotions and events which surround us." She enjoys writing mysteries, and recent novels include *Mystery of the Melted Diamonds*, *The Case of the Vanishing Villain*, and *The Case of the Lost Lookalike*.

Responding

1. **Personal Response** Would you like to try out swoodies and the slimmer? Why or why not?

2. **Literary Analysis** How would you describe the *tone* of this story?

3. **Theme Connection** Can you think of anything in our society that is like the swoodies? If so, do you see any potential dangers? Explain.

Language Workshop

Using Context Clues to Understand Jargon Author Carol Farley has made up some specialized terms, or jargon, for this science fiction story. Since she invented these words, we can't look them up in the dictionary, but we can guess their meanings by looking at the terms in context. For example, the story mentions the Health Brigade Corp several times. By reading what is said about it on pp. 264, 267, 269, and 271, we can infer that the Health Brigade Corp sounds like an organization that is responsible for everyone's health.

Here's another example, from p. 266.

. . . a chocolate cone dropped down, like a coffee cup from a kitcho machine.

From this description, we can guess that a kitcho machine is a machine in the kitchen that makes coffee.

Find at least three other examples of jargon in the story. Use context clues to write a possible definition for each term.

Writer's Portfolio

Are people being used by aliens? Or are swoodies and slimmers simply a harmless new fad? Write a follow-up story set six months later that describes what has happened in the meantime.

FLOYD SALAS

$\mathcal{S}$tealing

$\mathcal{L}$ARRY HAD GIVEN ME THE RIDE DOWNTOWN ON HIS bike. He was in the same fifth grade as me, although he was a head taller and a year older. He lived on Thirtieth Street and Chestnut, a short block from my house on Thirtieth and Adeline. He took me to Payless Market on Nineteenth and Telegraph. It was a huge warehouse-of-a-market, filled with different types of stores and stands, including a market with sundry goods. For some reason, we went in there and the next thing I knew, he was taking a pen out of a drawer, and I did, too. Then I followed him over to a side entrance where he ducked under the turnstile.

I squatted to duck down under the turnstile and sneak out without paying, when steel fingers clamped on my shoulder and I looked up to see a woman in dress clothes, pulling me back into the sundry goods section. Trapped in the pincers of her fingers, I was marched through the stalls, up some steep back stairs and into an office with wide windows that looked out over the entire store. We were right above the stand where the pens Larry and I had stolen were kept. There was a man up there who must have been watching all the time.

I was so scared, I shook. When she asked me my name, I lied and said, Floyd Sánchez, giving my mother's maiden name instead of Salas.

> ### Words to Know
>
> **sundry goods** (p. 274) various items, such as pens and paper, sewing notions, etc.
>
> **turnstile** (p. 274) a post with bars that turn, used to let people in or out of a place
>
> **pincers** (p. 274) a tool for gripping and holding tight, made like a scissors but with jaws instead of blades

She pointed to the floor beneath a high counter and said, "You sit down under there!" Which I did. Then she asked me what my religion was.

When I answered Catholic, she said, "Catholics don't steal."

I just stared at the floor. She made me sit on the floor under the counter for a long time. I didn't have the slightest idea what was going to happen to me, but I knew I was in deep trouble. I knew my mother was going to spank me and that I had committed a terrible wrong, even a sin, for stealing. I was so ashamed, I couldn't look up.

Finally the woman said, "You come out of there and stand over here!" I got up and stood in front of her desk. She sat behind it and made me empty my pockets, I guess to see if I'd stolen anything else. I had ten cents in my pocket, so I wasn't penniless. But there was also a test I'd taken in grammar school with my name, Floyd Salas, written across the top of it.

"Oh, you not only steal, but you lie, too," she said, and I felt my face light up with hot shame.

"How old are you?" she asked.

"Nine," I said.

"Are you sure?" she said.

I nodded my head, afraid to insist, even though I was nine and small for my age.

"What's your phone number?" she asked. When I gave it to her, she immediately picked up the phone and dialed the number. I remember she asked over the phone, "How old is he?" She listened for a moment, then said, "Seven!" and glared at me as if I had lied to her again. Evidently the person on the phone at home was trying to help me by saying I was younger than I was. She then handed me the phone.

"Hello!" I said, and when my sister Dorothy said, "Floyd! What's the matter?" I wailed, "Oh, Dorothy!" and burst out crying.

I was sobbing so loudly, the woman took the phone from me. I don't know what else she said, but she hung up the phone and looked at me. I was still sobbing, rubbing my eyes with the back of my hand, trying to hide my face. Finally she said, "You can go home now. But don't come here and steal ever again. Do you understand?"

I nodded, still sobbing, and walked out, following her pointing finger to the swinging gate that led down the narrow steps to the ground floor.

I hurried down Twentieth Street to San Pablo in the warm sun, my face feeling stiff from all the dried tears. I hurried north on the east side of the boulevard, past the giant, red granite cathedral of St. Francis Catholic Church, which made me feel guilty again. I'd committed a sin and knew it, and God would punish me for it. I turned my face away towards the Greyhound Bus Depot across the street, which as usual had a lot of people moving in and out of the front door. Then I looked ahead again, up toward Thirtieth Street, where I had to turn left to head home in a few short blocks. I was going to get my just deserts, for sure, from my mother—the second punishment, after the store detective grilling.

When I started across Twenty-Second Street, and crossed over the streetcar tracks where the electric B Train was bound across the Bay Bridge for San Francisco, I saw a kid I knew casually from Clawsen Grammar School sitting on his shoeshine kit. He was a brown Filipino kid named Vincent. He and his sister were the only Filipino kids in school. I was so glad to see someone I knew, I stopped to talk to him. Although we weren't friends, I told him what happened to me, saying I was probably going to get a spanking when I got home. He squinted up at me, through the strands of straight black hair that fell across his eyes, and nodded.

"Do you want a donut?" I asked.

He nodded again, so I stepped into a donut shop next

to the old-fashioned beerjoint on the corner and bought two big, sugar-glazed donuts for a nickel. I stepped back out and gave him one. I stood next to him until we both finished. Then, my face still stiff from the dried tears, I waved goodbye and started up San Pablo towards home.

I was getting gradually more and more scared the closer I got to the house, and I was trembling when I crossed Adeline on Thirtieth Street and saw my white house in the center of the block. It was a pretty house, solidly built, with love seats in the hallway and in the front room, wide rooms on the second story, with big walk-in closets and windows all around. It had been built in the twenties probably. But it didn't look pretty to me then. I was plain scared, and could barely reach out for the front doorknob when I crossed the porch.

As soon as I stepped into the big hallway, Dorothy rushed up to me and said, "What happened, Floyd?"

"I...I..." I couldn't finish because my mother stepped into the hall and, with a worried crease between her brows, stared at me through her rimless glasses, her green eyes shimmering with pale light. I started to cry again.

"Come on," my mother said and grabbed her purse from the dining room table and crossed to the coat rack to get her coat. "I'm going to find out what's going on right now!"

I cringed and started crying even more, knowing I was going to get whatever I deserved, but really dreaded having to face that woman detective again.

"You get your coat, too, Dorothy. We're going down there right now!"

"Oooooooh!" I moaned, getting a taste now of the final day when God would pass judgment on me.

Dorothy got her coat, too, and Mother turned and reached for the door, when Al came running down the stairs from the second floor. He grabbed my hand and ran up the stairs, pulling me after him, refusing to stop when my mother called, "Albert! Albert! Come down here!"

"He's already paid enough, Momma!" he called back and pulled me down the hall and into our bedroom, right at the front of the house. "It's okay, Floyd! It's okay! Just don't do it again," he said. He hugged me and rocked me back and forth. He was back with the family again after being in reform school for six months.

When my sobbing finally quieted down and my chest quit heaving, he asked, "Who took you down there?"

"Larry Andre," I said.

"It's all right for now," Al said, "but don't let anybody lead you into anything like that again."

"Okay," I said, breaking out into another sob, feeling like my chest was going to crack with wracking pain. Suddenly I heard my name being called, "Floyyyd! Floyyyyyd!" and Albert let go of me.

We both stepped to our second story window. I could see Larry out there on his bicycle, looking toward the front door below us, his brown curls falling onto his forehead.

"Did he take you downtown on his bike?" Al asked. I nodded, and he said, "Wait here," and left the room.

I saw him go out onto the porch below me and shout, "You get away from here, kid, and don't come around my little brother again." When Larry looked up at him with a pale, scared face, Al said, "You heard me! Get going!"

Larry didn't say anything. He just pushed off on his bike and quickly pumped out of sight. I felt sorry for losing a friend, but I really felt grateful to my brother, who came back up the stairs and said, "Come on downstairs now. Mom's fine. You're okay. Just learn something from it. Never steal again. You don't want to end up in a reform school like me, do you?"

"Nooooo," I said, squinting my eyes with the hot tears that rolled out again.

"Come on down, then," Al said and, taking my hand, he led me out the door and down the hall to the stairs, where I could hear my mother in the kitchen, closing the refrigerator door. When I walked into the kitchen, still scared, both Mom and my sister turned to look at me. Mom's face was pink from the heat in the kitchen, but her green eyes were gentle. Dorothy smiled, showing that one dimple in the one cheek. I looked over at my brother, who smiled at me, also.

About Floyd Salas

In his autobiography *Buffalo Nickel*, from which "Stealing" is taken, Floyd Salas describes his experiences growing up in California and Colorado during the Great Depression and World War II. Salas, who was a boxer and petty criminal in his youth, found himself in and out of juvenile hall and then jail during the early years of his life.

Salas began writing as a teenager. In college, he won writing fellowships that convinced him to pursue writing as a career. Many of his novels and poems focus on his early experiences with the dark world of drugs and prison.

Floyd Salas believes that boxing and writing are similar. He says, "both require the same basic traits of character: dedication, durability, and courage, as well as the need to be spiritually pure and humble if you want to do well."

Responding

1. **Personal Response** Floyd's mother wanted to take Floyd back to the store. Floyd's brother Al said Floyd had suffered enough. Who do you think was right?

2. **Literary Analysis** When the detective grabs Floyd, he says he feels trapped "in the pincers of her fingers." What does this *metaphor* convey about the experience?

3. **Theme Connection** What, if anything, do you think Floyd learned from this experience?

Language Workshop

More About Metaphors A metaphor describes one thing by seeming to say it is another thing. Question 2 above gives one example of a metaphor. On p. 274 of "Stealing," the phrase *steel fingers clamped on my shoulder* also contains a metaphor: fingers are being compared to a steel clamp. Metaphors can be hard to spot because, unlike similes, there are no connective words such as *like* or *as*.

Identify the metaphor in each sentence and tell what two things are being compared.

1. Larry flew out of the market.

2. The detective gave Floyd an icy stare.

3. Floyd's cheeks burned when he was caught telling a lie.

Writer's Portfolio

Floyd was caught when he tried to steal. What might have happened if he hadn't been caught? Record a conversation between Albert and Floyd, in which Floyd tells Albert about stealing the pen.

YOSHIKO UCHIDA

Becoming a "Nonalien"

from *The Invisible Thread*

"No COMPANY FOR LUNCH?" I ASKED, SURPRISED. It was Sunday, but there were only the four of us going home from church. It seemed strange, but I was glad for the peace and quiet. Finals were starting soon at the university, and I was anxious to have a quick lunch and go to the library to study.

As we were having lunch, an urgent voice suddenly broke into the program on the radio. Japan, the announcer said, had attacked Pearl Harbor.

"Oh, no!" Mama gasped. "It must be a mistake."

"Of course it is," Papa agreed.

He turned up the volume. It didn't sound like a mistake.

"It's probably the work of some fanatic," Papa insisted.

Not one of us believed it was war. Kay went with my parents to visit friends, and I went to the campus library to study. I didn't return until almost five o'clock. The minute I got home, I knew something was wrong. A strange man sat in our living room, and my father was gone.

Mama and Kay explained that two FBI men had taken my father for questioning. A third remained to guard us, intercepting all phone calls and preventing friends from coming to see us.

"We're prisoners in our own home," Kay said ominously. "The police even broke in and searched our house while we were out."

As upset as she was, in her usual thoughtful way, Mama was making tea for the FBI man in the kitchen. She always served tea to anyone who called, even the "Real Silk Lady," who came with her

YOSHIKO UCHIDA   **283**

satchel of silken samples to sell Mama stockings and undergarments.

"You're making tea for the FBI man?" I asked, indignant.

But Mama respected everybody regardless of the work

they did. The man who delivered our dry cleaning, the People's Bread man who sold doughnuts and bread from his truck, the boy who delivered rice and tofu from the Japanese grocery store, or the Watkins door-to-door salesman. She treated them all with equal respect and courtesy.

"He's only doing his job," Mama said now of the FBI man. "He's trying to be pleasant." And she carried a tray of tea things into the living room.

But I wasn't about to have tea with someone guarding us as though we were prisoners. I went to my bedroom and stayed there until the FBI man got instructions to leave.

When at last the three of us were alone, we made supper, but none of us felt like eating. Papa was gone, and we had no idea what happened to him or when he would be back. We finally went to bed, leaving the porch light on for him.

As I lay in bed in my cold, dark room, I heard the mournful wail of the foghorns on the bay. I felt a clammy fear come over me, as though I was at the bottom of a deep well and couldn't climb out.

My father didn't return that night or for the next three days. We had no idea where he was or what had happened to him. But Mama persuaded me to continue going to classes, and somehow I managed to get through my finals.

Five days after he was taken, we finally learned that

my father was being held at the Immigration Detention Quarters in San Francisco with about one hundred other Japanese men.

The FBI had apprehended all the leaders of the Japanese American community—businessmen, teachers, bankers, farmers, fishermen—and held them incommunicado.

The following day we got a postcard from Papa asking us to send his shaving kit and some clean clothing. We arranged for permission to visit him, and Kay drove us to San Francisco.

My heart sank when I saw the drab gray building that looked like a jail. And as though to confirm my impression, a guard brought Papa to the visiting room like a prisoner.

"Papa! Are you all right?"

He looked tired and haggard, but assured us that he was fine. The news he gave us, however, was terrible. All the men in his group were being sent in a few days to a prisoner-of-war camp in Missoula, Montana.

"Montana! Then we won't be able to visit you anymore."

"I know," Papa answered, "but we can write to each other. Now, girls, be strong, and take good care of Mama for me, will you?"

Kay and I began to cry as we said our good-byes and watched Papa go back down the bleak hallway. It was Mama who was the strong one.

From the moment we were at war with Japan, my parents (and all the Issei) had suddenly become "enemy aliens." They were not citizens because by law the United States prevented Asians from becoming naturalized citizens. Now Kay, as the oldest U.S. citizen, became head of our household.

She had graduated from Mills College in 1940 with a degree in early childhood education, but the only job she could find was as a nursemaid to a three-year-old white child. Her employers asked her to stay on in spite of the war, but I wondered why they felt compelled to say that. After all, Kay was still the same person, and she was an American, just as they were.

However, strange ideas seemed to be erupting in the minds of many Americans. I was astonished when a white friend of many years asked, "Didn't you have any idea it was going to happen?"

I was hurt that she had asked. Her question implied that we somehow knew of Japan's war plans simply because we were Americans of Japanese ancestry. It was a ridiculous assumption.

Eventually Kay left her job to devote all her time to managing our household affairs. Papa's bank account had been blocked immediately, and for a while we could withdraw only $100 a month for living expenses. She needed important papers from his safe-deposit box, but found that the FBI had confiscated all his keys.

> **Business Words**
>
> **safe-deposit box** (p. 286) a locked box used for storing valuables
>
> **premium** (p. 286) amount of money paid for insurance
>
> **income tax return** (p. 286) an annual report filed with the government that states how much money one has earned during the year
>
> **U. S. Defense Bonds** (p. 286) bonds sold by the U. S. government to raise money for the war

She needed to pay the premiums on his car and life insurance policies, file his income tax returns, and at his request, purchase U.S. Defense Bonds. It was a difficult job for Kay, trying to manage all the tasks that Papa had handled until then.

Papa wrote often, trying to help us manage without him, but his letters often arrived looking like lace doilies. The censors had cut out whatever they didn't want us to read.

"Don't forget to lubricate the car," Papa wrote. Or, "Be sure to have the roses pruned, brush Laddie every day, send Grandma her monthly check, and take our Christmas offering to church."

We could tell he was trying to anticipate all our problems from his snowbound camp in Montana. He also tried to cheer us up, and asked us to tell our church friends not to be too discouraged.

Still, it was hard not to worry. Japan was now the despised enemy, and every Japanese American became a target of the same hatred directed at Japan. It was not because we had done anything wrong, but simply because we *looked* like the enemy.

Once again, my Japanese face was going to cause me misery.

ONE EVENING I WENT OUT WITH SOME FRIENDS FOR A LATE evening snack to a restaurant where we'd often gone before. We hadn't been there long when an angry Filipino man came to our table. His fists were clenched, and his eyes flashed with anger.

"You know what your Jap soldiers are doing to my homeland?" he shouted. "They're killing my people!"

"But we're not from Japan," we said, trying to reason with him. "We're Americans!"

He continued to harass us, not listening to anything we said. Then having had his say, he left, still scowling. But he had ruined our evening, for we knew there were many others who hated us as much as he did. We left the restaurant quickly and went home in silence.

> **Words to Know**
>
> **sabotage** (p. 287) an act of destruction done to harm a nation's war effort
>
> **refute** (p. 287) prove wrong

I was frightened as I saw newspaper accounts accusing Japanese Americans of spying and sabotage in Hawaii. These rumors were later completely refuted, but at the time most Americans accepted them as the truth.

Soon racist groups began calling for a forced eviction of all Americans of Japanese ancestry along the West Coast. They called it an "evacuation"—a word implying removal for the protection of the person being removed— but actually it was an uprooting.

Hatred against Asians, however, was not new to California. It had existed for a hundred years. Laws that restricted immigration and land ownership already existed, and now groups who would benefit economically from our removal joined in the calls for a mass uprooting.

As new rumors spread, we grew more and more uneasy. Several of my classmates from out of town left the university to rejoin their families. And in Montana my father worried helplessly about what would happen to us.

We thought we should start packing some of our belongings, in case we were actually uprooted. One evening, as we were packing books into wooden crates, a friend stopped by to see us.

"What on earth are you doing?" he asked. "There will never be a mass evacuation. Don't you realize we're American citizens? The U.S. government would never intern its own citizens. It would be unconstitutional."

Words to Know

intern (p. 288) force to stay in a certain place

infiltrate (p. 288) become part of an organization or institution for the purpose of spying

Of course his facts were right. Still, we knew that the attorney general of California claimed, incorrectly, that Japanese Americans had "infiltrated . . . every strategic spot" in the state.

On the floor of the House of Representatives, Congressman John Rankin had shouted, "I say it is of vital importance that we get rid of every Japanese . . . Damn them! Let us get rid of them now!"

Our government did nothing to stop these hysterical outcries or to refute the false rumors. We learned many years later that although President Franklin D. Roosevelt had seen a State Department report testifying to the "extraordinary degree of loyalty" among the West Coast Japanese Americans, he chose instead to listen to the voices of the hatemongers.

On February 19, 1942, the President signed Executive Order 9066, which resulted in the forcible eviction of all Japanese, "aliens and non-aliens," from the West Coast of the United States. He stated that this was a military necessity, and because we did not know otherwise at the time, we believed him. The Supreme Court of the land sanctioned his decision.

> **Words to Know**
>
> **hatemonger** (p. 289) someone who spreads hatred
>
> **sanction** (p. 289) in this case, to support or approve
>
> **due process of law** (p. 289) following the proper steps stated by law
>
> **exclusion zone** (p. 290) an area within which certain people are not allowed

It was a sad day for all Americans of Japanese ancestry. Our government no longer considered us its citizens, simply referring to us as "nonaliens." It also chose to ignore the Fifth and Fourteenth Amendments to the Constitution that guaranteed "due process of law" and "equal protection under the law for all citizens." We were to be imprisoned in concentration camps without a trial or hearing of any kind.

"But we're at war with Germany and Italy, too," I objected. "Why are only the Japanese Americans being imprisoned?"

No one, including our government, had an answer for that.

Under the direction of Lieutenant General John L. DeWitt of the Western Defense Command, 120,000 men, women, and children of Japanese ancestry (two-thirds of whom were American citizens) were to be uprooted from their homes on the West Coast of the United States.

We were told we could "evacuate voluntarily" outside the military zone but most of us had no place to go. How could we suddenly pick up everything and move to a new and unknown location? Some of our friends moved to inland towns, but when the exclusion zone was later extended, they were uprooted once again and eventually interned in a camp anyway.

We felt like prisoners even before our actual eviction. We had to observe an 8:00 P.M. curfew and were not permitted to travel more than five miles beyond our home. We had to turn in all shortwave radios, cameras, binoculars, and firearms. We also had to register. Each family was given a number, and ours was 13453.

I shuddered when I read the headlines of our local paper on April 21. It read, "JAPS GIVEN EVACUATION ORDERS HERE." On May 1, we were to be sent to the Tanforan Racetrack, which had been hurriedly converted into an "Assembly Center."

"But how can we clear out our house in only ten days?" Mama asked desperately. "We've lived here for fifteen years!"

"I guess we just have to do it, Mama," Kay answered. "We can't argue with the U.S. Army."

Friends came to help us clear out our belongings. But no one could help us decide what to keep and what to discard. We had to do that for ourselves. We grew frantic as the days went by. We sold furniture we should have kept and stored things we should have thrown out.

Mama was such a saver. She had drawers and closets and cartons overflowing with memory-laden belongings. She saved everything from old string and wrapping paper to valentines, Christmas cards, clay paperweights, and drawings that Kay and I had made for her. She had dozens of photograph albums and guest books and packets of old letters from friends and family.

"How can I throw all this away?" she asked bleakly.

In the end she just put everything in trunks that we

stored at the Bekins Storage Company. We also stored there the furniture that was too large to be left with friends offering us space in their basements.

We put off until the last minute a decision none of us wanted to make. What were we going to do with our beloved Laddie? We knew no friends who could take him. Finally, it occurred to me to put an ad in the *Daily Californian* at the university.

"I am one of the Japanese American students soon to be evacuated," I wrote, "and have a male Scotch collie that can't come with me. Can anyone give him a home? If interested, please call me immediately at Berkeley 7646W."

The day my ad appeared, I was deluged with sympathetic calls, but we gave him to the first boy who called because he seemed kind and caring. We gave him Laddie's dog house, leash, brushes, favorite toy, and everything else he would need.

The boy promised he would write us at Tanforan to let us know how Laddie was doing. We each gave Laddie a hug and watched him climb reluctantly into the strange car.

"Be a good boy now, Laddie," I said. "We'll come back for you someday."

Mama, Kay, and I couldn't bear to go inside. We stood at the curb watching as the boy drove off. And we could still hear Laddie's plaintive barking even after the car turned the corner and we could no longer see it.

About Yoshiko Uchida

Yoshiko Uchida was born and raised near San Francisco, California, in a house full of books with a family that loved to read. It's not surprising that she began writing stories and keeping a journal when she was ten.

An American of Japanese heritage, Uchida identifies strongly with both cultures. Through her writing, she tries to encourage young people to be "caring human beings who don't think in terms of labels—foreigners or Asians or whatever—but think of people as human beings."

In her autobiography *The Invisible Thread*, from which "Becoming a 'Nonalien'" is taken, Uchida recounts her family's experience during World War II, when they were forced to live in an internment camp. Uchida's other award-winning books include *A Jar of Dreams, The Best Bad Thing,* and *The Happiest Ending.*

Responding

1. **Personal Response** How would you feel if you faced a situation like the one Yoshiko Uchida describes?

2. **Literary Analysis** How would you describe the *mood* of this selection?

3. **Theme Connection** Why do you think the forced relocation of Japanese Americans occurred? How could similar events be avoided in the future?

Language Workshop

Euphemisms A *euphemism* is the use of a mild or indirect expression in order to avoid a more direct, possibly unpleasant expression. Euphemisms are part of our everyday life, as when a death is referred to as someone "passing away." But some euphemisms are used for political reasons. For example, in recent times corporations have begun to use the euphemism "downsizing" when they eliminate large numbers of jobs.

Yoshiko Uchida tells us that the U. S. Government used the term "nonaliens" to refer to American citizens of Japanese ancestry. Tell why this euphemism might have been preferred. Then list a few more euphemisms you have heard.

Writer's Portfolio

Today the U. S. government has admitted that sending Japanese Americans to concentration camps during World War II was wrong, but at the time many people thought it was a good idea. Write an editorial about something happening right now that you believe is wrong or unjust, even though other people accept it.

JAMES MITSUI

Destination: Tule Lake
Relocation Center, May 20, 1942

She had raised the window
higher

than her head; then
paused

to lift wire spectacles,
wiping

sight back with a wrinkled
hand-

kerchief. She wanted to watch
the old

place until the train's passing
erased

the tarpaper walls and tin roof;
she had

been able to carry away
so little.

The fingers of her left
hand

worried two strings
attached

to a baggage tag
flapping

from her
lapel.

Holding Center, Tanforan Race Track
Spring 1942

—for Mine Okubo

Dinner was cold: one boiled potato,
a can of Vienna sausage
and rice with cinnamon & sugar.
Outside the fence
a dog barks in the cricket-filled night.
You stay in your horse stall,
sitting on a mattress stuffed with straw
and stare at white grass
growing up through the floor.
Hay, horse hair and manure
are whitewashed to the boards.
In the corner
a white spider is suspended
in the shadow of a white spider web.

About James Mitsui

During World War II, when James Mitsui was
very young, he and his family were forced to live
in an internment camp for Japanese Americans.
This experience is frequently explored in his
poetry. Now a high school English teacher, James
Mitsui lives in Seattle and has published several
books of poetry, including *Journal of the Sun* and
After the Long Train.

Responding

1. **Personal Response** What images from these two poems will stay with you for a while? Why?

2. **Literary Analysis** How do the *titles* of these poems help the reader understand what the poems are about?

3. **Theme Connection** What words and images in the poems indicate that something is not right?

Language Workshop

Using Adjectives Some writers simply gush with *adjectives*, while others hardly use any. James Mitsui belongs to the latter group—notice how he lets nouns and verbs do most of the work in his poems. When he does use adjectives, though, each one alerts your senses: a *cricket-filled* night, a *horse* stall, *tarpaper* walls and a *tin* roof.

Pick one of the following scenes and write a description in which you use adjectives sparingly but with maximum effect.

a fireworks display   the ocean at night

a busy intersection   a school hallway

Writer's Portfolio

As in "Becoming a 'Nonalien,'" the forced relocation of Japanese Americans during World War II is again the topic—but this time it is described through poetry. Pick another selection you have read in this unit and write a poem, song, or rap to go along with it.

Right or Wrong

PROJECTS

Roll Cameras

There's nothing movie audiences like better than a clash between good and evil. Imagine you are a Hollywood producer making a movie version of one of the selections you've just read. Begin by choosing the selection you want to work with. Then write a summary that describes what kind of movie you are making (thriller, romance, comedy, action movie, and so on), where it will be filmed, who will star in it, and what props and costumes will be needed. Choose a musician or musicians to compose your sound track. Finally, create an advertisement or movie poster— text and art—that will grab the attention of Hollywood and the world.

Debating the Issues

Who decides what's right and what's wrong? Was it right for the U. S. government to incarcerate Japanese Americans during World War II because of a supposed threat to national security? Was it wrong for Hannah and Crow to go to a funeral looking for a free meal? In small groups, plan a debate about an issue from one of the stories you read in Unit 5. Decide who in your group will argue for one side of the issue and who will argue for the other side. Stage your debate for the rest of the class.

Writing About Right or Wrong

Think of an issue that many teenagers face—drugs, staying in school, accepting differences in others, and so on. Write an essay that gives your point of view on the right way to handle the issue.

FURTHER READING

Doing the right thing isn't always easy, popular, or obvious. The characters in each of the following books have difficult choices to make.

The Chocolate War by Robert Cormier. Jerry Renault wages a lonely battle against the Vigils, a powerful secret society at his high school. But his rebellion could cost him everything.

Farewell to Manzanar by Jeanne Wakatsuki Houston and James D. Houston. During World War II, the U.S. government ordered that thousands of Japanese Americans be sent to internment camps. This book describes what happened during the three years that Jeanne Houston, a Japanese American, and her family lived in a camp called Manzanar.

Julius Caesar by William Shakespeare. This play raises a provocative question: Is it worse to betray your country or your friend?

The Pearl by John Steinbeck. When a Mexican pearl fisher finds a magnificent pearl, it is unclear whether good or bad fortune will come to him and his family.

Killing Mr. Griffin by Lois Duncan. No one likes Mr. Griffin, a high school English teacher who seems mean and unfair. When five students plan a practical joke to get back at him, none of them is prepared for the unexpected consequences.

Brave New World by Aldous Huxley. This futuristic novel describes a world where intelligence, physical appearance, and even romance are scientifically controlled.

UNIT 6

Journeys

When was the last time you traveled somewhere—whether across town or across the country? What did you find when you got there? Did you learn anything about yourself along the way?

Journeys are often significant moments in a person's life. Life itself can be thought of as a journey, even when there's no actual travel involved. Does your life seem to be a journey?

The characters in this unit must undertake a journey of one kind or another. As you read, think about how these characters are affected by the journeys they take. How are their lives different afterwards? How would you feel if you accompanied them in their travels?

The Road Goes Ever On and On

The Road goes ever on and on
    Down from the door where it began.
Now far ahead the Road has gone,
    And I must follow, if I can,
Pursuing it with eager feet,
    Until it joins some larger way
Where many paths and errands meet.
    And whither then? I cannot say.

THEODORE ROETHKE

Night Journey

Now as the train bears west,
Its rhythm rocks the earth,
And from my Pullman berth
I stare into the night
While others take their rest.
Bridges of iron lace,
A suddenness of trees,
A lap of mountain mist
All cross my line of sight,
Then a bleak wasted place,
And a lake below my knees.
Full on my neck I feel
The straining at a curve;
My muscles move with steel,
I wake in every nerve.
I watch a beacon swing
From dark to blazing bright;
We thunder through ravines
And gullies washed with light.
Beyond the mountain pass
Mist deepens on the pane;
We rush into a rain
That rattles double glass.
Wheels shake the roadbed stone,
The pistons jerk and shove,
I stay up half the night
To see the land I love.

AUDRE LORDE

A Trip on the Staten Island Ferry

Dear Jonno
there are pigeons who nest
on the Staten Island Ferry
and raise their young
between the moving decks
and never touch
ashore.

Every voyage is a journey.

Cherish this city
left you by default
include it in your daydreams
there are still   secrets
in the streets
even I have not discovered
who knows if the old men
shining shoes on the Staten Island Ferry
carry their world   in that box
slung across their shoulders
if they share their lunch
with the birds flying
back and forth
on an endless journey
if they ever find their way
back home.

About J.R.R. Tolkien

J.R.R. Tolkien grew up in England and taught languages for many years at Oxford University. He was fascinated with myths and fairy tales and the idea of journeys. His love of such stories greatly influenced his famous books *The Hobbit* and *The Lord of the Rings* trilogy, which all involve great journeys.

About Theodore Roethke

Theodore Roethke's family owned a greenhouse, and Roethke grew up with a deep love of nature. Though he struggled with mental illness and alcoholism, Roethke worked hard at perfecting his poetry, and his poems continue to influence many other writers. His books include *The Waking*, *Words for the Wind*, and *The Far Field*.

About Audre Lorde

Audre Lorde loved poetry as a child and began writing in eighth grade. Many of her poems were about her personal experiences as an African American woman and her long battle with cancer. Before her death, Lorde wrote numerous books of poetry, including *The Black Unicorn* and *The Marvelous Arithmetics of Distance*.

Responding

1. **Personal Response** Which of these poems says the most to you? Why?

2. **Literary Analysis** Read "Night Journey" aloud. Notice the *rhythm* in the poem. What does the poet do to achieve that rhythm?

3. **Theme Connection** Compare journeys that are described in these poems. How are the journeys different? How are they the same?

Language Workshop

Rhyme scheme You can figure out if a poem has a *rhyme scheme*—a pattern of rhyming words. Assign each line of the poem a letter of the alphabet. Give lines with last words that rhyme the same letter. For example, the rhyme scheme of "The Road Goes Ever On and On" is *a b a b c d c d.*

Figure out the rhyme scheme of "Night Journey." Does this poem have a regular pattern like "The Road Goes Ever On and On"? How does the rhyme scheme affect the poem?

Writer's Portfolio

What makes a poem effective? Write a critical review of one or more of these poems. Tell which images stand out the most for you and why. If you think the poem has any weaknesses, explain what they are. Be prepared to share your review in a class discussion on poetry.

DUANE BigEagle

The Journey

I HAD KNOWN THE TRAIN ALL MY LIFE. ITS WAILING roar rushed through my dreams as through a tunnel and yet I had never even been on one. Now I was to take one on a two-thousand-kilometer journey halfway into a foreign country!

This particular adventure was my fault, if you can call being sick a fault. Mama says finding fault is only a way of clouding a problem and this problem was clouded enough. It began when I was thirteen and I still have tuberculosis scars on my lungs but this illness was more than tuberculosis. The regular doctors were mystified by the fevers and delirium that accompanied a bad cough and nausea. After six months of treatment without improvement they gave up.

Papa carried me on his back as we left the doctor's office and began our walk to the barrio that was our home. Mama cried as she walked and Papa seemed weighted by more than the weight of my thinned-down frame. About halfway home Papa suddenly straightened up. I was having a dizzy spell and almost slipped off his back but he caught me with one

About the People in This Story

Raoul and his family live in Mexico. The Yaqui Indians (p. 309) are a tribe living in parts of Mexico, Arizona, and California. Papa refers to the old Papago trails across the desert. The Papago Indians, also known as the Tohono O'odham, live in northern Mexico and the southwestern United States.

hand and shouted, "Aunt Rosalie! What a fool I am! Aunt Rosalie Stands Tall!" Papa started to laugh and to dance around and around on the dirt path in the middle of a field.

"What do you mean?" cried Mama as she rushed around with her hands out, ready to catch me if I fell. From the look on her face, the real question in her mind was more like, Have you gone mad? "Listen, woman," said Papa, "there are some people who can cure diseases the medical doctors can't. Aunt Rosalie Stands Tall is a medicine woman of the Yaqui people and one of the best! She'll be able to cure Raoul! The only problem is she's married to an Indian in the United States. But that can't be helped, we'll just have to go there. Come on, we have plans to make and work to do!"

The planning began that day. We had very little money, but with what we had and could borrow from Papa's many friends there was just enough for a child's ticket to the little town in Oklahoma where Rosalie lived. I couldn't be left alone in a foreign country so Papa decided simply to walk. "I'll take the main highway north to the old Papago trails that go across the desert. They'll also take me across the border undetected. Then I'll head east and north to Oklahoma. It should be easy to catch occasional rides

DUANE BigEagle   **309**

once I get to the U.S. When I arrive I'll send word for Raoul to start."

Papa left one fine spring morning, taking only a blanket, a few extra pairs of shoes, bow and arrows to catch food, and a flintstone for building fires. Secretly I believe he was happy to be traveling again. Travel had always been in his blood. As a young man, Papa got a job on a sailing ship and traveled all over the world. This must have been how he learned to speak English and also how he met Mama in the West Indies. Myself, I was still sixty kilometers from the town I was born in and even to imagine the journey I was about to take was more than my fevered brain could handle. But as Mama said, "You can do anything in the world if you take it little by little and one step at a time." This was the miraculous and trusting philosophy our family lived by, and I must admit it has usually worked.

Still, the day of departure found me filled with a dread that settled like lead in my feet. If I hadn't been so lightheaded from the fevers, I'm sure I would have fallen over at any attempt to walk. Dressed in my best clothes which looked shabby the minute we got to the train station, Mama led me into the fourth-class carriage and found me a seat on a bench near the windows. Then she disappeared and came back a minute later with a thin young man with sallow skin and a drooping Zapata mustache. "This is your second cousin, Alejandro. He is a conductor on this train and will be with you till you get to Juarez; you must do whatever he says."

At that time, the conductors on trains in Mexico were required to stay with a train the entire length of its journey which perhaps accounted for Alejandro's appearance. He did little to inspire my confidence in him. In any case, he disappeared a second later and it was time for Mama to go

Words to Know

sallow (p. 310) having a sickly, yellowish color

Zapata mustache (p. 310) Emiliano Zapata, a hero of the Mexican Revolution, had a thick dark mustache.

too. Hurriedly, she reminded me that there was money in my coat to buy food from the women who came onto the train at every stop and that there was a silver bracelet sewn into the cuff of my pants to bribe the guards at the border. With one last tearful kiss and hug, she was gone and I was alone. The train started with a jerk which knocked me off my bench and I began my journey upside down in a heap on top of my crumpled cardboard suitcase. I didn't even get a chance to wave goodbye.

I soon got used to the jerking starts of the train, and unsmiling Alejandro turned out to be a guardian angel which was fortunate because my illness began to get worse as the journey went along. Many times I awoke to find Alejandro shuffling some young thief away from my meager possessions or buying me food at the last stop before a long stretch of desert. He would bring me things too, fresh peaches and apples and leftover bread and pastries from the first-class carriages where he worked. Once, in the middle of the desert he brought me a small ice-cold watermelon, the most refreshing thing I'd ever tasted—who knows where he got it?

To this day, I'm not sure exactly which of the things I saw through the window of the train were real and which were not. Some of them I know were not real. In my delirium, a half-day's journey would pass in the blink of an eye. Often I noticed only large changes in the countryside, from plains to mountains to desert. Broad valleys remain clearly in my mind and there were many of these. Small scenes, too, remain—a family sitting down to dinner at a candle-lit table in a hut by a river. And a few more sinister ones—once between two pine trees I caught a glimpse of one man raising a large club to strike another man whose back was turned. I cried out but there was nothing to be done, the train was moving too fast on a downgrade and probably couldn't have been stopped. But then, did I really see them at all? My doubt was caused by the girl in the dark red dress.

I think I began to see her about halfway through the journey to Juarez. She was very beautiful, high cheekbones, long black hair and very dark skin. She was about my height and age or maybe a little older. Her eyes were very large and her mouth seemed to have a ready smile. The first time I saw her, at a small station near a lake, she smiled and waved as the train pulled away. Her sensuality embarrassed me and I didn't wave back. I regretted it immediately. But she was back again the next day at a station in the foothills of the mountains, this time dressed in the white blouse and skirt that the Huichol women wear.

> ### Terms to Know
> **Huichol** (p. 312) The Huichol Indians live in the Mexican states of Jalisco and Nayarit.
> **Sierra Madre Oriental** (p. 312) the eastern range of the Sierra Madre mountain chain
> **crescent-shaped** (p. 312) shaped like a quarter moon

She became almost a regular occurrence. Sometimes she was happy, sometimes serious and most of the time she was wearing the dark red dress. Often I would only see her in passing; she'd be working in a field and raise up to watch the train go by. Gradually, my condition grew worse. My coughing fits grew longer and I slept more so I began not to see the girl so much, but the last time I saw her really gave me a shock. The mountains of the Sierra Madre Oriental range are very rugged and are cut in places by deep gorges called barrancas. The train was in one of these gorges on a ledge above the river and was about to go around a bend. For some reason, I looked back the way we had come and there, imbedded in the mountain with her eyes closed, was the face of the girl, thirty feet high! For the first time, I noticed the small crescent-shaped scar in the middle of her lower lip.

The vision, or whatever it was, quickly disappeared as the train rounded the curve. I sank back on to the bench with a pounding heart and closed my eyes. I must have slept or perhaps I fell into a coma because I remember very little of the last part of the trip. I awoke once while Alejandro was carrying me across the border and delivering me to a friend of his on the train to Dallas. How I got from Dallas to Oklahoma I may never know because I remember nothing. But it happened. And finally, I awoke for a minute in my father's arms as he carried me off the train.

Then, there was a sharp pain in the center of my chest. And a pounding. Rhythmic pounding. A woman's voice began to sing in a very high pitch. My eyes opened of themselves. At first I couldn't make it out, arched crossing lines, flickering shadows. I was in the center of an oval-shaped lodge built of bent willow limbs covered with skins and lit by a small fire. A tall woman came into view; she was singing and dancing back and forth. Somehow I knew this was Rosalie Stands Tall, the medicine woman. The pain hit me again and I wanted to get away but hands held me still.

Papa's voice said in my ear, "She is calling her spirit helpers, you must try and sit up." I was sitting up facing the door of the lodge. There was a lizard there and he spoke in an old man's voice, words I couldn't understand. Rosalie sang again and there was a small hawk there. The pain rose up higher in my chest. There was a coyote in the door and his words were tinged with mocking laughter. The pain rose into my throat. There was a small brown bear in the door, his fur blew back and forth in the wind. The pain rose into the back of my mouth. I felt I needed to cough. Rosalie put two porcupine quills together and bound them with leather to make a pair of tweezers. She held my lips closed with them, painfully tight. A pair of wings beat against the top of the lodge. I needed badly to cough. There was something hot in my mouth, it was sharp, it was hurting my mouth, it needed to come out! IT WAS OUT!

I awoke in bed in a small room lit by a coal-oil lamp. There was a young woman with her back to me preparing food by the side of the bed. She had very long black hair. She put the tray down on the table beside the bed. As she turned to leave the room, I saw a small crescent-shaped scar in the middle of her lower lip. I started to call her back but there was no need. I knew who she was. An immense peacefulness settled over me. It was warm in the bed. Papa sat on the other side of the bed. He seemed very happy when I turned and looked at him. He said softly, "Raoul, you have changed completely. You're not anymore the young boy left in Mazatlán." I wanted to tell him everything! There was so much to say! But all I could get out was, "Yes, I know, Papa, I've come on a journey out of childhood." And then I went to sleep again.

About Duane BigEagle

The son of a Cherokee mother and an Osage father, Duane BigEagle grew up on an Indian reservation in Oklahoma. He says, "As an American Indian youth, I was taught to value a connection with the

 land which sustains our lives. I learned early on that individuality, creativity, self-expression, and love of beauty are essential to the survival of a whole and healthy person."

Before Duane BigEagle began writing seriously, he worked in lumber mills, fisheries, and on a ranch in California. He now writes and teaches poetry and American Indian studies to high school and college students in California.

Responding

1. **Personal Response** Have you ever taken a journey that meant a lot to you? How was your journey like the one described in the story? How was it different?

2. **Literary Analysis** Raoul sees the girl in the red dress during his journey and when he arrives in Oklahoma. What do you think she *symbolizes* for him?

3. **Theme Connection** Raoul says he has taken a journey out of childhood. How will his life be different now?

Language Workshop

Establishing a Mood At the beginning of this story, the narrator says that the roar of the train "rushed through my dreams as through a tunnel. . . ." By mentioning dreams in the very first paragraph, author Duane BigEagle creates a mood of dreaminess and unreality that lasts through the whole story. List at least three other passages in the story that express a dreamlike mood.

Writer's Portfolio

As the narrator describes the train ride to Juarez, he gives many details about what he observes inside and outside the train. Picture in your mind one of the trips you make on a regular basis—the bus ride to school or the route to a grandparent's home, for example. Write a detailed description of everything that happens during one of these trips.

GARY PAULSEN

Stupid

from *Woodsong*

$\mathcal{D}$IFFERENT DOGS OF COURSE HAVE DIFFERENT tempers. Some are more short-tempered than others, but on one occasion I had a whole team mad at me.

It made for a wild ride.

The thing is, it started gently enough. My leader was a sweet dog named Cookie and I had six dogs, all cheerful. It was on the trapline. I had checked several sets and the weather had turned sour. By late afternoon there was a full storm blowing snow so hard it was impossible to see where we were going.

The dogs always know direction but this was before I learned to trust them—learned to understand that lead dogs know more than the person on the sled. Afraid I would get lost in the storm, I challenged every decision. If Cookie wanted to go left, I wanted to go right, if she wanted to go right, I wanted to go left or straight ahead.

Each time she persisted, overriding my commands, I scolded her for fighting me, and each time I would find later that she was right.

Still I did not learn and I continued to challenge them, often causing the team to get tangled. In time they grew sick of my idiocy. When I went up to pull them over, floundering in the deep snow, they ignored me, tried to shrug away my hand. Still trying to be partially polite, they let me know I was being a *putz*, and still I persisted.

Finally I went too far.

We were running along the top edge of a long ridge, higher and higher. The wind was tearing at us. I had my head buried in my parka hood and couldn't even see the

> ### *About Dogsledding*
>
> A *trapline* (p. 317) is a series of animal traps set out over a distance. The trapper visits the traps on a regular basis to see what has been caught. The *lead dog* is the dog in the front position who sets the pace for the rest of the team. The *gangline* (p. 319) is the line the dogs are harnessed to in order to pull the sled. The *snowhook* (p. 319) is a hook that is tied to the sled. When thrust into the snow or hooked around a tree or other solid object, the snowhook keeps the sled from moving forward. The *runners* (p. 319) are the wooden or metal blades under the sled that glide over the snow.

front end of the team.

But I was sure I knew the ridge, knew where we were, felt that I had been there before.

I was absolutely, dead wrong.

The team went slower and slower until they were walking, lugging up the middle of the ridge and—perhaps after a quarter of a mile—they stopped. I yelled at them to turn right ("Gee" is the command for right, "Haw" for left). I knew where we were now—was sure of it—but Cookie tried to turn them left, down a long, shallow incline.

I became furious at their mutiny, swore, yelled at the team, then stomped forward, grabbed Cookie by the back of her harness and half-pulled, half-threw her off to the right.

She vanished in the driving snow and wind, moving angrily in the direction I had thrown her. The team followed her, and I jumped on the sled as it went by.

For one or two seconds it was all right. I stood on the brake and held the sled back and we slithered down the hill.

Then it all blew apart. With a great lurch I felt the sled fly out into empty space and drop beneath me. I barely had time to fall backward and go into a tuck before I hit the side of a nearly vertical incline and began to tumble.

I flapped and rolled for what seemed like hours, end over end. I heard the dogs falling beneath me, the sled rolling over and over, and all the gear and food being tossed out, crashing around me.

With a resounding thump the whole pile—sled, dogs, gear, and me, upside down—plummeted into a heap in the bottom of what seemed to be a deep gully.

It was impossible for a moment to understand what had happened. There was not a place where I ended and the dogs and junk began. One dog—named Lad—had his nose jammed squarely in my mouth, another was in my armpit. The sled was on top of me, and if you'd asked me my

Words to Know

resounding (p. 318) loud

plummet (p. 318) to drop

gully (p. 318) a small ravine

name I couldn't have told you.

Cookie had knowingly taken the team over the edge of a sharp drop. It was something she never would have done on her own, but I had pushed and griped and hollered too much and she thought it time to give me a lesson.

If I wanted to be stupid, if I persisted in being stupid, if I just couldn't resist being stupid, then she figured I had it coming and she wouldn't hold me back.

It was a good lesson.

But it wasn't over yet. I stood and shook the snow out of my clothes—it was actually packed in my ears—and tipped the sled upright. It took me fifteen minutes to find all the gear and repack the sled and the dogs watched me quietly the whole time.

When the sled was loaded I set to work on the dogs. They were an unholy mess, tangled so badly the gangline was in knots.

The dogs were . . . strange. While I worked to untangle them, it was almost as if I weren't there, as if a robot were working on them. They were pleasant enough, but they did not make eye contact with me. They looked straight ahead while I untangled them. They almost, but not quite, ignored me. Even the dogs that would normally be jumping all over me held back.

It was eerie, quiet even with the wind blowing over the top of the gully. But after a moment I dismissed it as all in my head and went back to the sled.

I pulled the snowhook and stood on the runners.

And the whole team lay down.

They did not drop instantly. But each and every dog, as if by a silent command from Cookie, dug a bit and made a bed and lay down in the snow and went to sleep. I tried every way I knew to get them to run. Fed them, begged them, bit their ears, but they completely ignored me. I wasn't even there.

They didn't get up for eighteen hours.

I had gone over the line.

In the storm, in the pushing and yelling and driving, I had passed the point where they would accept me, run for me, pull for me, and they told me there in that gully. In that wild place they told me so that I would understand that they were the team, they were all of it, and if I ignored them or treated them wrong I would know it.

Finally I pulled out my sleeping bag and made a camp of sorts and heated some tea and dozed and drank tea and thought of how it is to be stupid.

And later, when they felt I'd had enough—late the next day while I was still in the sleeping bag—Cookie stood and shook the snow off. The rest of the dogs did the same, shook and marked the snow. I got out of the bag and fed them and packed and stood on the sled and they pulled up and out of the gully like a runaway train. They pulled up and into the sun and loped all the way home in great joy and glee; joy they were happy to share with me. Unless I grew stupid again.

About Gary Paulsen

The son of an Army officer, Gary Paulsen had to move a lot as a boy, changing schools constantly: "It was a miserable life. School was a nightmare

because I was unbelievably shy, and terrible at sports. I had no friends, and teachers ridiculed me." What saved him was a librarian who introduced him to the world of books: "It was as though I had been dying of thirst and the librarian had handed me a five-gallon bucket of water. I drank and drank."

Paulsen has worked as a rancher, engineer, singer, teacher, editor, actor, and archer. His many books include *Hatchet*, *The Monument*, and *Woodsong*.

Responding

1. **Personal Response** Would you like to run a dog team? Why or why not?

2. **Literary Analysis** What is the moment of greatest suspense, or the *climax* of this story?

3. **Theme Connection** What did Gary Paulsen learn about himself and his dogs on this trip?

Language Workshop

Compound Predicates Gary Paulsen packs a lot of action into a few pages. One way he keeps things moving is by writing sentences with compound predicates — in other words, sentences with more than one verb. For example, he writes:

I became furious at their mutiny, swore, yelled at the team, then stomped forward, grabbed Cookie by the back of her harness and half-pulled, half-threw her off to the right.

Seven verbs! Look at how much action takes place in that sentence. Find two more examples in the selection of sentences with compound predicates. Then write two sentences of your own that have compound predicates.

Writer's Portfolio

Gary Paulsen's writing is full of interesting and sometimes amusing observations about animals. Write about an animal you have observed—perhaps the family cat, a sea lion at the zoo, or the sparrow at your birdfeeder. What details did you notice about the animal? Were your previous ideas about this animal changed by what you observed?

D O R E E N   R A P P A P O R T

The River of Ice

"WE NEED THE MONEY, AND ELIZA'LL FETCH A GOOD price. She's young, and a good looker and a good worker."

Eliza's master's words stunned her. He was selling her. Not that she hadn't always known it was a possibility. Like all slaves, she lived with the gnawing reality that at any moment she could be sold and uprooted from her loved ones. But Eliza's owners had always been so kind to her that she had lulled herself into forgetting reality. Their kindness had vanished with their need for money. Within a few days Eliza would be separated from her two-year-old daughter, Caroline.

She knew what she had to do. She couldn't let anyone take Caroline from her. She couldn't lose this child. She had already buried two others.

She waited patiently all day for the darkness and the quiet. She had done her chores efficiently but not too efficiently, not wanting to draw attention to herself. She had listened to her mistress' talking, ignored what she was supposed to ignore, nodded where she was expected to nod and answered when she was expected to answer. She had carefully controlled her every facial gesture and tone of voice so she wouldn't give away her angry feelings, so that her owners wouldn't suspect that she had overheard their plan to sell her.

Now it was almost time. Caroline was asleep, wrapped in a blanket made from saved scraps of wool. Eliza was tired too, but she didn't dare sleep. She needed to leave a few hours before daylight so she could cross the river when it was light. If she gave in to her weariness, she might not get up in time. She lay awake, thinking about the journey ahead.

When she thought it was time, she scooped Caroline up from the floor and took her in her arms. "Be good, darling, don't cry now," she whispered, worried that the other children and the adults in the cabin would awaken.

She tiptoed out of the cabin. When she stepped outside, the night air bit into her face. She pulled the

An invoice of ten negroes sent this day to John B Williamson by Geo Kremer named & cost as follows

- To wit - Betsey Kackley . . . . . . $ 410. 00
  Nancy Aulick 515. 00
  Harry & Helen Miller . . .1200. 00
  Mary Kootz 600. 00
  Betsey Ott? 560. 00
  Isaac & Fanny Brent . 992. 00
  Lucinda Luckett 467. 50
  George Smith 510. 00
Amount of my traveling expences & boarding 5 254. 50
of lot N° 9 not included in the other bills .. 39. 50
Kremers expences Transporting lot N9 to chic[?] 51. 00
Carryall hire .. 6 00
$ 5351. 00

I have this day delivered the above named negroes costing includeing my expences and other expences five thousand three hundred & fifty dollars this May 26th 1835

John. W. Pittman
I did intend to leave Nancy child but she made such a damned fuss I had to let her take it I could of got fifty Dollars for so you must add forty Dollars to the above

blanket farther over Caroline's head and looked up at the sky. There was the single star, the one that pointed the way to freedom. She followed it down to the other stars, grouped together like a drinking gourd.

About the Drinking Gourd

This constellation—also known as Ursa Major, or the Big Dipper—includes the North Star. Escaping slaves, who were safer traveling by night, followed the Drinking Gourd north toward freedom.

"If I thirsty before I cross the river to freedom, I drink from the sky." She laughed silently at her joke.

There was no sound but her feet quietly touching the cold ground as she walked the five miles through the woods toward the river. She knew all about the river, the long, narrow river that separated the slave state of Kentucky from the free state of Ohio. She'd heard stories of slaves who swam or rowed across it. Eliza had dreamed of crossing that river ever since she was old enough to realize she was a slave. She had talked with other slaves about what it would be like to be free, but she had never thought she would be brave enough to escape. But all that had changed today. Today, with her master's words, she had found a courage she hadn't known she possessed.

Crossing would be easy. The river was always frozen over at this time of year. Her feet, clad in thin-soled shoes, were cold now and would be even colder by the time they touched free ground, but that was a small price to pay for freedom. She pulled Caroline closer and ran along the narrow path that led to the river.

In less than two hours, at daylight, she spotted the river. She raced eagerly toward it. When she reached the riverbank, she saw that the ice had started to thaw. It was broken up some and was slowly drifting by in large cakes. Her heart sank. Crossing was impossible now. She would have to hide and wait for the cold night wind to swoop down and freeze the water some more.

Her eyes searched in both directions for a sign of shelter, for a place where she might rest while she waited for the river to freeze again. She had heard there were free colored folks living along the river who helped runaways. There were a few cabins in the distance. But how would she know which cabin held friends? She wouldn't, but she would have to take a chance.

She pulled the blanket away to reassure herself that Caroline was still sleeping. "Thank you, Lord, for keepin' her still." Then she ran down the path alongside the river. It was a while before she came to a small cabin, not much bigger than the cabin that she had shared with ten others. Black smoke was rising out of its chimney. Dare she stop and ask for help? Her eyes scanned the landscape again. There was no place to hide near the river. And no place in the woods. And even if she could find a place, Caroline might not survive in the freezing cold. What choice did she have? Her master would soon discover she was gone and start tracking her down.

She lifted her head to the sky. "Dear Lord, help me."

She knocked gently on the cabin door. No answer. She knocked again more vigorously. The door opened hesitantly. A short man, with frizzy gray hair and skin black as ebony, nodded at her. It was the kind of gentle greeting black folks often gave each other on their way to Sunday service.

"Mornin'," he said in a quiet voice. His friendly eyes fixed on the bundle that was her daughter.

Eliza swallowed and whispered, "We need a place to stay till nightfall."

"Welcome," he said, hurrying her into the one-room cabin. The cabin had a small table, two chairs, and straw matting on the floor near the hearth to sleep on. There was a roaring fire in the hearth.

"I'm George, and that's my wife Rosetta." His wife, a pleasant-looking woman with cocoa skin like Eliza's, was stirring something in a large pot over the fire. She beckoned for Eliza to come and sit near her.

Eliza squatted down on the straw and held Caroline

gently in her lap, hoping not to disturb her sleep. Rosetta ladled out a liquid from the pot and handed it to Eliza. The broth was warm and nourishing. George brought Eliza a blanket and told her to stretch out. Before she knew it, she was asleep. She spent most of the day sleeping by the fire.

When she awakened, it was almost twilight. George was gone. Rosetta was feeding soup to Caroline. Eliza waited until Caroline had sipped the last spoonful. Then she took her daughter in her arms, planted kisses all over her face, and rocked her back and forth. Caroline drifted into sleep again.

"Where are you from?" Rosetta asked. Eliza told her story. Rosetta told Eliza that she was a freeborn colored but George had been born a slave. She had worked hard and saved the money to buy his freedom.

"But if you free, why you stay in Kentucky?" asked Eliza.

Rosetta smiled gently. "'Cause there are more like you, wantin' to cross the river. And they need shelter till they get cross. So we stay and wait and help."

The door opened, and George hurried in. Eliza knew from his worried eyes that she was not safe. "The slave hunters are out. Goin' from cabin to cabin askin' about you."

It was too dangerous to stay any longer. Eliza had to cross the river now or she would be captured. She stood up with Caroline in her arms. She nodded her silent thanks to Rosetta and George and raced out the cabin door toward the river.

With a sinking heart, Eliza realized that there was even more water between the massive ice chunks. She looked back at the cabin, then at the river path in either direction. There were figures in the distance hurrying toward her. Her eyes followed the river to the other side. "It not that far," she whispered to Caroline, trying to encourage herself. "And when we get there, we gonna be free." She looked upward to the sky. "Lord, we need you." She took Caroline's arms and wrapped them around her neck. "Hold on tight, and don't let go, 'less I tell you," she whispered.

Eliza stepped onto the ice. It was solid. She stepped across a large chunk onto another. That was solid too. And then another. She rushed forward to the next chunk. The ice was giving way. She could feel the weight of her body threatening to pull her down into the water. She leaped onto another chunk. Cold water came rushing up to her ankles.

On the other side of the river she saw a man standing at the shoreline. Eliza leaped onto another chunk. And then another. "We gonna get there," she said to herself as she felt the water rising above her ankles.

A minute later the water reached up to her knees. "Lord, Lord." Soon the water would start to cover Caroline. She was only thirty feet or so from freedom. The water rushed up to her chest.

"Mama, mama," Caroline screamed as the water began to cover her.

"Let go, baby." With her left hand Eliza undid Caroline's arms from around her neck. With her right hand she grabbed a chunk of ice. Then she slid Caroline onto the piece of ice. Caroline screamed louder as the ice touched her back. "I here, baby," Eliza shouted, grabbing the ice chunk with both hands and kicking her feet hoping to propel herself and the ice with Caroline on it farther toward the shore.

She was only ten feet or so from the shore. Caroline's screams filled Eliza's ears. The icy water was beginning to numb Eliza. "Lord, we so close." She kicked even harder. The chunk of ice with Caroline on it was almost at the riverbank. Eliza was only a couple of feet from shore. The man grabbed Caroline off the ice, and Eliza pulled herself onto the shore.

ELIZA'S PURSUERS WATCHED PASSIVELY FROM THE RIVERBANK on the Kentucky side as she and her daughter stepped onto free soil. The man at the riverbank took Eliza and

Caroline to the home of antislavery sympathizers, who gave them food and dry clothing. That night Eliza and her daughter began their trip by the Underground Railroad to Canada.

Author's Note: This story was recounted in Reminiscences of Levi Coffin. *Coffin's antislavery activities earned him the nickname President of the Underground Railroad; Coffin and his wife, Catherine, sheltered over 3,000 runaways at their home in Newport (now Fountain City), Indiana.*

Eliza's escape was written up in many antislavery newspapers. Her courage and desperation so moved Harriet Beecher Stowe that she made her a central character called Eliza in her anti-slavery novel Uncle Tom's Cabin. *While Coffin, in telling this story, referred to Eliza Harris as the runaway, other accounts led me to believe that perhaps this was not her real name. I chose the name Caroline for her daughter.*

About Doreen Rappaport

Doreen Rappaport has made it her goal to write about "untold stories in history." For example,

her book *Living Dangerously: American Women Who Risked Their Lives for Adventure* is a collection of biographies of women who accomplished great feats, such as climbing the highest mountain in Peru, overcoming handicaps to run a marathon, and leading an African safari.

Doreen Rappaport's other award-winning books include *The Boston Coffee Party, Trouble at the Mines,* and *American Women: Their Lives in Their Words.*

Responding

1. **Personal Response** Do you think you could have done what Eliza did? Tell why or why not.

2. **Literary Analysis** A *dialect* is a way of speaking that is characteristic of a particular group of people. Why do you think the author had Eliza speak in dialect?

3. **Theme Connection** Eliza took a serious risk when she attempted her journey toward freedom. What factors helped make that journey a success?

Language Workshop

Fact v. Fiction "The River of Ice" is a fictionalized account of a true story. Although the author couldn't know exactly what happened so long ago, she combined the facts she found through research with details supplied by her imagination.

Tell which of the following details from the story were probably found through research and which were probably the product of the author's imagination.

1. Eliza and her daughter lived in the slave state of Kentucky.

2. Eliza couldn't sleep the night before she escaped with her daughter.

3. Eliza gained her freedom by crossing the river to Ohio.

Writer's Portfolio

Twelve years have passed. Eliza and Caroline are in Canada, but many other African Americans are still living in slavery in the United States. Be Caroline and write a letter to President Abraham Lincoln in which you tell him why slavery is wrong.

LENSEY NAMIOKA

The Inn of Lost Time

In feudal Japan, the *samurai* were professional warriors who spent many years perfecting their skills in the martial arts. These soldiers, who followed a strict code of honor, usually worked for the wealthiest and most powerful nobles and warlords. In this story, a *ronin* (an unemployed samurai) describes an unusual incident he witnessed many years earlier while working for a wealthy merchant.

"Will you promise to sleep if I tell you a story?" said the father. He pretended to put on a stern expression.

"Yes! Yes!" the three little boys chanted in unison. It sounded like a nightly routine.

The two guests smiled as they listened to the exchange. They were wandering ronin, or unemployed samurai, and they enjoyed watching this cozy family scene.

The father gave the guests a helpless look. "What can I do? I have to tell them a story, or these little rascals will give us no peace." Clearing his throat, he turned to the boys. "All right. The story tonight is about Urashima Taro."

Instantly the three boys became still. Sitting with their legs tucked under them, the three little boys, aged five, four, and three, looked like a descending row of stone statuettes. Matsuzo, the younger of the two ronin, was reminded of the wayside half-body statues of Jizo, the God of Travelers and Protector of Children.

Behind the boys the farmer's wife took up a pair of iron chopsticks and stirred the ashes of the fire in the charcoal brazier. A momentary glow brightened the room. The lean faces of the two ronin, lit by the fire, suddenly looked fierce and hungry.

The farmer knew that the two ronin were supposed to use their arms in defense of the weak. But in these troubled times, with the country torn apart by civil wars, the samurai didn't always live up to their honorable code.

Then the fire died down again and the subdued red light softened the features of the two ronin. The farmer relaxed and began his story.

The tale of Urashima Taro is familiar to every Japanese. No doubt the three little boys had heard their father tell it before—and more than once. But they listened with rapt attention.

Words to Know

brazier (p. 332) a large metal pan that holds burning charcoal or coal

desolate (p. 332) unhappy

decrepit (p. 333) broken down, weakened by old age

poignant (p. 333) painful

＊

URASHIMA TARO, A FISHERMAN, RESCUED A TURTLE FROM some boys who were battering it with stones. The grateful turtle rewarded Taro by carrying him on his back to the bottom of the sea, where he lived happily with the Princess of the Undersea. But Taro soon became homesick for his native village and asked to go back on land. The princess gave him a box to take with him but warned him not to peek inside.

When Taro went back to his village, he found the place quite changed. In his home he found his parents gone, and living there was another old couple. He was stunned to learn that the aged husband was his own son, whom he had last seen as a baby! Taro thought he had spent only a pleasant week or two undersea with the princess. On land, seventy-two years had passed! His parents and most of his old friends had long since died.

Desolate, Taro decided to open the box given him by the princess. As soon as he looked inside, he changed in an instant from a young man to a decrepit old man of more than ninety.

✳

AT THE END OF THE STORY THE BOYS WERE CLOSE TO TEARS. Even Matsuzo found himself deeply touched. He wondered why the farmer had told his sons such a poignant bedtime story. Wouldn't they worry all evening instead of going to sleep?

But the boys recovered quickly. They were soon laughing and jostling each other, and they made no objections when their mother shooed them toward bed. Standing in order of age, they bowed politely to the guests, and then lay down on the mattresses spread out for them on the floor. Within minutes the sound of their regular breathing told the guests that they were asleep.

Zenta, the older of the two ronin, sighed as he glanced at the peaceful young faces. "I wish I could fall asleep so quickly. The story of Urashima Taro is one of the saddest that I know among our folk tales."

The farmer looked proudly at his sleeping sons. "They're stout lads. Nothing bothers them much."

The farmer's wife poured tea for the guests and apologized. "I'm sorry this is only poor tea made from coarse leaves."

Zenta hastened to reassure her. "It's warm and heartening on a chilly autumn evening."

"You know what I think is the saddest part of the Urashima Taro story?" said Matsuzo, picking up his cup and sipping the tea. "It's that Taro lost not only his family and friends, but a big piece of his life as well. He had lost the most precious thing of all: time."

The farmer nodded agreement. "I wouldn't sell even one year of my life for money. As for losing seventy-two years, no amount of gold will make up for that!"

Zenta put his cup down on the floor and looked curiously at the farmer. "It's interesting that you should say that. I had an opportunity once to observe exactly how much gold a person was willing to pay for some lost years of his life." He smiled grimly. "In this case the man went as far as one gold piece for each year he lost."

"That's bizarre!" said Matsuzo. "You never told me about it."

"It happened long before I met you," said Zenta. He drank some tea and smiled ruefully. "Besides, I'm not particularly proud of the part I played in that strange affair."

"Let's hear the story!" urged Matsuzo. "You've made us all curious."

The farmer waited expectantly. His wife sat down quietly behind her husband and folded her hands. Her eyes looked intently at Zenta.

"Very well, then," said Zenta. "Actually, my story bears some resemblance to that of Urashima Taro. . . ."

✳

IT HAPPENED ABOUT SEVEN YEARS AGO, WHEN I WAS A green, inexperienced youngster not quite eighteen years old. But I had had a good training in arms, and I was able to get a job as a bodyguard for a wealthy merchant from Sakai.

As you know, wealthy merchants are relatively new in our country. Traditionally the rich have been noblemen, landowners, and warlords with thousands of followers. Merchants, considered as parasites in our society, are a despised class. But our civil wars have made people unusually mobile and stimulated trade between various parts of the country. The merchants have taken advantage of this to conduct businesses on a scale our fathers could not imagine. Some of them have become more wealthy than a warlord with thousands of samurai under his command.

The man I was escorting, Tokubei, was one of this new breed of wealthy merchants. He was trading not only with outlying provinces but even with the Portuguese from across the sea. On this particular journey he was not carrying much gold with him. If he had, I'm sure he would have hired an older and more experienced bodyguard. But if the need should arise, he could always write a message to his clerks at home and have money forwarded to him. It's important to remember this.

The second day of our journey was a particularly grueling one, with several steep hills to climb. As the day was drawing to its close, we began to consider where we should spend the night. I knew that within an hour's walking was a hot-spring resort known to have several attractive inns.

But Tokubei, my employer, said he was already very tired and wanted to stop. He had heard of the resort, and knew the inns there were expensive. Wealthy as he was, he did not want to spend more money than he had to.

While we stood talking, a smell reached our noses, a wonderful smell of freshly cooked rice. Suddenly I felt ravenous. From the way Tokubei swallowed, I knew he was feeling just as hungry.

We looked around eagerly, but the area was forested and we could not see very far in any direction. The tantalizing smell seemed to grow and I could feel the saliva filling my mouth.

"There's an inn around here, somewhere," muttered Tokubei. "I'm sure of it."

We followed our noses. We had to leave the well-traveled highway and take a narrow, winding footpath. But the mouth-watering smell of the rice and the vision of fluffy, freshly aired cotton quilts drew us on.

The sun was just beginning to set. We passed a bamboo grove, and in the low evening light the thin leaves turned into little golden knives. I saw a gilded clump of bamboo shoots. The sight made me think of the delicious dish they would make when boiled in soy sauce.

We hurried forward. To our delight we soon came to a clearing with a thatched house standing in the middle. The fragrant smell of rice was now so strong that we were certain a meal was being prepared inside.

Standing in front of the house was a pretty girl beaming at us with a welcoming smile. "Please honor us with your presence," she said, beckoning.

There was something a little unusual about one of her hands, but, being hungry and eager to enter the house, I did not stop to observe closely.

You will say, of course, that it was my duty as a bodyguard to be suspicious and to look out for danger. Youth and inexperience should not have prevented me from wondering why an inn should be found hidden away from the highway. As it was, my stomach growled, and I didn't even hesitate but followed Tokubei to the house.

Before stepping up to enter, we were given basins of water to wash our feet. As the girl handed us towels for drying, I saw what was unusual about her left hand: she had six fingers.

Tokubei had noticed it as well. When the girl turned away to empty the basins, he nudged me. "Did you see her left hand? She had—" He broke off in confusion as the girl turned around, but she didn't seem to have heard.

The inn was peaceful and quiet, and we soon discovered the reason why. We were the only guests. Again, I should have been suspicious. I told you that I'm not proud of the part I played.

Tokubei turned to me and grinned. "It seems that there are no other guests. We should be able to get extra service for the same amount of money."

> ### About Japanese Inns
>
> In feudal Japan, guests at an inn would sleep on the floor on cotton quilts, or futons. Meals would be eaten with chopsticks while sitting on cushions at low tables. Sliding doors or painted screens would divide up the space and provide privacy.

The girl led us to a spacious room which was like the principal chamber of a private residence. Cushions were set out for us on the floor and we began to shed our traveling gear to make ourselves comfortable.

The door opened and a grizzled-haired man entered. Despite his vigorous-looking face his back was a little bent and I guessed his age to be about fifty. After bowing and greeting us he apologized in advance for the service. "We have not always been innkeepers here," he said, "and you may find the accommodations lacking. Our good intentions must make up for our inexperience. However, to compensate for our inadequacies, we will charge a lower fee than that of an inn with an established reputation."

Tokubei nodded graciously, highly pleased by the words of our host, and the evening began well. It continued well when the girl came back with some flasks of wine, cups, and dishes of salty snacks.

While the girl served the wine, the host looked with interest at my swords. From the few remarks he made, I gathered that he was a former samurai, forced by circumstances to turn his house into an inn.

Words to Know

accommodations (p. 336) lodging and food

inadequacies (p. 337) deficiencies, shortcomings

Having become a bodyguard to a tight-fisted merchant, I was in no position to feel superior to a ronin turned innkeeper. Socially, therefore, we were more or less equal.

We exchanged polite remarks with our host while we drank and tasted the salty snacks. I looked around at the pleasant room. It showed excellent taste, and I especially admired a vase standing in the alcove.

My host caught my eyes on it. "We still have a few good things that we didn't have to sell," he said. His voice held a trace of bitterness. "Please look at the panels of these doors. They were painted by a fine artist."

Tokubei and I looked at the pair of sliding doors. Each panel contained a landscape painting, the right panel depicting a winter scene and the left one the same scene in late summer. Our host's words were no idle boast. The pictures were indeed beautiful.

Tokubei rose and approached the screens for a closer look. When he sat down again, his eyes were calculating. No doubt he was trying to estimate what price the paintings would fetch.

After my third drink I began to feel very tired. Perhaps it was the result of drinking on an empty stomach. I was glad when the girl brought in two dinner trays and a lacquered container of rice. Uncovering the rice container, she began filling our bowls.

Again I noticed her strange left hand with its six fingers. Any other girl would have tried to keep that hand hidden, but this girl made no effort to do so. If anything, she seemed to use that hand more than her other one when she served us. The extra little finger always stuck out from the hand, as if inviting comment.

The hand fascinated me so much that I kept my eyes on it, and soon forgot to eat. After a while the hand looked blurry. And then everything else began to look blurry. The last thing I remembered was the sight of Tokubei shaking his head, as if trying to clear it.

When I opened my eyes again, I knew that time had passed, but not how much time. My next thought was that it was cold. It was not only extremely cold but damp.

I rolled over and sat up. I reached immediately for my swords and found them safe on the ground beside me. *On the ground?* What was I doing on the ground? My last memory was of staying at an inn with a merchant called Tokubei.

The thought of Tokubei put me into a panic. I was his bodyguard, and instead of watching over him, I had fallen asleep and had awakened in a strange place.

I looked around frantically and saw that he was lying on the ground not far from where I was. Had he been killed?

I got up shakily, and when I stood up my head was swimming. But my sense of urgency gave some strength to my legs. I stumbled over to my employer and to my great relief found him breathing—breathing heavily, in fact.

When I shook his shoulder, he grunted and finally opened his eyes. "Where am I?" he asked thickly.

It was a reasonable question. I looked around and saw that we had been lying in a bamboo grove. By the light I guessed that it was early morning, and the reason I felt cold and damp was because my clothes were wet with dew.

"It's cold!" said Tokubei, shivering and climbing unsteadily to his feet. He looked around slowly, and his eyes became wide with disbelief. "What happened? I thought we were staying at an inn!"

His words came as a relief. One of the possibilities I had considered was that I had gone mad and that the whole episode with the inn was something I had imagined. Now I knew that Tokubei had the same memory of the inn. I had not imagined it.

But why were we out here on the cold ground, instead of on comfortable mattresses in the inn?

"They must have drugged us and robbed us," said Tokubei. He turned and looked at me furiously. "A fine bodyguard you are!"

There was nothing I could say to that. But at least we were both alive and unharmed. "Did they take all your money?" I asked.

Tokubei had already taken his wallet out of his sash and was peering inside. "That's funny! My money is still here!"

This was certainly unexpected. What did the innkeeper and his strange daughter intend to do by drugging us and moving us outside?

At least things were not as bad as we had feared. We had not lost anything except a comfortable night's sleep, although from the heaviness in my head I had certainly slept deeply enough—and long enough too. Exactly how much time had elapsed since we drank wine with our host?

All we had to do now was find the highway again and continue our journey. Tokubei suddenly chuckled. "I didn't even have to pay for our night's lodging!"

As we walked from the bamboo grove, I saw the familiar clump of bamboo shoots, and we found ourselves standing in the same clearing again. Before our eyes was the thatched house. Only it was somehow different. Perhaps things looked different in the daylight than at dusk.

But the difference was more than a change of light. As we approached the house slowly, like sleepwalkers, we saw that the thatching was much darker. On the previous evening the thatching had looked fresh and new. Now it was dark with age. Daylight should make things appear brighter, not darker. The plastering of the walls also looked more dingy.

Tokubei and I stopped to look at each other before we went closer. He was pale, and I knew that I looked no less frightened. Something was terribly wrong. I loosened my sword in its scabbard.

We finally gathered the courage to go up to the house. Since Tokubei seemed unable to find his voice, I spoke out. "Is anyone there?"

After a moment we heard shuffling footsteps and the front door slid open. The face of an old woman appeared. "Yes?" she inquired. Her voice was creaky with age.

What set my heart pounding with panic, however, was not her voice. It was the sight of her left hand holding on to the frame of the door. The hand was wrinkled and crooked with the arthritis of old age—and it had six fingers.

I heard a gasp beside me and knew that Tokubei had noticed the hand as well.

The door opened wider and a man appeared beside the old woman. At first I thought it was our host of the previous night. But this man was much younger, although the resemblance was strong. He carried himself straighter and his hair was black, while the innkeeper had been grizzled and slightly bent with age.

"Please excuse my mother," said the man. "Her hearing is not good. Can we help you in some way?"

Tokubei finally found his voice. "Isn't this the inn where we stayed last night?"

The man stared. "Inn? We are not innkeepers here!"

"Yes, you are!" insisted Tokubei. "Your daughter invited us in and served us with wine. You must have put something in the wine!"

The man frowned. "You are serious? Are you sure you didn't drink too much at your inn and wander off?"

"No, I didn't drink too much!" said Tokubei, almost shouting. "I hardly drank at all! Your daughter, the one with six fingers in her hand, started to pour me a second cup of wine . . ." His voice trailed off, and he stared again at the left hand of the old woman.

"I don't have a daughter," said the man slowly. "My mother here is the one who has six fingers in her left hand, although I hardly think it polite of you to mention it."

"I'm getting dizzy," muttered Tokubei and began to totter.

"I think you'd better come in and rest a bit," the man said to him gruffly. He glanced at me. "Perhaps you wish to join your friend. You don't share his delusion about the inn, I hope?"

"I wouldn't presume to contradict my elders," I said carefully. Since both Tokubei and the owner of the house were my elders, I wasn't committing myself. In truth I didn't know what to believe, but I did want a look at the inside of the house.

The inside was almost the same as it was before but the differences were there when I looked closely. We entered the same room with the alcove and the pair of painted doors. The vase I had admired was no longer there, but the doors showed the same landscapes painted by a master. I peered closely at the pictures and saw that the colors looked faded. What was more, the left panel, the one depicting a winter scene, had a long tear in one corner. It had been painstakingly mended, but the damage was impossible to hide completely.

Tokubei saw what I was staring at and he became even paler. At this stage we had both considered the possibility that a hoax of some sort had been played on us. The torn screen convinced Tokubei that our host had not played a joke: the owner of a valuable painting would never vandalize it for a trivial reason.

As for me, I was far more disturbed by the sight of the sixth finger on the old woman's hand. Could the young girl have disguised herself as an old crone? She could put rice powder in her hair to whiten it, but she could not transform her pretty straight fingers into old fingers twisted with arthritis. The woman here with us now was genuinely old, at least fifty years older than the girl.

It was this same old woman who finally gave us our

> ### Words to Know
>
> **hoax** (p. 341) a mischievous trick
>
> **vandalize** (p. 341) destroy willfully or senselessly
>
> **trivial** (p. 341) not important
>
> **crone** (p. 341) an old woman

greatest shock. "It's interesting that you should mention an inn, gentlemen," she croaked. "My father used to operate an inn. After he died, my husband and I turned this back into a private residence. We didn't need the income, you see."

"Your . . . your . . . f-father?" stammered Tokubei.

"Yes," replied the old woman. "He was a ronin, forced to go into innkeeping when he lost his position. But he never liked the work. Besides, our inn had begun to acquire an unfortunate reputation. Some of our guests disappeared, you see."

Even before she finished speaking, a horrible suspicion had begun to dawn on me. Her *father* had been an innkeeper, she said, her father who used to be a ronin. The man who had been our host was a ronin turned innkeeper. Could this mean that this old woman was actually the same person as the young girl we had seen?

I sat stunned while I tried to absorb the implications. What had happened to us? Was it possible that Tokubei and I had slept while this young girl grew into a mature woman, got married, and bore a son, a son who is now an adult? If that was the case, then we had slept for fifty years!

The old woman's next words confirmed my fears. "I recognize you now! You are two of the lost guests from our inn! The other lost ones I don't remember so well, but I remember *you* because your disappearance made me so sad. Such a handsome youth, I thought, what a pity he should have gone the way of the others!"

A high wail came from Tokubei, who began to keen and rock himself back and forth. "I've lost fifty years! Fifty years of my life went by while I slept at this accursed inn!"

The inn was indeed accursed. Was the fate of the other guests similar to ours? "Did anyone else return as we did, fifty years later?" I asked.

The old woman looked uncertain and turned to her son. He frowned thoughtfully. "From time to time wild-looking people have come to us with stories similar to

> ### Words to Know
> **keen** (p. 342) cry out in mourning
> **accursed** (p. 342) under a curse, doomed

yours. Some of them went mad with the shock."

Tokubei wailed again. "I've lost my business! I've lost my wife, my young and beautiful wife! We had been married only a couple of months!"

A gruesome chuckle came from the old woman. "You may not have lost your wife. It's just that she's become an old hag like me!"

That did not console Tokubei, whose keening became louder. Although my relationship with my employer had not been characterized by much respect on either side, I did begin to feel very sorry for him. He was right: he had lost his world.

As for me, the loss was less traumatic. I had left home under extremely painful circumstances, and had spent the next three years wandering. I had no friends and no one I could call a relation. The only thing I had was my duty to my employer. Somehow, some way, I had to help him.

"Did no one find an explanation for these disappearances?" I asked. "Perhaps if we knew the reason why, we might find some way to reverse the process."

The old woman began to nod eagerly. "The priestess! Tell them about the shrine priestess!"

"Well," said the man, "I'm not sure if it would work in your case. . . ."

"What? What would work?" demanded Tokubei. His eyes were feverish.

"There was a case of one returning guest who consulted the priestess at our local shrine," said the man. "She went into a trance and revealed that there was an evil spirit dwelling in the bamboo grove here. This spirit would put unwary travelers into a long, unnatural sleep. They would wake up twenty, thirty, or even fifty years later."

"Yes, but you said something worked in his case," said Tokubei.

The man seemed reluctant to go on. "I don't like to see you cheated, so I'm not sure I should be telling you this."

"Tell me! Tell me!" demanded Tokubei. The host's reluctance only made him more impatient.

"The priestess promised to make a spell that would

undo the work of the evil spirit," said the man. "But she demanded a large sum of money, for she said that she had to burn some very rare and costly incense before she could begin the spell."

At the mention of money Tokubei sat back. The hectic flush died down on his face and his eyes narrowed. "How much money?" he asked.

The host shook his head. "In my opinion the priestess is a fraud and makes outrageous claims about her powers. We try to have as little to do with her as possible."

"Yes, but did her spell work?" asked Tokubei. "If it worked, she's no fraud!"

"At least the stranger disappeared again," cackled the old woman. "Maybe he went back to his own time. Maybe he walked into a river."

Tokubei's eyes narrowed further. "How much money did the priestess demand?" he asked again.

"I think it was one gold piece for every year lost," said the host. He hurriedly added, "Mind you, I still wouldn't trust the priestess."

"Then it would cost me fifty gold pieces to get back to my own time," muttered Tokubei. He looked up. "I don't carry that much money with me."

"No, you don't," agreed the host.

Something alerted me about the way he said that. It was as if the host knew already that Tokubei did not carry much money on him.

Meanwhile Tokubei sighed. He had come to a decision. "I do have the means to obtain more money, however. I can send a message to my chief clerk and he will remit the money when he sees my seal."

"Your chief clerk may be dead by now," I reminded him.

"You're right!" moaned Tokubei. "My business will be under a new management and nobody will even remember my name!"

"And your wife will have remarried," said the old

woman, with one of her chuckles. I found it hard to believe that the gentle young girl who had served us wine could turn into this dreadful harridan.

"Sending the message may be a waste of time," agreed the host.

"What waste of time!" cried Tokubei. "Why shouldn't I waste time? I've wasted fifty years already! Anyway, I've made up my mind. I'm sending that message."

"I still think you shouldn't trust the priestess," said the host.

That only made Tokubei all the more determined to send for the money. However, he was not quite resigned to the amount. "Fifty gold pieces is a large sum. Surely the priestess can buy incense for less than that amount?"

"Why don't you try giving her thirty gold pieces?" cackled the old woman. "Then the priestess will send you back thirty years, and your wife will only be middle-aged."

While Tokubei was still arguing with himself about the exact sum to send for, I decided to have a look at the bamboo grove. "I'm going for a walk," I announced, rising and picking up my sword from the floor beside me.

The host turned sharply to look at me. For an instant a faint, rueful smile appeared on his lips. Then he looked away.

Outside, I went straight to the clump of shoots in the bamboo grove. On the previous night—or what I perceived as the previous night—I had noticed that clump of bamboo shoots particularly, because I had been so hungry that I pictured them being cut up and boiled.

The clump of bamboo shoots was still in the same place. That in itself proved nothing, since bamboo could spring up anywhere, including the place where a clump had existed fifty years earlier. But what settled the matter in my mind was that the clump looked almost exactly the way it did when I had seen it before, except that every shoot was about an inch taller. That was a reasonable amount for bamboo shoots to grow overnight.

Overnight. Tokubei and I had slept on the ground here overnight. We had not slept here for a period of fifty years.

Once I knew that, I was able to see another inconsistency: the door panels with the painted landscapes. The painting with the winter scene had been on the *right* last night and it was on the *left* this morning. It wasn't simply a case of the panels changing places, because the depressions in the panel for the handholds had been reversed. In other words, what I saw just now was not a pair of paintings faded and torn by age. They were an entirely different pair of paintings.

But how did the pretty young girl change into an old woman? The answer was that if the screens could be different ones, so could the women. I had seen one woman, a young girl, last night. This morning I saw a different woman, an old hag.

The darkening of the thatched roof? Simply blow ashes over the roof. The grizzled-haired host of last night could be the same man who claimed to be his grandson today. It would be a simple matter for a young man to put gray in his hair and assume a stoop.

And the purpose of the hoax? To make Tokubei send for fifty pieces of gold, of course. It was clever of the man to accuse the shrine priestess of fraud and pretend reluctance to let Tokubei send his message.

I couldn't even feel angry toward the man and his daughter—or mother, sister, wife, whatever. He could have killed me and taken my swords, which he clearly admired. Perhaps he was really a ronin and felt sympathetic toward another one.

When I returned to the house, Tokubei was looking resigned. "I've decided to send for the whole fifty gold pieces." He sighed.

"Don't bother," I said. "In fact we should be leaving as soon as possible. We shouldn't even stop here for a drink, especially not of wine."

Tokubei stared. "What do you mean? If I go back home, I'll find everything changed!"

"Nothing will be changed," I told him. "Your wife will be as young and beautiful as ever."

"I don't understand," he said. "Fifty years. . . ."

"It's a joke," I said. "The people here have a peculiar sense of humor, and they've played a joke on us."

Tokubei's mouth hung open. Finally he closed it with a snap. He stared at the host, and his face became first red and then purple. "You—you were trying to swindle me!" He turned furiously to me. "And you let them do this!"

"I'm not letting them," I pointed out. "That's why we're leaving right now."

"Are you going to let them get away with this?" demanded Tokubei. "They might try to swindle someone else!"

"They only went to this much trouble when they heard of the arrival of a fine fat fish like you," I said. I looked deliberately at the host. "I'm sure they won't be tempted to try the same trick again."

✳

"AND THAT'S THE END OF YOUR STORY?" ASKED MATSUZO. "You and Tokubei just went away? How did you know the so-called innkeeper wouldn't try the trick on some other luckless traveler?"

Zenta shook his head. "I didn't know. I merely guessed that once the trick was exposed, they wouldn't take the chance of trying it again. Of course I thought about revisiting the place to check if the people there were leading an honest life."

"Why didn't you?" asked Matsuzo. "Maybe we could go together. You've made me curious about that family now."

"Then you can satisfy your curiosity," said Zenta, smiling. He held his cup out for more tea, and the farmer's wife came forward to pour.

Only now she used both hands to hold the pot, and for the first time Matsuzo saw her left hand. He gasped. The hand had six fingers.

"Who was the old woman?" Zenta asked the farmer's wife.

"She was my grandmother," she replied. "Having six fingers is something that runs in my family."

At last Matsuzo found his voice. "You mean this is the very house you visited? This is the inn where time was lost?"

"Where we *thought* we lost fifty years," said Zenta. "Perhaps I should have warned you first. But I was almost certain that we'd be safe this time. And I see that I was right."

He turned to the woman again. "You and your husband are farmers now, aren't you? What happened to the man who was the host?"

"He's dead," she said quietly. "He was my brother, and he was telling you the truth when he said that he was a ronin. Two years ago he found work with another warlord, but he was killed in battle only a month later."

Matsuzo was peering at the pair of sliding doors, which he hadn't noticed before. "I see that you've put up the faded set of paintings. The winter scene is on the left side."

The woman nodded. "We sold the newer pair of doors. My husband said that we're farmers now and that people in our position don't need valuable paintings. We used the money to buy some new farm implements."

She took up the teapot again. "Would you like another cup of tea?" she asked Matsuzo.

Staring at her left hand, Matsuzo had a sudden qualm. "I—I don't think I want any more."

Everybody laughed.

About Lensey Namioka

Although she was born in China, Lensey Namioka has spent most of her life in the United States. She says, "For my writings I draw heavily on my Chinese cultural heritage and on my husband's Japanese cultural heritage." Some of her books, including *Island of Ogres* and *The Coming of the Bear*, continue the saga of Zenta and Matsuzo. She attributes her interest in the feudal period in Japan to her father-in-law.

Responding

1. **Personal Response** If you were Tokubei, how would you react to the news that fifty years have passed? Would you pay to go back in time? Explain.

2. **Literary Analysis** In the beginning of "The Inn of Lost Time," the farmer tells his boys about the legend of Urashima Taro. How does the farmer's story *foreshadow*, or hint at, the events that happen later?

3. **Theme Connection** Zenta says he was "a green, inexperienced youngster" when he traveled with Tokubei as a bodyguard. What do you think Zenta learned from that first trip with Tokubei?

Language Workshop

Commas in Compound Sentences Compound sentences have two or more independent clauses, which are often linked with one of these conjunctions: *and, yet, but, or, nor,* and *so.* Usually a comma is needed right before the conjunction. Notice how commas are used in this compound sentence from the story:

The inn was peaceful and quiet, and we soon discovered the reason why.

Correct the punctuation in the following sentences.

1. Tokubei frequently traveled to distant parts of the country and he expected his bodyguard to protect him.

2. Zenta was worried but, he hid his fears from Tokubei.

Writer's Portfolio

Imagine that you are a traveler who visits the "Inn of Lost Time" before Tokubei and Zenta stop there. Record a few entries in your travel diary that describe what happens to you during your stay.

WALTER DEAN MYERS

The Legacy

Malcolm Little was born in Omaha, Nebraska, on May 19, 1925. A series of tragedies split his family apart, and as a teenager Malcolm gradually drifted into a life on the street. But while serving time in prison for robbery, Malcolm became a convert of the Nation of Islam, a religious organization for African Americans that is based on the beliefs of Islam. Malcolm left behind his old way of life, and, following a Nation of Islam tradition, he took the last name "X" as a symbol of his lost African name. Malcolm X quickly rose to a position of national leadership within the Nation of Islam, but political differences eventually led him to break away from the organization. On February 21, 1965, Malcolm X was assassinated while delivering a speech at the Audubon Ballroom in Harlem.

WHO WAS MALCOLM X, AND WHAT IS HIS LEGACY? Malcolm's life seems so varied, he did so many things over the far too short thirty-nine years of his life, that it almost appears that there was not one Malcolm at all, but four distinct people. But in looking at Malcolm's life, in examining the expectations against what he actually did, we see a blending of the four Malcolms into one dynamic personality that is distinctively American in its character. For only a black man living in America could have gone through what Malcolm went through.

The first Malcolm was Malcolm the child, who lived in Nebraska and Michigan. He lived much like a million other black boys born in the United States. He was loved by two parents, Earl and Louise Little. From them he learned about morality, and decency, and the need to do well in school. His parents gave him a legacy of love, but also a legacy of pride.

Malcolm saw his father, a Baptist minister, at the meetings of the Universal Negro Improvement Association, saw him speaking about the black race, and about the possibility of justice. From what the young Malcolm saw, from what he experienced as a young child, one might have expected him, upon reaching maturity, to become a religious man and an activist for justice, as was his father.

Even when Earl Little was killed, Louise Little tried to hold the family together. Malcolm started school and did well. His mother saw to it that he did his assignments, and there was no doubt that Malcolm was bright. Bright children often understand their gifts, and it is possible that Malcolm understood his early on. He said in his autobiography that he had not given a lot of thought to what he wanted to do with those gifts when he was asked by a teacher in the eighth grade. A lawyer, he ventured.

Malcolm had not known exactly what he wanted to do with his talents, but he understood that the talents he possessed were valued in his schoolmates. The teacher said to him that it was not practical for him to be a lawyer, because he was black. The teacher probably thought of himself as being a realist. There is no use misleading Malcolm, he probably thought. Where does a black teenaged boy go, to what does he turn if he is not allowed the same avenues of value as his white friends?

The second Malcolm answers that question. The black teenager goes among his own people, and searches among the values of his peers for those he can use. So Malcolm bought the zoot suit, with the gold chain dangling against the pants leg. He bought the wide-brimmed hat and learned the hip jargon of the street, the same way teenagers today buy the gold chains and sneakers that cost enough to feed a family for a week. Malcolm was a human being, and human beings need to be able to look into the mirror and see something that pleases them. What had value in the American society that Malcolm knew? The conk had value, burning your hair until it was tortured enough to approximate the appearance of a white man's hair.

Malcolm said that he wanted to be a lawyer, to use his

> ### Words to Know
>
> **zoot suit** (p. 352) a stylish men's suit, popular in the 1940s, featuring a long coat and baggy trousers that narrowed at the cuff
>
> **conk** (p. 352) a hair treatment that straightened hair by applying harsh chemicals to it

mind. He was told that no, he couldn't do that because he was black. Perhaps it wouldn't have made any difference what the teacher had said. As was the case with so many black teenagers, Malcolm's family, now with only the mother to support it, would not have been able to afford college for him.

Malcolm toughened himself. Malcolm used his mind. If he couldn't use it to study law, he would use it in street hustles. He used it in making money the way people in the inner cities who don't have "downtown" jobs make money. Eventually he used it to commit burglaries. Some societies never learn that to make a person socially responsible you must first include him or her in your society. Malcolm's career as a petty criminal, much sensationalized in the autobiography he never got to read, ended quickly when he was caught, tried, and sentenced to eight to ten years in prison.

The second Malcolm, the one using his wits to survive on the streets, skirting both sides of the law, might have continued after he was released if it were not for the Nation of Islam. Elijah Muhammad claimed that he lifted Malcolm up and saved him from a life of degradation. Nothing was more truthful. The Nation of Islam, with its strict moral codes, its religion, its understanding, forgiveness, and even celebration of black men who had fallen by the wayside, was the garden from which the third Malcolm emerged.

> **People to Know**
>
> **Elijah Muhammad** (p. 353) an early leader of the Nation of Islam
>
> **Jomo Kenyatta** (p. 354) an African political leader and the president of Kenya from 1964-1978
>
> **Marcus Garvey** (p. 356) an African American leader during the 1920s who launched a movement to return to Africa
>
> **El Hajj Malik el Shabazz** (p. 358) After Malcolm X made his pilgrimage to Mecca, he took this as his new name.

Here now was Malcolm the religious man, the activist, the thinker, the man who stood up for his people, who confronted the forces of injustice in America at a time when black people were being beaten in the streets, were being publicly humiliated and even killed. Here was a Malcolm who offered himself as the voice of the defeated, the manliness of a people who badly needed manliness.

And he was a worker. He organized and preached. He cajoled and threatened. He attacked racism with the biting tone of the absolute cynic, vowing to attain freedom by any means necessary and with any sacrifice. He understood, as few other leaders did, that there were people like himself in the streets, and in the prisons, who had contributions to make. He included people in the struggle for human rights in America who had never before been included. This was the third Malcolm.

Malcolm grew. He grew away from the Nation of Islam, and away from the separatist philosophy of that organization. The Nation of Islam had returned to him the wings that had been taken from him because of his color, and Malcolm, the fourth Malcolm, found himself able to fly.

Words to Know

separatist (p. 354) someone who believes people of different religions or cultures should live separated from one another

atheism (p. 354) the belief that there is no God

What one would have expected, or at least hoped for, on meeting the wide-eyed boy in the Pleasant Grove Elementary School, was that he would one day touch the edge of greatness. It is what we wish for all children. The fourth Malcolm—the one with his head slightly bowed as he listened to Jomo Kenyatta, the great African leader, the one learning firsthand about the liberation of the African continent so that he could liberate his own—had touched the edge of that greatness.

Malcolm's life was about growth, about the intensely changing man that moved from thievery to honesty, from being a racial separatist to searching for true brotherhood, and from atheism to Islam.

But his life was also about the return to the idealism of his childhood. The world of the child, before he or she is exposed to racism, before he or she is conditioned to react to the hurts inflicted on him or her, is one of acceptance and love. Malcolm had grown, and in that growing had learned to accept those people, regardless of race or nationality, who accepted and loved him.

Malcolm spoke for the voiceless, for the people from whom not even some black leaders wanted to hear. He spoke for the jobless, and for the homeless. He spoke for the young men whose hard bodies, bodies that could perform miracles on inner-city basketball courts, were not wanted in America's offices. He spoke for the millions of black Americans who saw themselves as a minority in a world in which most of the inhabitants were people of color like themselves. He spoke for the men and women who had to turn too many other cheeks, had to fight off too many insults with nothing but smiles.

Malcolm had walked in their shoes, and they knew it when they heard him speak.

Thurgood Marshall, civil rights lawyer and, later, Supreme Court justice, understood the court system and the importance of having a legal basis for protest. He understood that for years racists and their supporters could simply hide behind the issue of legality, claiming that the only reason schools were segregated, the only reason housing was denied blacks, the only reason it was difficult to vote in certain places, was because of certain laws that had been on the books for years, and then work to prevent changes in the law.

Martin Luther King, Jr., knew the power of public persuasion. Racists and bigots wanted to look as if they were in the right. They wanted their families and friends to think that they were protecting southern women, or law and order, or even something as vague as a "way of life." He understood that nonviolence, in the wake of police dogs, and fire hoses, would attract a favorable world opinion of African Americans.

But Malcolm, coming from the awareness of the Garvey tradition, and coming from the same street corners on which he would later "fish for the dead," having experienced the same hunger, the same frustrations, even the same jails as poor blacks did, understood something else as well: that all the goals of the mainstream civil rights movement, the civil rights laws, school integration, voting rights, none of these would have meaning if African Americans still thought of themselves as a racially crippled people, if they still walked with their heads down because they were black.

In the last year of his life, having grown away from the Nation of Islam, and having made a spiritual pilgrimage to Mecca, Malcolm was moving both to a new and an old place. He was moving more solidly into Pan-Africanism, the territory that his father had explored over forty years before.

Malcolm's message is remembered by many people who find comfort and inspiration in it today. One of them is the African American poet Wopashitwe Mondo Eyen we Langa, who wrote the poem "Great Bateleur." A bateleur is a reddish-brown eagle found in Africa. It is notable for its acrobatic flying style and its ferocious cry as it dives to capture its prey.

Great Bateleur

we were pigeons, Malcolm
congregating at the park benches of america
to peck at the crumbs of america's wealth
but you were a bateleur
you did not coo at men's feet
gratefully bobbing your head for cast away scraps

we were wrens and sparrows
good survivors
good at nervous flight
from any sound or sight of fearsome threat
we could not
would not
hold our ground and fight
perhaps you feared like us
but you did not quiver
but thrust forward sharp talons boldly
yours were not the frantic chirpings
of timidity and self-doubt
but the righteous clamor of indignation

we were ducklings waddling in shame
thinking ourselves ugly
seeking disguise in feathers that were foreign to us
but you hid yourself from no one
but sailed in the daylight
stretching your wings to soar

we were those who begged, Malcolm
who could not find courage
nor faith in ourselves
who could not peer into reflecting pools
nor look each other in the face
and see the beauty that was ours
but for you, Malcolm
but for you, Great Bateleur
Eagle of Africa
still your spirit flies.

Perhaps history will tell us that there were no wrong strategies in the civil rights movement of the sixties. That all factors involved, the pray-ins, the legal cases, the marches, the militancy, were all vital to the time, that each had its place. Undoubtedly, too, as current needs color memories of distant events, we will bring different concepts from that period of American history, and different voices. One voice that we will not forget is that of El Hajj Malik el Shabazz, the man we called Malcolm.

About Walter Dean Myers

Walter Dean Myers grew up in New York City, where he remembers "the bright sun on Harlem streets, the easy rhythms of black and brown bodies moving along the tar and asphalt pavement." Myers liked to read as a boy but wasn't especially interested in books until his fifth grade teacher tore  up his comic and handed him a stack of good books.

In high school, his father helped him buy a typewriter, which he used to write short stories and poems. By the time Myers had completed his service in the Army, he knew he wanted to be a writer: "Writing, being a writer, is wonderful. I love it more than anything else in the world."

Myers has written many books for young adults, including *Scorpions*, *The Outside Shot*, and *Fallen Angels*.

Responding

1. **Personal Response** What were your impressions of Malcolm X before reading this selection? What are your impressions now?

2. **Literary Analysis** The poem "Great Bateleur" compares Malcolm X to an African eagle. How is Malcolm X like the bateleur? What does this *figurative language* reveal about Malcolm X?

3. **Theme Connection** Malcolm X's life can be described as a journey. Compare that journey with one of the other journeys you have read about in this unit. What do the two journeys have in common? How are they different?

Language Workshop

Suffixes *-ness* and *-less* When the suffixes *-ness* and *-less* are added to words, they change the meaning of the words. The suffix *-ness* means "the condition of being." For example, the word *greatness* means "the condition of being great." The suffix *-less* means "without" or "incapable of being." The word *homeless*, for example, means "being without a home."

Find at least four more examples in "The Legacy" of words that end with *-less* or *-ness*. Write a brief definition of each of the words.

Writer's Portfolio

Walter Dean Myers explains how Malcolm X changed and grew over the course of his life. Choose an issue in your life. Describe how you feel about it now, and predict what your attitude toward this issue will be in ten and in thirty more years.

Journeys

PROJECTS

Dramatic Moments

The journeys you have read about in this unit all have their "dramatic moments." Working in small groups, choose one or more of these moments and reenact them for your class. You may want to write additional dialogue for the characters, and think of props you can use to suggest the setting.

Songs of the Road

All around the world, people have composed songs and poems about unusual journeys. With a group, write a song or poem that describes one of the journeys you have read about in this unit. Perform your song or poem for the class.

Writing About Journeys

Think of a memorable journey you have taken. It could be a real journey, like a trip to the mountains, or a figurative one, like your "journey" from kindergarten to the grade you're in now. Write an essay that compares your journey to that of one of the characters in this unit. What did you each learn from your journey? What obstacles, if any, did each of you encounter along the way? Were either of you changed by your journey?

FURTHER READING

When one journey ends, you can plan another. Continue your travels with the following selections.

The Old Man and the Sea by Ernest Hemingway. When a gigantic marlin takes the bait, an old fisherman hooks the catch of his life. As the marlin fights for its life by pulling the fishing boat far out to sea, the old man's fishing trip becomes a journey of the soul.

Homecoming by Cynthia Voigt. When their mother abandons them, thirteen-year-old Dicey Tillerman takes charge of her younger sister and two brothers. Together they set off on a long and possibly futile journey toward the home of a grandmother they've never met.

The Odyssey by Homer. After the Trojan Wars, Odysseus has many adventures on his long voyage before he reaches home and is reunited with his wife.

The Coming of the Bear by Lensey Namioka. Zenta and Matsuzo continue their adventures when their boat is washed ashore in the land of the Ainu.

Call of the Wild by Jack London. During the Alaskan gold rush, a stolen dog learns that only the fittest can survive in harsh world of the Klondike. As Buck is transformed from a mild pet to a rugged, fearless work dog, he finds it hard to resist the lure of the wilderness.

Dogsong by Gary Paulsen. Russel, a fourteen-year-old Inuit boy, travels across the Alaskan tundra to get away from home and his own unhappiness.

GLOSSARY

abscess (ab′ ses) *n.* collection of fluid resulting from an infection

abuse (ə byüz′) *v.* use harsh and insulting language

abutment (ə but′ mənt) *n.* support for an arch or bridge

accelerate (ak sel′ ə rāt′) *v.* speed up

accommodations (ə kom′ ə dā′ shənz) *n.* lodging and food

accursed (ə ker′ sid) *adj.* under a curse; doomed

aerobics (er′ ō′ biks) *n.* type of exercise that increases the body's use of oxygen and strengthens the heart

afghan (af′ gan) *n.* shawl or blanket that is knitted or crocheted

allegiance (ə lē′ jəns) *n.* loyalty

alliterate (ə lit′ ə rāt′) *v.* use words with the same sound repeatedly

amid (ə mid′) *prep.* surrounded by

ancestry (an′ ses′ trē) *n.* line of descent from ancestors

angina pectoris (an ji′ nə   pek′tər is) *n.* serious condition of the heart involving chest pains and breathing difficulty

anguish (ang′ gwish) *n.* extreme pain; great suffering

animatedly (an′ ə mā′ tid lē) *adv.* in a lively way

apprentice (ə pren′ tis) *n.* person learning a trade or art; beginner

arabesque (ar′ ə besk′) *n.* a pose on one leg with the other leg extended horizontally behind

ardent (ärd′ nt) *adj.* very enthusiastic; eager

arrest (ə rest′) *v.* stop

articulate (är tik′ yə lāt) *v.* express clearly

Assiniboin (ə sin′ ə boin′) *n.* Plains Indian tribe whose members now live primarily in Montana and the Canadian provinces of Alberta and Saskatchewan

atheism (ā′ thē iz′ əm) *n.* belief that there is no God

audible (ô′ də bəl) *adj.* loud enough to be heard

avenge (ə venj′) *v.* take revenge; get back at

avert (ə vert′) *v.* turn away

ball and chain slang term referring to marriage as a trap or burden

barrio (bär′ ē ō) *n.* Spanish word for neighborhood

battalion (bə tal′ yən) *n.* military unit of soldiers

bearing (ber′ ing) *n.* way of standing, sitting, walking, or behaving

belligerency (bə lij′ ər ən sē) *n.* stubborn hostility

bellow (bel′ ō) *v.* make a loud, roaring noise

beribbon (bi rib′ ən) *v.* adorn or decorate with ribbons

berth (berth) *n.* place to sleep on a ship, train, or plane

bespectacled (bi spek′ tə kəld) *adj.* wearing glasses

beveled (bev′ əld) *adj.* curved or slanted

binge (binj) *n.* eating spree; bout of indulgence

bionic (bī on′ ik) *adj.* having both biological and electronic parts

biscuit-polished polished with a biscuit

bland (bland) *adj.* smoothly agreeable and polite; dull

bleak (blēk) *adj.* bare; desolate; dismal

boomerang (bü′ mə rang′) *n.* curved piece of wood that, when thrown, returns to the thrower

bore (bôr) *v.* drill a hole; penetrate

brazen (brā′ zn) *adj.* bold; shameless

brazier (brā′ zhər) *n.* large metal pan that holds burning charcoal or coal

brooding (brüd′ ing) *adj.* worried and gloomy

Brylcreem (bril′ krēm) *n.* brand name of a hair gel that makes hair shiny

buck the system rebel; refuse to go along

cajole (kə jōl′) *v.* persuade by pleasant words or flattery; coax

callused (kal′ əst) *adj.* hardened from constant pressure or friction. Also **calloused**.

capitalist (kap′ ə tə list) *n.* person who supports a capitalist form of government; wealthy person

casually (kazh′ ü əl ē) *adv.* informally; irregularly

cataract (kat′ ə rakt′) *n.* cloudy film in the eye that can cause blindness

chaperone (shap′ ə rōn) *v.* act as an older guide or companion to ensure safety and proper behavior

cherish (cher′ ish) *v.* hold dear; care for

clad (klad) *adj.* clothed

cleaver (klē′ vər) *n.* cutting tool with a large, heavy blade and a short handle

clique (klik) *n.* small, exclusive group of people

clone (klōn) *n.* an exact copy of an original form

coddle (kod′ l) *v.* treat tenderly; pamper

commando (kə man′ dō) *n.* soldier trained to make brief surprise raids in enemy territory

compel (kəm pel′) *v.* urge with force

confiscate (kon′ fə skāt) *v.* seize by authority; take and keep

conformist (kən fôr′ mist) *n.* someone who goes along with the rules

conk (kongk) *n.* hair treatment that straightens hair by applying harsh chemicals to it

conniving (kə nīv′ ing) *adj.* secretly plotting or doing something wrong

crescent-shaped shaped like a quarter moon

cringe (krinj) *v.* crouch in fear

crone (krōn) *n.* old woman

cubbyhole (kub′ ē hōl′) *n.* small, enclosed place

davenport (dav′ ən pôrt) *n.* long, upholstered sofa

decrepit (di krep′ it) *adj.* broken down; weakened by old age

default (di fôlt′) *n.* in place of or in the absence of

defense mechanism self-protective reaction

degradation (deg′ rə dā′ shən) *n.* dishonorable or lowered condition

delirium (di lir′ ē əm) *n.* temporary disorder of the mind that occurs during fevers

desolate (des′ ə lit) *adj.* unhappy; empty

dishevelment (də shev′ əl mənt) *n.* state of disorder; messiness

disparity (dis par′ ə tē) *n.* difference; being unalike

disperse (dis pėrs′) *v.* scatter; go off in different directions

doily (doi′ lē) *n.* small piece of linen, lace, paper, or plastic, usually with small holes, used as a decoration under objects on a table or shelf

downcast (doun′ kast′) *adj.* sad; discouraged

downgrade (doun′ grād′) *n.* downward slope

drab (drab) *adj.* lacking brightness or color; dull

dribble (drib′ əl) *v.* bounce a ball

due process of law following the proper steps stated by law

earnest (ėr′ nist) *adj.* strong and firm in purpose; serious

eavesdrop (ēvz′ drop′) *v.* listen to a conversation that one is not supposed to hear

eligibility (el′ ə jə bil′ ə tē) *n.* fitness to be chosen

encrusted (en krust′ əd) *adj.* decorated with a layer of costly material

est (est) *n.* acronym for Erhard Seminar Training, a program of psychological therapy developed by Werner Erhard that stresses self-fulfillment

evacuation (i vak′ yü ā′ shən) *n.* withdrawal or removal

exclusion zone area within which certain people are not allowed

execute (ek′ sə kyüt) *v.* carry out; perform

extraterrestrial (ek′ strə tə res′ trē əl) *adj.* outside the earth; from outer space

extricate (ek′ strə kāt) *v.* set free from; release

exude (eg züd′) *v.* give forth; emit

exultantly (eg zult′ nt lē) *adv.* triumphantly; rejoicingly

fanatic (fə nat′ ik) *n.* person who is carried away beyond reason because of feelings or beliefs, especially in matters of religion or politics

faultlessly (fôlt′ lis lē) *adv.* perfectly

fetish (fet′ ish) *n.* material object regarded with great affection, reverence, or superstition

finesse (fə nes′) *n.* graceful skill

fixated (fik′ sāt əd) *adj.* very interested in or attached to

flask (flask) *n.* small bottle

flicker (flik′ ər) *v.* move quickly or lightly

flintstone (flint′ stōn′) *n.* very hard granular quartz used with steel to start fires

flounder (floun′ dər) *v.* struggle awkwardly without making much progress

fluted (flü′ tid) *adj.* having long, round grooves

foreman (fôr′ mən) *n.* person in charge of a group of workers or of some part of a factory

forge (fôrj) *v.* move forward slowly but steadily

forthright (fôrth′ rīt′) *adj.* straightforward; direct

fortnight (fôrt′ nīt) *n.* two weeks

fraud (frôd) *n.* fake; cheater; imposter

freeze (frēz) *v.* become motionless

garnish (gär′ nish) *v.* withhold part of a paycheck to pay a debt

gawk (gôk) *v.* stare rudely or stupidly

grimy (grī′ mē) *adj.* covered with grime; very dirty

gripe (grīp) *v.* complain

grizzled (griz′ əld) *adj.* gray

groomed (grümd) *adj.* well cared for; made to look attractive

grudging (gruj′ ing) *adj.* giving unwillingly

grueling (grü′ ə ling) *adj.* very tiring

gruesome (grü′ səm) *adj.* causing fear or horror

gruffness (gruf′ nes) *n.* rough, rude, or unfriendly manner

guard (gärd) *v.* in sports, to try to keep another player from scoring

gully (gul′ ē) *n.* narrow gorge; small ravine; ditch

haggard (hag′ ərd) *adj.* looking worn from pain, fatigue, worry, hunger, etc.

hamlet (ham′ lit) *n.* small village

hammerlock (ham′ ər lok′) *n.* wrestling hold in which an opponent's arm is twisted and held behind the opponent's back

harbor (här′ bər) *v.* have and keep in mind

harridan (har′ ə dən) *n.* bad-tempered old woman

harried (har′ ēd) *adj.* worried; having lots of problems

hatemonger (hāt′ mon′ gər) *n.* someone who spreads hatred

hoax (hōks) *n.* mischievous trick

hokey (hō′ kē) *adj.* slang term that means trivial, silly, or fake

holler (hol′ ər) *v.* cry out or shout loudly

Huichol (wē chōl′) *n.* Indian tribe whose members live mainly in the Mexican states of Jalisco and Nayarit

humanoid (hyü′ mə noid) *n.* being that has human qualities

husky (hus′ kē) *adj.* big and strong

hypocrite (hip′ ə krit) *n.* person who is not sincere; pretender

idiocy (id′ ē ə sē) *n.* great stupidity

immovable (i mü′ və bəl) *adj.* cannot be moved

inadequacy (in ad′ ə kwə sē) *n.* deficiency; shortcoming

incendiary bomb bomb that is made to start fires

incline (in′ klin) *n.* slope

incoherently (in′ kō hir′ ənt lē) *adv.* with no logical connection of ideas

income tax return annual report filed with the government that states how much money one has earned during the year

incommunicado (in′ kə myü′ nə kä′ dō) *adj.* without any way of communicating with others

incurably (in kyur′ ə blē) *adv.* not able to be cured

indignant (in dig′ nənt) *adj.* angry at something that is unfair or wrong

inevitable (in ev′ ə tə bəl) *adj.* sure to happen; unavoidable

infest (in fest′) *v.* spread or swarm in large numbers

infiltrate (in′ fil trāt) *v.* become part of an organization or institution for the purpose of spying

innumerable (i nü′ mər ə bəl) *adj.* too many to count

inquisition (in′ kwə zish′ ən) *n.* thorough investigation or questioning

inseparable (in sep′ ər ə bəl) *adj.* constantly together

intensify (in ten′ sə fi) *v.* strengthen and increase

intently (in tent′ lē) *adv.* with much interest

intercept (in′ tər sept′) *v.* stop or prevent

interject (in′ tər jekt′) *v.* insert abruptly; throw in between other things

interminable (in tėr′ mə nə bəl) *adj.* long and tiring; endless

intern (in tėrn′) *v.* force to stay in a certain place

intuition (in′ tü ish′ ən) *n.* knowing or understanding without using reason

iota (ī ō′ tə) *n.* tiny part or amount

Issei (ē′ sā′) *n.* first-generation immigrants who were born in Japan

jar (jär) *v.* shock

jargon (jär′ gən) *n.* language used by a special group or members of the same profession

jostle (jos′ əl) *v.* shove; push; crowd against

keen (kēn) *v.* cry out in mourning

laboriously (lə bôr′ ē əs lē) *adv.* with great effort

laceration (las′ ə rā′ shən) *n.* wound; rough tear

lacquered (lak′ ərd) *adj.* painted with shellac or varnished

laden (lād′ n) *adj.* loaded

lapel (lə pel′) *n.* part of the front of a coat folded back just below the collar

legacy (leg′ ə sē) *n.* something that has been handed down from someone who came before

leotard (lē′ ə tärd) *n.* tight-fitting, one-piece garment often worn during exercises

leper (lep′ ər) *n.* person who has leprosy, a contagious disease that damages the skin and nerves and can cause numbness, paralysis, and deformity

leverage (lev′ ər ij) *n.* bargaining power

linger (ling′ gər) *v.* stay or go slowly, as if unwilling to leave

literally (lit′ ər ə lē) *adv.* actually

lounge (lounj) *v.* pass time lazily or at one's ease

louse (lous) *n.* small bloodsucking insect that infests the hair or skin of people and animals

lubricate (lü′ brə kāt) *v.* apply oil, grease, or other substance to make something run smoothly

lyre (lir) *n.* ancient stringed musical instrument somewhat like a small harp

lyric (lir′ ik) *n.* short poem expressing personal emotion

makeshift (māk′ shift′) *adj.* used temporarily as a substitute

malleable (mal′ ē ə bəl) *adj.* easily shaped or influenced

malnutrition (mal′ nü trish′ ən) *n.* lack of proper nutrition

manicure (man′ ə kyur) *n.* trimming and cleaning of the fingernails

manicured (man′ ə kyürd) *adj.* carefully tended or trimmed

maudlin (môd′ lən) *adj.* sentimental in a weak, silly way

meager (mē′ gər) *adj.* poor or scanty

Member of Parliament elected official who serves on Parliament, the term for the highest lawmaking body in Canada, Great Britain, and some other countries

menacingly (men′ is ing lē) *adv.* threateningly

mess (mes) *n.* slang for a cute, stylish, or extraordinary person

meter (mē′ tər) *n.* poetic rhythm

miffed (mift) *adj.* offended; irritated

mill (mil) *v.* move in a confused group

minstrel (min′ strəl) *n.* musician

minutiae (mi nü′ shē ē) *n.* very small matters

miser (mi′ zər) *n.* someone who loves money and hates to share it

mobile (mō′ bəl) *adj.* able to move around easily

momentarily (mō′ mən ter′ ə lē) *adv.* for a moment

morose (mə rōs′) *adj.* gloomy; sullen

mute (myüt) *v.* soften; make dull

nauseatingly (nô′ zē āt′ ing lē) *adv.* sickeningly

nonmotorized (non′ mō′ tə rizd) *adj.* run without a motor

nuance (nü′ äns) *n.* shade of expression, meaning, feeling, etc.

obnoxious (əb nok′ shəs) *adj.* very disagreeable; offensive

ode (ōd) *n.* lyric poem full of noble feeling expressed with dignity

offstage (ôf′ stāj′) *adj., adv.* away from or behind a stage

ogle (ō′ gəl) *v.* look at with desire; stare at

ominous (om′ ə nəs) *adj.* unfavorable; threatening

ominously (om′ ə nəs lē) *adv.* threateningly

optical recorder machine that records visual images: for example, a camera

outcast (out′ kast′) *n.* one who has been rejected by his or her peer group

outlying (out/ li/ ing) *adj.* lying outside the boundary; far from the center

overpass (ō/ vər pas/) *n.* bridge over a road or railroad

parasite (par/ ə sīt) *n.* someone or something that lives off of others

patronizing (pā/trə nīz ing) *adj.* condescending or haughty

perplexity (pər plek/ sə tē) *n.* confusion

perverse (pər vėrs/) *adj.* obstinately opposing what is wanted, reasonable, or required

petty (pet/ ē) *adj.* having little importance or value; small

philosophy (fə los/ ə fē) *n.* system or way of thinking that guides life and decisions

piazza (pē az/ ə) *n.* large porch

pig wallow mudhole that a pig lies in

pincers (pin/ sərz) *n.* tool for gripping and holding tight, made like a scissors but with jaws instead of blades

piston (pis/ tən) *n.* flat, round piece of wood or metal, fitting closely inside a tube or hollow cylinder in which it is moved back and forth, often by the force of vapor combustion or steam

pivot (piv/ ət) *v.* turn or swing around without taking a step

placate (plā/ kāt) *v.* soothe or satisfy the anger of

placid (plas/ id) *adj.* calm; peaceful

pliant (plī/ ənt) *adj.* bending easily; flexible

plummet (plum/ it) *v.* plunge or drop

ply (plī) *v.* work at

poetical (pō et/ ə kəl) *adj.* showing beautiful or noble language, imagery, or thought

poignant (poi/ nyənt) *adj.* painful

pointer (poin/ tər) *n.* hint; tip; suggestion

posted (pōst/ əd) *v.* put along a route

precocious (pri kō/ shəs) *adj.* developed earlier than usual in knowledge or skill

preen (prēn) *v.* show pride in oneself; show off

prefabricated (prē fab/ rə kāt əd) *adj.* prepared in advance at a factory with standardized parts

prejudiced (prej/ ə dist) *adj.* unjust or unfair, based on personal feelings

premium (prē/ mē əm) *n.* amount of money paid for insurance

prime (prīm) *adj.* best time, stage, or state

privation (prī vā/ shən) *n.* lack of the comforts or necessities of life

propel (prə pel/) *v.* drive or push forward

prune (prün) *v.* cut off useless or undesirable twigs or branches

psyched (sikt) *adj.* mentally ready

punctuate (pungk/ chü āt) *v.* give point or emphasis to

qualm (kwäm) *n.* doubt

quaver (kwā/ vər) *n.* a shaking or trembling, especially of the voice

rant and rave scold violently

ravage (rav/ ij) *v.* damage greatly; destroy

rebound (rē/ bound/) *n.* in basketball, a ball that bounces off the backboard or basket rim after a shot has been attempted

recollection (rek/ ə lek/ shən) *n.* memory

refute (ri fyüt/) *v.* prove to be false or incorrect

relegate (rel/ ə gāt) *v.* put into a lower condition or position

relentless (ri lent/ lis) *adj.* merciless; unyielding

remedy (rem/ ə dē) *n.* cure or means of curing a problem or disease

remit (ri mit´) *v.* send money

resignedly (ri zīn´ əd lē´) *adv.* with an attitude of acceptance; giving up without complaint

resounding (ri zoun´ ding) *adj.* sounding loudly; ringing

retrace (ri trās´) *v.* go or trace back over

reverie (rev´ ər ē) *n.* dreamy thoughts

revitalize (rē vī´ tə līz) *v.* put new life into; restore

riddled (rid´ ld) *adj.* spread throughout; filled with

rig (rig) *n.* truck

riser (rī´ zər) *n.* long, low platform

rival (rī´ vəl) *n.* competitor; one who competes for the same thing as another

ronin (rō´ nin) *n.* person trained as a samurai in the military class in feudal Japan, but who was not in the service of any master

rueful (rü´ fəl) *adj.* sorrowful

ruefully (rü´ fəl lē) *adv.* unhappily; with sorrow

rummage (rum´ ij) *v.* search by moving things about in a disorderly way

sabotage (sab´ ə täzh) *n.* act of destruction done to harm a nation's war effort

sadistic (sə dis´ tik) *adj.* cruel; taking pleasure in causing others pain

safe-deposit box locked box used for storing valuables

salami (sə lä´ mē) *n.* kind of thick sausage often flavored with garlic

salivary (sal´ ə ver´ ē) *adj.* producing saliva

sallow (sal´ ō) *adj.* having a sickly, yellowish color

samurai (sam´ u ri) *n.* member of the military class in feudal Japan

sanction (sangk´ shən) *v.* support or approve

sassiness (sas´ ē nes) *n.* pertness; self-confidence

satchel (sach´ əl) *n.* small bag for carrying clothes

saunter (sôn´ tər) *v.* stroll; walk leisurely

sensuality (sen´ shü al´ ə tē) *n.* sensual nature; enjoyment of the pleasures of the senses

separatist (sep´ ər ə tist) *n.* someone who believes people of different religions or cultures should live separated from one another

sequence (sē´ kwəns) *n.* order of events; succession

serial (sir´ ē əl) *n.* movie shown as a series, one part at a time

shakedown (shāk´ doun´) *n.* taking of someone's money by force

shamble (sham´ bəl) *v.* walk awkwardly or unsteadily

shard (shärd) *n.* broken piece or fragment

sibling (sib´ ling) *n.* brother or sister

Sierra Madre Oriental eastern range of the Sierra Madre mountain chain

slam dunk in basketball, to slam a ball through a basket from above

sociopathic (so´ sē ə path´ ik) *adj.* antisocial; having no sense of responsibility toward others

span (span) *n.* part of a bridge that runs between the supports

spot (spot) *n.* spotlight; bright light

sputter (sput´ ər) *v.* speak confusedly

statuette (stach´ ü et´) *n.* small statue

staunch (stônch) *adj.* strong and firm; loyal and steadfast

stevedore (stē´ və dôr) *n.* person employed at a port to load and unload ships

stiff (stif) *n.* slang for a dead body

stricken (strik´ ən) *adj.* banished or removed from; hit, wounded, or affected by a weapon, disease, trouble, sorrow, and so on

subdued (səb düd´) *adj.* toned down; softened

subside (səb sīd´) *v.* die down; lessen

subversive (səb vėr´ siv) *adj.* tending to undermine, overthrow, or destroy tradition

sullen (sul´ ən) *adj.* gloomy; dismal; quietly angry

sundry goods various items, such as pens and paper, sewing notions, and other odds and ends

swindle (swin´ dl) *v.* cheat

sympathetic (sim´ pə thet´ ik) *adj.* sharing another's sorrow or trouble; having the same feelings

sympathizer (sim´ pə thīz´ ər) *n.* person who shares or agrees with a feeling or opinion

tantrum (tan´ trəm) *n.* fit of bad temper

thicket (thik´ it) *n.* thick, dense mass

threshold (thresh´ ōld) *n.* doorway; beginning point

throes (thrōz) *n.* great pain; agony

tofu (tō´ fü) *n.* cheeselike food consisting of curds coagulated from soy milk

totter (tot´ ər) *v.* stand or walk with shaky, unsteady steps

treachery (trech´ ər ē) *n.* breaking of faith; disloyalty

trifle (trī´ fəl) *v.* play with

trivial (triv´ ē əl) *adj.* not important

tuberculosis (tü bėr´ kyə lō´ sis) *n.* infectious disease affecting various tissues of the body, most often the lungs

turnstile (tėrn´ stīl´) *n.* post with bars that turn, used to let people in or out of a place

twingy (twinj´ ē) *adj.* involving individual sharp pains

U.S. Defense Bonds bonds sold by the U.S. government to raise money for war

ultimate (ul´ tə mit) *adj.* greatest possible

uneasily (un ēz´ i lē) *adv.* with restlessness or discomfort

unison (yü´ nə sən) *n.* harmonious combination; agreement

unwary (un wer´ ē) *adj.* careless; unguarded

upend (up end´) *v.* turn over; set on end

vague (vāg) *adj.* not definitely or clearly expressed

vandalize (van´ dl īz) *v.* destroy willfully or senselessly

verandah (və ran´ də) *n.* large porch

vindictive (vin dik´ tiv) *adj.* wanting to take revenge

wage (wāj) *v.* carry on

waive (wāv) *v.* give up

wheezy (hwē´ zē) *adj.* having a hissing or whistling sound as with difficult breathing

whereby (hwer bī´) *conj.* by which

whitewash (hwīt´ wosh´) *v.* cover up faults or mistakes

wily (wī´ lē) *adj.* sly; crafty and deceiving

wisp (wisp) *n.* thin, little thing

womanishness (wum´ ə nish nəs) *n.* for young girls, behavior that seems too old for their age

wrath (rath) *n.* very great anger; rage

wriggle (rig´ əl) *v.* twist and turn

Zen (zen) *n.* Japanese form of Buddhism that emphasizes meditation and intuition as means of achieving spiritual enlightenment

zoot suit stylish men's suit, popular in the 1940s, featuring a long coat and baggy trousers that narrowed at the cuff

ACKNOWLEDGMENTS

vi Foreword by Robert Cormier © 1994 by ScottForesman, Glenview, Illinois.

viii, ix, and *xi* Thomas Wolfe, *The Web and the Rock.* Harper, 1939.

2 "Growing Up" by Gary Soto from *Baseball in April and Other Stories* by Gary Soto, pages 121–134. Copyright © 1990 by Gary Soto. Reprinted by permission of Harcourt Brace & Company.

12 Quotes by Gary Soto from Donald R. Gallo, *Speaking for Ourselves, Too;* Urbana IL: The National Council of Teachers of English, 1993, page 196; and from *Contemporary Authors,* Volume 125; Detroit: Gale Research Center, 1989, p. 425.

14 "Mildred" by Colby Rodowsky from *Connections: Short Stories* by Donald R. Gallo, Editor, pages 95–104. Copyright © 1989 by Colby Rodowsky. Used by permission of Delacorte Press, a division of Bantam Doubleday Dell Publishing Group, Inc.

24 Quote by Colby Rodowsky from Gallo, *Speaking for Ourselves, Too,* page 172.

26 *Hum It Again, Jeremy* by Jean Davies Okimoto. Copyright © 1990 by Jean Davies Okimoto. Reprinted by permission of Ruth Cohen, Inc.

44 Quote by Jean Davies Okimoto from Gallo, *Speaking for Ourselves, Too,* page 152.

46 "Be-ers and Doers" from *The Leaving and Other Stories* by Budge Wilson, 171–189. Text copyright © 1990 by Budge Wilson. Reprinted by permission of Philomel Books and Stoddart Publishing Co. Limited, Don Mills, Ont.

60 "The Last Word" by Judith Ortiz Cofer is reprinted with permission from the publisher of *Silent Dancing: A Partial Remembrance of a Puerto Rican Childhood* (Houston: Arte Publico Press—University of Houston, 1990), pages 153–156.

63 "My Father in the Navy" by Judith Ortiz Cofer from *Triple Crown.* Copyright © 1987 by the Bilingual Press/Editorial Bilingüe (Arizona State University, Tempe, AZ). Reprinted by permission of the Bilingual Press/Editorial Bilingüe. Quote by Judith Ortiz Cofer from *Contemporary Authors: New Revision Series,* Volume 32. Detroit: Gale Research Center, 1991, page 89.

70 "On the Bridge" by Todd Strasser from *Visions* by Donald R. Gallo, Editor, pages 122–128. Copyright © 1987 by Todd Strasser. Used by permission of Dell Books, a division of Bantam Doubleday Dell Publishing Group, Inc.

78 Quote by Todd Strasser from *Something About the Author,* Volume 45. Detroit: Gale Research Center, 1986, page 199.

80 "Beauty: When the Other Dancer Is the Self" by Alice Walker from *In Search of Our Mothers' Gardens* by Alice Walker, pages 384–393. Copyright © 1983 by Alice Walker. Reprinted by permission of Harcourt Brace & Company.

90 Quote by Alice Walker from *SATA* 31, pages 177–178.

92 "Beautiful & Cruel" by Sandra Cisneros from *The House on Mango Street* by Sandra Cisneros, pages 88–89. Copyright © 1984 by Sandra Cisneros. Published in the United States by Vintage Books, a division of Random House, Inc., New York and in hardcover by Alfred A. Knopf, a division of Random House, Inc., New York in 1994. Reprinted by permission of Susan Bergholz Literary Services, New York.

94 "Maybe" by Eve Merriam from *If Only I Could Tell You* by Eve Merriam, page 48. Copyright © 1983 by Eve Merriam. Reprinted by permission of Marian Reiner.

95 "I, Too" by Langston Hughes from *Selected Poems* by Langston Hughes. Copyright 1926 by Alfred A. Knopf, Inc. and renewed 1954 by Langston Hughes. Reprinted by permission of the publisher.

96 Quote by Eve Merriam from *CANR* 29, page 296.

98 "Dancer" by Vickie Sears from *Simple Songs* by Vickie Sears. Copyright © 1990 by Vickie Sears. Reprinted by permission of Firebrand Books, Ithaca, New York, 14580.

106 "Being Alive" from *Heartbeats and Other Stories* by Peter D. Sieruta, pages 109–130. Copyright © 1989 by Peter D. Sieruta. Reprinted by permission of HarperCollins Publishers.

122 Quotes by Peter Sieruta from *Publishers Weekly,* December 22, 1989.

128 "Priscilla and the Wimps" by Richard Peck from *Sixteen: Short Stories* by Donald R. Gallo, ed., pages 42–45. Copyright © 1984 by Richard Peck. Used by permission of Dell Books, a division of Bantam Doubleday Dell Publishing Group, Inc.

134 From *Dear America: Letters Home from Vietnam,* edited by Bernard Edelman, pages 109, 110-111, 127-128, 237 and 238-239. Copyright © 1985 by The New York Vietnam Veterans Memorial Commission. Reprinted by permission.

146 From *Anne Frank: The Diary of a Young Girl* by Anne Frank, pages 237-238. Copyright 1952 by Otto H. Frank. Used by permission of Doubleday, a division of Bantam Doubleday Dell Publishing Group, Inc. and Vallentine Mitchell Publishers.

152 "Future Tense" by Robert Lipsyte from *Sixteen: Short Stories* by Donald R. Gallo, ed., pages 60–69. Copyright © 1984 by Robert Lipsyte. Used by permission of Dell Books, a division of Bantam Doubleday Dell Publishing Group, Inc.

162 Quote by Robert Lipsyte from Donald R. Gallo, *Speaking for Ourselves.* Urbana, IL: The National Council of Teachers of English, 1990, pages 122–123.

164 "The Harringtons' Daughter" by Lois Lowry from *A Gathering of Flowers: Stories About Being Young in America,* edited by Joyce Carol Thomas, pages 23–34. Copyright © 1990 by Joyce Carol Thomas. Reprinted by permission of HarperCollins Publishers.

172 Quotes by Lois Lowry from Gallo, *Speaking for Ourselves, Too,* pages 125–126.

178 "Checkouts" by Cynthia Rylant from *A Couple of Kooks: And Other Stories About Love* by Cynthia Rylant, pages 21–28. Copyright © 1990 by Cynthia Rylant. Used by permission of Orchard Books, New York.

184 Quote by Cynthia Rylant from *SATA* 50, page 186.

186 "Protestants Cry, Too" by Robert Cormier from *Eight Plus One* by Robert Cormier, pages 97–113. Copyright © 1967 by Robert Cormier. Reprinted by permission of Pantheon Books, a division of Random House, Inc.

202 Quotes by Robert Cormier from Gallo, *Speaking for Ourselves,* page 57; and from *SATA* 45, page 65.

204 "King of the Roller Rink" from *Paradise Cafe and Other Stories* by Martha Brooks, pages 18–24. Copyright © 1988 by Martha Brooks. Reprinted by permission of Little, Brown and Company and Thistledown Press Ltd.

210 Quotes by Martha Brooks from *SATA* 68, page 41.

212 "So Close" from *The Land I Lost: Adventures of a Boy in Vietnam* by Huynh Quang Nhuong, pages 62–68, 70–71. Copyright © 1982 by Huynh Quang Nhuong. Reprinted by permission of HarperCollins Publishers.

220 "I Hate You, Wallace B. Pokras" by Ellen Conford from *If This Is Love, I'll Take Spaghetti* by Ellen Conford, pages 89–100. Copyright © 1983 by Ellen Conford. Reprinted with the permission of Four Winds Press, an Imprint of Macmillan Publishing Company.

228 Quotes by Ellen Conford from *SATA* 68, page 57; and from Gallo, *Speaking for Ourselves,* page 53.

230 "What to Reply When Someone Wonders" by Claire Barliant from *Open Fist: An Anthology of Young Illinois Poets* edited by Anne Schultz, page 46. Copyright © 1993 by Claire Barliant. Reprinted by permission of the author.

231 "Mixed Singles" from *Sports Pages* by Arnold Adoff, page 52. Copyright © 1986 by Arnold Adoff. Reprinted by

permission of HarperCollins Publishers.
232 "Kidnap Poem" by Nikki Giovanni from *The Women and the Men* by Nikki Giovanni. Copyright © 1970, 1974, 1975 by Nikki Giovanni. Reprinted by permission of William Morrow and Company, Inc.
234 Quote by Claire Barliant used by permission of the author. Quote by Arnold Adoff from *SATA* 57, page 11. Quote by Nikki Giovanni from *SATA* 24, page 120.
240 "Waters of Gold" from *Tongues of Jade* by Laurence Yep, pages 107–117. Copyright © 1991 by Laurence Yep. Reprinted by permission of HarperCollins Publishers.
248 Quote by Laurence Yep from *SATA* 69, page 231.
250 "I, Hungry Hannah Cassandra Glen . . ." by Norma Fox Mazer from *Sixteen: Short Stories* by Donald R. Gallo, ed., pages 2–13. Copyright © 1984 by Norma Fox Mazer. Used by permission of Dell Books, a division of Bantam Doubleday Dell Publishing Group, Inc.
262 Quote by Norma Fox Mazer from *SATA* 67, page 134.
264 "Lose Now, Pay Later" by Carol Farley from the book, *2041: Twelve Stories About the Future by Top Science Fiction Writers*, selected and edited by Jane Yolen, pages 39–48. Copyright © 1991 by Carol Farley. Reprinted by permission of GRM Associates, Inc., Agents for Carol Farley.
272 Quote by Carol Farley from *CANR* 25, page 123.
274 Excerpt from *Buffalo Nickel: A Memoir* by Floyd Salas is reprinted with permission from the publisher of *Buffalo Nickel: A Memoir* (Houston: Arte Publico Press—University of Houston, 1992), pages 27–30.
280 Quote by Floyd Salas from *CA* 119, page 304.
282 "Becoming a 'Nonalien'" from *The Invisible Thread* by Yoshiko Uchida, pages 63–71. Copyright © 1991 by Yoshiko Uchida. Used by permission of the publisher, Julian Messner/A Division of Silver Press, Inc., Simon & Schuster, Englewood Cliffs, N.J.
292 Quote by Yoshiko Uchida from *SATA* 53, page 156.
294 "Destination: Tule Lake Relocation Center, May 20, 1942" by James Masao Mitsui from *After the Long Train* by James Masao Mitsui. Copyright © 1986 by James Masao Mitsui. Reprinted by permission of The Bieler Press.
296 "Holding Center, Tanforan Race Track, Spring 1942" by James Masao Mitsui from *After the Long Train* by James Masao Mitsui. Copyright © 1986 by James Masao Mitsui. Reprinted by permission of The Bieler Press.
302 "The Road Goes Ever On and On" from *The Fellowship of the Ring* by J.R.R. Tolkien. Copyright © 1954, 1965 by J.R.R. Tolkien, © renewed 1982 by Christopher R. Tolkien, Michael H.R. Tolkien, John F.R. Tolkien and Priscilla M.A.R. Tolkien. Reprinted by permission of Houghton Mifflin Company and HarperCollins Publishers. All rights reserved.
313 "Night Journey" from *The Collected Poems of Theodore Roethke* by Theodore Roethke. Copyright 1940 by Theodore Roethke. Used by permission of Doubleday, a division of Bantam Doubleday Dell Publishing Group, Inc.
304 "A Trip on the Staten Island Ferry" by Audre Lorde from *Undersong*, Chosen Poems Old and New, Revised Edition, by Audre Lorde. Copyright © 1992, 1982, 1976, 1973, 1970, 1968 by Audre Lorde. Reprinted by permission of W.W. Norton & Company, Inc.
308 "The Journey" by Duane BigEagle from *Earth Power Coming: Short Fiction in Native American Literature*, Navajo Community College Press. Copyright © 1983 by Duane BigEagle. Reprinted by permission of the author.
314 Quote by Duane BigEagle reprinted by permission of the author. Copyright © 1994.
316 From *Woodsong* by Gary Paulsen, pages 66–70. Copyright © 1990 by Gary Paulsen. Reprinted with the permission of Bradbury Press, an Affiliate of Macmillan, Inc.
320 Quotes by Gary Paulsen from *SATA* 54, page 78.

322 "The River of Ice" from *Escape from Slavery: Five Journeys to Freedom* by Doreen Rappaport, pages 3–10, 12–13, and 110. Copyright © 1991 by Doreen Rappaport. Reprinted by permission of HarperCollins Publishers.
328 Quotes by Doreen Rappaport reprinted by permission of HarperCollins Publishers.
330 "The Inn of Lost Time" by Lensey Namioka. Copyright © 1989 by Lensey Namioka. Reprinted by permission of Ruth Cohen, Inc.
348 Quote by Lensey Namioka from *SATA* 27, page 154.
350 "The Legacy" by Walter Dean Myers from *Malcolm X: By Any Means Necessary* by Walter Dean Myers, pages 182–184, 186–188 and 190–192. Copyright © 1993 by Walter Dean Myers. Reprinted by permission of Scholastic, Inc.
356 "Great Bataleur" by Wopashitwe Mondo Eyen we Langa from *Malcolm X: By Any Means Necessary* by Walter Dean Myers, pages 190–191. Reprinted by permission of Wopashitwe Mondo Eyen we Langa.
358 Quotes by Walter Dean Myers from *SATA* 41, page 153; and from Gallo, *Speaking for Ourselves*, page 149.

PHOTOGRAPHS
x N. Frank/Viesti & Associates **2** Chip & Rosa Peterson **12** Courtesy Carolyn Soto **15** Elyse Lewin/The Image Bank **24** Courtesy of the author **26–27** Daniel Grogan/Uniphoto **44** Courtesy of the author **47** Dorothy Kerper Monnelly/Stock Boston **58** Courtesy of the author **61** Courtesy of the author **64** Courtesy/Arte Publico Press **68** Superstock **70–71** ©Richard Price/Westlight **78** Courtesy Dell Publishing **81** National Museum of American Art, Washington D. C./Art Resource **90** Jean Weisinger 1991/Courtesy Harcourt, Brace & Jovanovich **92** The Carson Collection **96t** Rubin Guzman **96c** Courtesy Macmillan Children's Book Group **96b** UPI/Bettmann **99** ©John Running **104** Courtesy Firebrand Books **107** Dennis Degnan/Photo Bank, Inc. **122** Courtesy of the author **126** UPI/Bettmann **129** Owen Franken/Stock Boston **132** Don Lewis/Dell Publishing **135** Bill Strode/Black Star **142** Ellen Leary/Courtesy of the author **147** Anne Frank Foundation **150t** Curt Koehler/Harold Leventhal Management, Inc. **150b** Anne Frank Foundation **152** The Carson Collection **162** Courtesy HarperCollins **165** Mike Mazzaschi/Stock Boston **172** Courtesy Houghton Mifflin **176** UPI/Bettmann **178–179** ©Mike Chesser **184** Courtesy Orchard Books **187** Photofest **202** Courtesy Bantam Publishing **210** Courtesy Thistledown Press Ltd. **212** *The Land I Lost: Adventures of a Boy in Vietnam* by Huynh Quang Nhuong. Illustrated by Vo-Dinh Mai/HarperCollins Children's Books **221** Yvonne Hemsey/Gamma-Liaison **231** ©Bob Thomas/Tony Stone Images **233** Francis de Richemond/The Image Works **234t** Diana Solis **234c** Barbara Goldberg **238** Doug Munuez/Stock Boston **241** Julien Bryan **248** K. Yep/Courtesy HarperCollins **251** Copyright Estate of André Kertész. All rights reserved **262** Courtesy Bantam, Doubleday, Dell Publishing **265** ©Carol Kaplan **272** Courtesy of the author **275** Nancy D'Antonio/Photo Researchers **280** Courtesy Arte Publico Press **282-283** UPI/Bettmann Newsphotos **292** Deborah Storms/Courtesy Macmillan Publishing Co. **294** War Relocation Authority **296** Courtesy Lilly Mitsui **300** Heiniger/Photo Researchers **304–305** John Elk III/Stock Boston **306t** Photograph by Snowdon/Camera Press **306b** ©Dagmar Schultz/Courtesy Charlotte Sheedy **308** Lee Walden/Tony Stone Images **314** John Burgess/Courtesy of the author **316** J. Christopher/The New Image Stock Photo Agency, Inc. **323** Library of Congress **328** Russell Dian **330–331** Tony Stone Images **348** Richard McNamee/Courtesy HarperCollins Publishers **351** AP/Wide World Photos **358** Courtesy Scholastic

INDEX